CRUSH THE CELL

CRUSH THE CELL

How to Defeat Terrorism Without Terrorizing Ourselves

MICHAEL A. SHEEHAN

CROWN PUBLISHERS NEW YORK

Author's Note: The photo on the dust jacket of this book was taken by a video camera in the London underground train system on July 21, 2005. It depicts one of the terrorist cell members who carried out the second subway plot (which failed following the successful attack two weeks before in the same system). The man is seen running in the station after his backpack bomb failed to detonate in a subway car. At NYPD, the man's "New York" sweatshirt got our attention. But we were never able to confirm if the shirt was a fashion decision for what he thought would be his last day on earth, a political statement directed at us, or mere coincidence.

Published in the United States by Crown Publishers, an imprint of the Crown Publishing Group, a division of Random House, Inc., New York.
www.crownpublishing.com

Library of Congress Cataloging-in-Publication Data
Sheehan, Michael A.
Crush the cell : how to defeat terrorism without terrorizing ourselves / Michael Sheehan.—1st ed.
p. cm.
Includes bibliographical references and index.
1. Terrorism—United States—Prevention. 2. Terrorism—Government policy—United States. 3. Terrorism—Psychological aspects. 4. Terrorists—Psychology. I. Title.
HV6432.S497 2008
363.325'16—dc22 2007048444

ISBN 978-0-307-38217-7

Printed in the United States of America

DESIGN BY LEONARD W. HENDERSON

10 9 8 7 6 5 4 3 2 1

First Edition

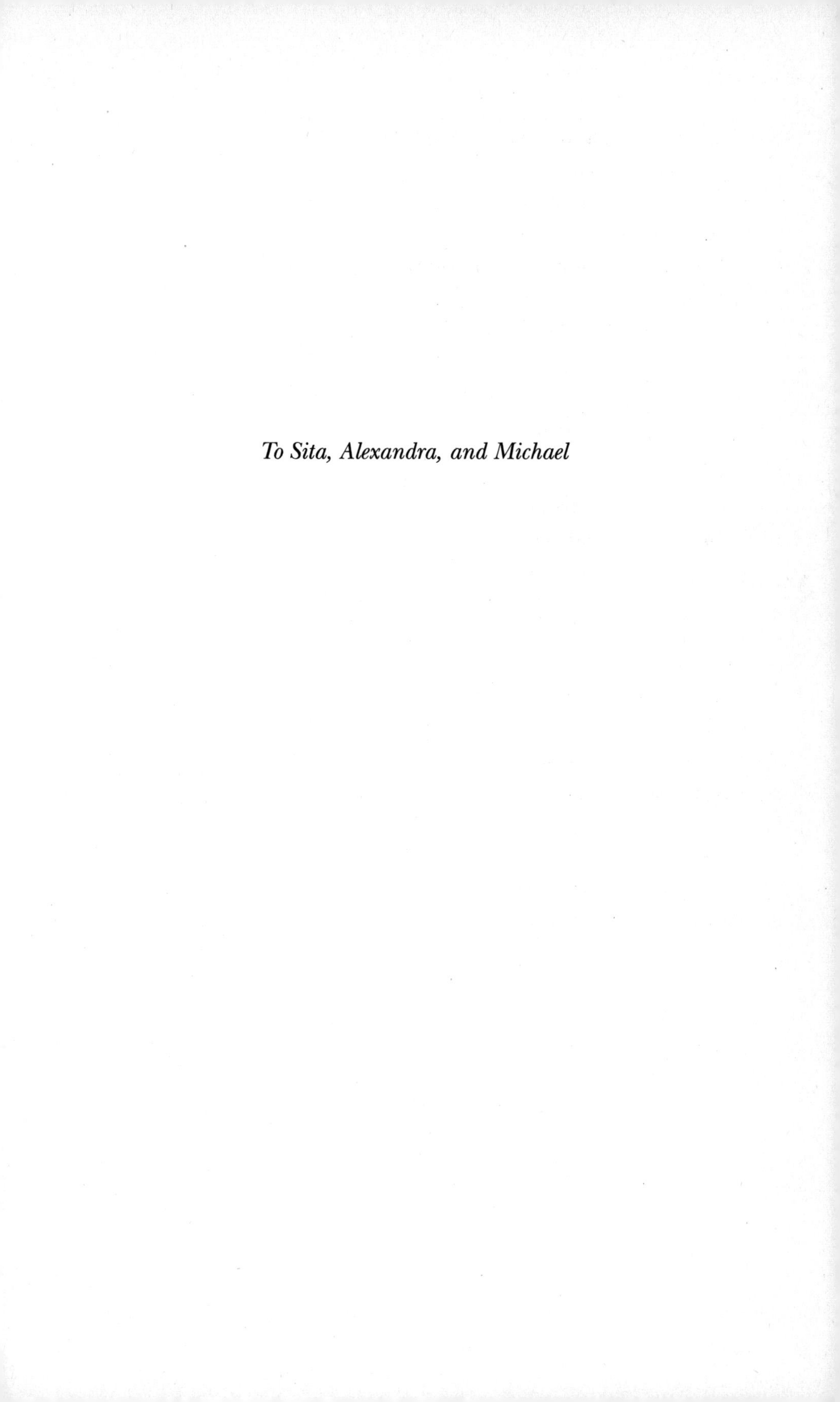

To Sita, Alexandra, and Michael

Contents

Part 2

Introduction

Terrorism Unplugged

THE TERRORISM ATTACKS of September 11, 2001, changed the way Americans look at national security. This new lens on the world is, in some ways, clearer than ever. But in other ways it has become distorted and blurred. In the aftermath of 9/11, Americans were keenly aware of the vulnerability of the U.S. homeland; now we take comfort in not having been hit again. Are we leaning on a false sense of security—or is the worst truly behind us? This book attempts to provide answers to questions such as this in plain language and without any hidden agendas. In this firsthand account of more than twenty years of counterterrorism work, I hope to present the terrorist threat in the most realistic light possible.

Anti-American terrorist activity has not abated since 9/11; overwhelming evidence points to the contrary. We're safe today for one primary reason: America has thus far been able to detect and crush the cells that would do us harm *before* they could fulfill their purpose. The clandestine cell is the essential building block of a terrorist operation. Effective terrorist cells are usually very small and tightly managed, generally comprising three or four people and rarely involving more than ten or twenty. When they get bigger, cells become much more vulnerable to penetration by law enforcement or detection by alert citizens. The 9/11 operation was conducted by four cells composed of about three to five people per cell, all of which were led by Mohamed Atta. Only Atta knew about all four cells. This highly disciplined group operated without being detected and achieved its tragic effect because our nation was asleep to the threat it posed.

Any terrorist cell is difficult to stop once it has devised a plan and assembled a weapon without detection. We live in an open, democratic society with attractive targets everywhere. We can and should protect our most critical infrastructure, and I'll discuss the best ways to do that as we proceed. However, all people and places can't be protected at all times—even in a fortress state, which nobody wants. Rather than adopting a bunker mentality, we must address the issue of terrorism at its source. Ideally, we should work toward changing the dynamic that drives a young man to kill for the sake of a radical cause, but changing that equation will take at least a generation. In the interim, we'll face a significant number of terrorists who are committed to doing us harm. Hence, the immediate and paramount goal of U.S. counterterrorism policy should be to detect and dismantle terrorist cells before they can attack.

Rather than attempting to eliminate every terrorist from the face of the earth, we need a policy that focuses on strategic terrorism, which is the real threat to our national interest. Terrorism is deemed *strategic* only when a terrorist organization exhibits the capability to sustain multiple conventional attacks over time, or develop and deploy a single catastrophic attack with a weapon of mass destruction. Only a strategic attack can change our way of life. Lone-wolf attacks such as those of Olympic Park bomber Eric Rudolph and Oklahoma City bomber Timothy McVeigh are tragic onetime events and shouldn't be confused with strategic attacks. In the immediate aftermath of one of these tactical attacks, we should mourn the loss of innocent life, then concentrate on finding, arresting, and trying the perpetrators. But these isolated events shouldn't fundamentally distort our lives or redefine our national security posture.

Don't Self-Terrorize

Tactical terrorist attacks can change our way of life only if we choose to terrorize ourselves, thereby giving what is in fact an isolated incident strategic dimensions. A terrorist attack is normally conducted by the weak and humiliated as an act of desperation against a superior military foe. As implied in the word *terrorism,* those who engage in that practice employ their enemy's fears and insecurities as part of their weaponry. Terrorists depend on an overreaction to scale up the impact of whatever they've done. If we overreact, then we afford the enemy disproportionate power. In this regard, we should take a lesson from Israel and the United Kingdom. Both countries have experienced more than their fair share of terrorist activity, but with experience comes wisdom. The Israelis and British don't allow a terrorist attack to have an impact beyond the immediate blasting area of the explosion. They clean up the attack area quickly, mourn their dead appropriately and without excessive fanfare, care for the injured, and get back to normal life. Politicians, pundits, and civic leaders are relatively mute compared to their hyperventilating counterparts on American talk radio and cable TV.

If a bomb explodes tomorrow in a New York City subway car, how should we react? In the first minutes after the attack, we should assume that there'll be other attacks (for that is al Qaeda's modus operandi). The trains should be shut down and thoroughly searched for additional bombs and bombers. However, it's essential to get the trains running again as soon as possible, no later than the very next morning rush hour. Commercial aviation was stopped for four days after 9/11, but hindsight has revealed that this was unnecessary. If terrorists attempt to disable our transportation infrastructure again, we must deny them that satisfaction. We must minimize the impact of the attack on our lives. Of course, extra security is appropriate, but we must not shut down entirely, as we did following 9/11. It's crucial to maintain our national composure in the wake of a terrorist attack.

In light of how overreacting plays into the terrorists' hands, those who in the wake of an attack promote hysteria to gain political advantage or raise network ratings should be held accountable for the havoc they wreak. Politicians and pundits who run to the microphones with frightening pronouncements should be condemned.

Regardless of their political leanings, they're usually inaccurate or flat wrong.

Many people think that tempering the national response to a terrorist event is impossible; they assume that we're not like the British and the Israelis. I disagree. We're slowly learning. As we saw in the aftermath of the horrific shooting spree at Virginia Tech, the media frenzy surrounding an event must be contained lest we give a madman his last wish for infamy and inadvertently inspire copycats. Initially, the media couldn't resist twenty-four-hour coverage of that horrible carnage—and indeed, it was an important news story. But after plastering Cho Seung-Hui's self-produced multimedia manifesto all over the networks for a day or two, most media executives realized they were serving the killer's wishes and pulled the images. It's a step in the right direction. In their response to domestic terror, the American media has begun to realize the significant impact they have on our national safety. I think Americans can and will learn to measure our responses to international terrorism as well, and in so doing effectively disarm those who seek to destroy us.

That said, let me be clear: we must never underestimate the very real threat of radical Islamic terrorism, led by al Qaeda. I've spent the better part of the past thirty years in counterterrorism work, and I'm fully aware of the special dangers this phenomenon poses. Our enemies have demonstrated both the intent and the capability to do us grave harm, and their leaders have repeatedly proven themselves impervious to reason. We must never bend to their will. Instead, we must prevent them from gaining the ability to sustain conventional bomb attacks or acquire a weapon of mass destruction. We do this by methodically strangling the terrorists' organizations around the globe, primarily through intelligence operations—not through large-scale warfare or massive social programs. Undercover agents, informant networks, and phone and e-mail intercepts are the most effective weapons we have.

We've made significant progress in containing the strategic threat from al Qaeda since 9/11. Thus far, they've failed to hit in the U.S. homeland again, and their impact on Western nations has been limited to two attacks by associated franchises in London and

Madrid. But the broader movement is alive and well; it's attempting now to rebuild a strategic capability. The reemergence of al Qaeda in western Pakistan is especially troubling. The bomb-making capability being developed in Iraq is also frightening, as is the unrest in Islamic enclaves from Birmingham, England, to Jakarta, Indonesia. I'm sure al Qaeda's leaders are preparing their next attack right now. We must stay one step ahead of them.

Fighting terrorism is not unlike fighting a cancer: early detection is crucial, followed by aggressive eradication of the offending cells. Crushing the cell requires an offensive strategy, but defensive, deterrent, and response strategies are also important. Some critical infrastructure, such as commercial aviation, requires special security measures with a "zero defects" approach. In other words, there's no room for error in protecting our nation's most vulnerable and valuable assets. But defensive strategies must be carefully thought through so they don't bankrupt our treasury while providing only marginal increases in security.

What Have We Learned Since 9/11?

Before 9/11, we underestimated al Qaeda's lethal determination. We also completely failed to recognize that they were planning direct attacks on American soil. Previous attacks on our foreign embassies and the USS *Cole* were conducted far away from home. Americans were largely detached from these tragedies and seemed to forget about them as soon as the dust settled. Americans were comforted by the arrest of Algerian-born, bin Laden–trained terrorist Ahmed Ressam as he attempted to cross the Canadian border with a carload of explosives in December 1999, but we failed to heed this important interdiction as a portent of things to come. How did we miss the signs that a very lethal threat was creeping closer? We simply underestimated the geographic reach of al Qaeda and its ability to operate in the United States, and we misread a changing, globalized world that requires a much more effective unification of domestic and international intelligence. For these and other reasons, we were asleep to the al Qaeda threat, allowing the terrorists to strike a tremendous blow on September 11, 2001.

After underestimating the threat prior to 9/11, the overreaction that followed was predictable, but not inevitable. By failing to understand the context of the organization, its very strengths and weaknesses, we magnified our mental image of terrorists as bogeymen. We thought they were hiding under every rock with a cunning lethality that would allow them to strike at our open society with virtual impunity. The anthrax attack that came shortly afterward fueled the nation's fears and feelings of vulnerability. The thought of a terrorist group getting its hands on a weapon of mass destruction became even more daunting. But just as we failed to recognize the scope of al Qaeda's reach prior to 9/11, we were unable to see the clear limitations of the organization after the fact. Nobody would have dared to predict that six years later, longer than the entire Atlantic and Pacific campaigns of World War II, al Qaeda would not have had an opportunity to attack us again. It was impossible to know that they'd be absolutely unable to conduct even one follow-up attack or even forge a credible plot (in which an actual weapon was acquired or constructed) within the United States.

But the overestimation of al Qaeda's power caused major problems for the United States, not the least of which has helped propel us into the Iraq war. Fear that Iraq was developing a weapon of mass destruction became sufficiently unbearable to President Bush and Congress that they launched and supported a preemptive war based on a poorly defined threat. Senior members of the Bush administration (either by honest mistake or purposeful manipulation) exaggerated intelligence and drew an erroneous link between the September 11 attack and Iraq in order to pursue a separate agenda: the elimination of Saddam Hussein. Meanwhile, Congress foisted on the administration two ill-conceived massive governmental expansions: the Department of Homeland Security and the new intelligence superbureaucracy of the Office of the Director of National Intelligence. The resulting massive increase in homeland security action, chasing of phantom threats, and protection of unlikely targets deflected America's attention from the real work at hand: finding and crushing terrorist cells at home and abroad.

Part 1 of this book attempts to properly define the real and current threats posed by al Qaeda, lone wolves, Hezbollah, and Iran. Part 2 takes the reader inside the world of counterterrorism, drawing on experiences I've had with the U.S. Army Special Forces, the State Department, the White House, the United Nations, and the New York City Police Department (NYPD). It also outlines and evaluates counterterrorism strategies since 9/11. My goal is to distinguish between real threats and hype, and to separate the most effective ways to defeat terrorism from the more wasteful and unproductive strategies.

Writing this book involved some professional risk. Terrorism experts, by nature, tend to overstate the threat, or at least take the safe route in prophesying an imminent, 9/11-scale attack. No terrorism expert or government leader wants to appear soft on terrorism. It's always safer to predict the worst; if nothing happens, the exaggerators are rarely held accountable for their nightmare scenarios. In fact, since 9/11 most predictions have been terribly wrong. Every summer there's terrorist "chatter," and every summer the same doomsayers predict the worst. One day they'll be right (even a broken clock is right twice a day), but when they are, we should keep in mind the many, many dark scenarios that never played out.

Admittedly, fearmongering is good business for terrorism consultants. By conjuring threats to our ports, our suburban shopping malls, and our agro-industry, terrorism consultancies thrive. I've chosen to resist that temptation. Yes, the threat of terrorism is real and enduring. I expect further attacks in the United States. I'm also very concerned about the steady growth of radical pockets around the world, particularly in Europe. But in the best interest of our national security, I always try to be balanced and accurate in my threat assessments.

It's time to set the record straight. Those who say we've entered World War III are not to be taken seriously. This *isn't* World War III. It's ridiculous to equate the rise of radical Islamic terrorist groups with World War III. Consider that World War II was advanced by two of the world's largest and most powerful economic and military states, Germany and Japan. Half of the free world was occupied by hostile troops, children were evacuated from London, and Stalingrad was under siege throughout the winter of 1942–43. Tens of millions were killed, maimed, or displaced, and six million Jews were systematically murdered by the Nazis—all within a period of about four years. As of the date of this book's publication, America hasn't been attacked in six years. The Islamic terrorists are nasty and brutish, but by no estimation do they match the caliber of our enemies in World War II. The primary terrorist threat, al Qaeda and its associated groups, has not controlled a single country since they lost the Afghan sanctuary provided by the Taliban regime.

I live in New York City, the prime terrorist target. And I'm staying here. I choose to make my home here not out of a false sense of bravado but because I've conducted a thorough assessment of our safety. If I felt my family was at risk, I'd move out to the suburbs immediately—or, if the danger seemed particularly menacing, to the foothills of Montana. It's undoubtedly safer there (although homeland security funding doesn't reflect this), but I sleep secure each night in Manhattan knowing that the terrorists aren't invincible; they can be deterred and stopped.

When they do strike again, I'm hopeful we can manage the attack appropriately. In this regard I'm more confident than most. As a terrorism analyst for NBC News, I'm very impressed with the professionalism and knowledge of the senior news staff there, including *Nightly News* anchor Brian Williams. I trust that NBC News won't hype a terrorist attack to get ratings, but will cover it in a sober-minded and appropriate manner. I also know analysts and producers at ABC, CBS, Fox, and CNN, and I believe that they'll do the same. I'm less convinced about some of the other cable shows and talk radio.

For the time being, my family and I will remain in New York City. I won't move to Montana. I won't send my children to the countryside, as Londoners did in 1942, to avoid being killed in the next bomb attack. But I've also promised a great many of my fellow New Yorkers over the past six years that I'll let them know if I surmise that it is time to depart the number one al Qaeda target.

PART I

The Terrorist Threat:

Reality versus Hype

Chapter 1

Al Qaeda: Killers and Bunglers

WHY HAS AL QAEDA not attacked us again since the eleventh of September, 2001? This is the question I am most frequently asked. New York City mayor Michael Bloomberg asked me this question when he interviewed me for the job of deputy commissioner of NYPD's Bureau of Counter Terrorism. I've heard it at conferences, meetings, and dinner tables from New York to Chicago to Seattle. Those who ask it usually have their own theories and attack scenarios based on assumptions about how al Qaeda operatives think. For example, they imagine the terrorists could hit ten malls simultaneously on a Sunday afternoon with ten small bombs and devastate our national economy. Or they could blast a dirty bomb in a container in one of our ports and shut down international commerce. They could even drive a truck bomb into Times Square on New Year's Eve and paralyze the nation with fear.

Why don't they do it? After all, we live in an open society with relatively easy access from abroad—just look at the Mexican border, where millions of illegal immigrants flow into our country every year. The average citizen hears horror stories of still-uncoordinated terrorist watch lists and looks on in dismay as a blue-haired grandmother is turned upside down and frisked at an airport in Topeka, while a bearded terrorist remains free to move through JFK International Airport on a crowded Sunday afternoon.

So why hasn't al Qaeda hit us again since 9/11? My answer can be somewhat unsettling to some: they haven't attacked again because, thus far, they haven't been able to. They aren't waiting for a special day or a bigger target. They've simply been unable to bring another terrorist plot to fruition on American soil. We've seen various plots exposed before they could unfold, including one to blow up the jet fuel pipeline heading into JFK. In the JFK case the plot was, in fact, much more difficult to conduct than that terrorist cell could handle. But if al Qaeda could hit us tomorrow, they would—and I wouldn't be shocked if they did. However, al Qaeda is much smaller and less effective than we supposed in the aftermath of September 11, especially in the United States.

This assertion angers some and befuddles others, but it raises the following question: how can an organization that was so destructive on September 11 be so ineffective since then? As hard as it is to explain to Americans, many Muslims around the world find it unbelievable that the most powerful nation on earth could allow such a ragtag group to destroy so many lives and so much property. Many are convinced that the attacks were staged by the Central Intelligence Agency (CIA) and Israeli intelligence as a pretext for invading the Middle East and controlling its oil. Is this crazy? From their perspective, the proof is self-evident: we're sitting on Middle East oil in Iraq and we haven't been attacked again since. Of course the notion of the United States staging an attack on itself is pure fantasy, but other theories are equally wrong: the terrorists aren't distracted by Iraq; we remain the primary target; they aren't holding back. They'll attack when they're ready, for real terrorists operate in real time.

Al Qaeda succeeded on 9/11 for two reasons: first, America was asleep to the threat they posed, and second, everything went remarkably well that day for an unusually disciplined al Qaeda cell. The devastation exceeded even its planners' wildest dreams. For the terrorists, it was, in many ways, a perfect storm. But al Qaeda has been under relentless pressure since that terrible day.

It's become clear that even at the time of the attack they had a very small operational capability in the West and were usually not very adept in their craft. When I say this to some audiences, misinterpretation often leads to downright hostility. But the fact remains that for six years since 9/11 they've been unable to deliver a second punch. This doesn't mean they won't strike again. In fact, I expect them to, and I suspect they're trying to pursue even more deadly weapons.

Prior to 9/11, my colleagues at the State Department teased me about my fixation on al Qaeda, an organization that had succeeded in simultaneously blowing up two of our embassies in East Africa. I may have been a bit shrill and hardheaded at times, but even then, I never underestimated the determination and lethality of this loosely linked band of killers. Now more than ever before, we must relentlessly track their every move and crush them before they can make a move toward us. Left to their devices, they'll be back to kill us in increasing numbers. Even under pressure, they remain dedicated and resourceful killers. But we must also remember that they're bound by their own limitations. Knowing al Qaeda's limitations is as important as knowing their capabilities.

On September 11, 2001, I wasn't actively working in counterterrorism; I was at the United Nations in peacekeeping. But after the attack, I knew I had to get back into counterterrorism. In June 2003, I began what was to become a three-year commitment to protecting the city of New York as deputy commissioner of counterterrorism. Every morning at nine o'clock, I met with NYPD commissioner Raymond Kelly and my good friend Dave Cohen, the head of NYPD intelligence. Kelly, Cohen, and I all came to New York with a lot of experience at the federal level, and each day we brought it all to work with us. As we focused on what we considered the imminent threats to the city of New York, we reviewed intelligence from the Central Intelligence Agency, the National Security Agency (NSA), and the Federal Bureau of Investigation (FBI), looking for the implications for New York City from every possible angle. My operating assumption was that there was a Mohamed Atta–like cell operating beneath our radar screens every day, poised to attack the city. We studied past attacks and assumed the bad guys were dreaming up new and more innovative ways to kill New Yorkers. We never discounted a single threat or possible scenario. It was a race against time—us against that cell.

NYPD pursued every lead that came into our call centers, no matter how small. Sometimes, even if the lead was a dead end, it would put us in contact with somebody out on the street who became another listening post for NYPD. And we had plenty of people to be concerned about; the radical movements and their violent tendencies were alive and well in the New York City area. After three years of intensely tracking violent groups in New York City and across the country, I'm convinced there are those who, if properly led and organized, will attack us again.

But even in 2003, less than two years after 9/11, I told Kelly and Cohen that I thought al Qaeda was simply not very good. They were a small and determined group of killers, but under the withering heat of the post-9/11 environment, they were simply not getting it done. I said what nobody else was saying: we underestimated al Qaeda's capabilities before 9/11 and overestimated them after. This seemed to catch both Kelly and Cohen a bit by surprise, and I agreed not to discuss my feelings in public. The likelihood for misinterpretation was much too high. I also didn't discuss this with my team in NYPD counterterrorism; I didn't want to allow any doubt that we were in a race against time to protect the city from an imminent threat. That remained my commitment every day I was on the job at NYPD, and will remain my frame of mind for at least another ten to twenty years. I assumed they were still coming after us, every day, and I wouldn't have been surprised to get that dreaded call saying that the city had been attacked again. But I also knew that many terrorism experts, administration officials, and media pundits were grossly exaggerating the threat.

Exaggerating al Qaeda's power isn't tantamount to playing it safe. It only clouds our view of this already clandestine enemy and contributes to the psychological terror that they hope to invoke. We need to know our enemies better than they know themselves. My intent in assessing al Qaeda as both killers and bunglers is to represent them as they are, not as I fear they may be or wish they were. My goal is to stay one step ahead of the enemy and, as I did when I was a foot soldier in the U.S. Army Special Forces, I can do that only if I know exactly where they are at all times. If I *don't* know exactly where they are, I have to keep them under broad pressure, both to keep them off balance and buy time until I can find and defeat them. So, where are they now and what are they doing? They're working hard to rebuild cells that, under U.S. military pressure, have lost their leadership and safe havens. They're more committed than ever to remaining undetected as they prepare to attack again.

As stated previously, I reject the notion that al Qaeda is waiting for the "big one" or holding back an attack. Close study of their historical modus operandi does not support this theory. A terrorist cell capable of attacking doesn't sit and wait for some more opportune moment. It's not their style, nor is it in the best interest of their operational security. Delaying an attack gives law enforcement more time to detect a plot or penetrate the organization (suicide operations in particular have a limited shelf life). Al Qaeda can at times be patient, as they demonstrated in Yemen in the year 2000, waiting until a U.S. warship returned to the port of Aden to attack it with a boat bomb. After the first attempt in January of that year failed, they reassembled their bomb and waited until October to hit the USS *Cole* as it came into the harbor. But they didn't wait a day longer than necessary. They didn't wait for a special date, and they were under some pressure from the central leadership of al Qaeda to expedite the attack (as was Mohamed Atta prior to the 9/11 attacks).

Al Qaeda is feeling the heat for its inaction, as evidenced by the group's partnership with now-deceased Jordanian terrorist Abu Musab al-Zarqawi. When bin Laden and his deputy, Ayman al-Zawahiri, forged an awkward operational alliance with Zarqawi in late 2004 it was merely a marriage of convenience. The thuggish Zarqawi, leader of an obscure, small-time insurgent group in Iraq called Tawhid and Jihad, was looking for international stature. Bin Laden and Zawahiri were desperate to link al Qaeda with somebody who was actually killing Americans, something they'd failed to do with any success since they were chased out of Afghanistan in November 2001.

I still fully expect al Qaeda to attack us again in the United States, perhaps even before this book hits the bookstores. But that won't diminish the fact that they've had great difficulty operating here since 9/11, and it's very important to keep this in perspective when they do hit again. Although an attack may be inevitable if not imminent, it doesn't have to be a major attack or a sustained campaign. If we remain focused and smart, we can minimize al Qaeda's capability. This should be our primary goal. Promises to completely eradicate the threat are not only unrealistic, they set up false expectations and increase the likelihood of an overreaction if al Qaeda does slip through the cracks.

America Sleeps Before 9/11

August 7, 1998, doesn't strike the average American as a day of infamy the way September 11, 2001, does, but in counterterrorism (CT) circles it is known as the day al Qaeda attacked not one but two American embassies in East Africa. At the time, I was working in the State Department in the office that handled UN peacekeeping, including the Balkans. I was in Rome on August 7 attending the wedding of my friend Jamie Rubin, the spokesman for Secretary of State Madeleine Albright, to award-winning international CNN correspondent Christiane Amanpour. The wedding came during the middle of an assignment I was working in Sarajevo concerning the latest Balkan crisis, and was a welcome diversion from that grim task. Ambassador Richard Holbrooke, the special envoy to the Balkans and architect of the Dayton agreement on Bosnia, was also attending. He was surrounded by administration officials, journalists, and other luminaries as they discussed the most dominant crises du jour.

At that time, terrorism was usually considered a backwater issue that would burst onto the scene every few years and then reliably fade back into the second tier of national security issues. "Real" foreign policy experts and intelligence professionals were focused on the big players and hot issues: Russia, European affairs, the Middle East peace crisis, and China. The Pentagon has always been focused on fighting and winning the nation's big wars. At the time terrorism, insurgency, and "low-intensity conflict" were seen as distractions from this principal mission. In Congress, terrorism was handled by a few members in the highly compartmentalized intelligence committee—inside baseball for a small subset of the Washington scene. Moreover, terrorism offered scant opportunities for congressional pork—there were no huge counterterrorism factories or military bases. The private sector also failed to take much notice. For national security officials and their friends in the mammoth defense companies, counterterrorism meant handfuls of Special Forces and intelligence operatives, not huge contracts and billion-dollar programs. Al Qaeda and Osama bin Laden were known to only a few, some of whom were with me at the Rubin-Amanpour wedding that fateful day.

As word spread through the cocktail party that there'd been an attack on our embassies in Kenya and Tanzania, nobody really knew what to make of it. Secretary Albright, who'd just landed at Rome International Airport on her way to the wedding, immediately returned to Washington to handle the embassy crisis. I knew my friend and former boss Richard Clarke would also be very busy at the White House sorting out a response with his small group of terrorism experts in Washington. I was shocked and angry like everyone else, but since I was working on the Balkans, I was instructed to continue my mission to Sarajevo. At that time, I had no idea that this attack would bring me back into the world of counterterrorism, which I'd entered eighteen years prior as a Green Beret during the Iran hostage crisis.

The embassy attack was well coordinated and devastating. Two U.S. outposts—in Nairobi, Kenya, and Dar es Salaam, Tanzania—had been blasted by massive truck bombs. This wasn't a new phenomenon; a U.S. Air Force barracks in Saudi Arabia had been bombed only two years before by local Hezbollah agents with Iranian support. However, the East African attacks were against an official but *civilian* target. Due to bungling on the part of several of the terrorist operatives immediately before and after the attack, it was determined within days that this plot was the handiwork of an organization, little known outside of the intelligence community, called al Qaeda.

When I returned from the Balkans about ten days later, Secretary Albright called me up to her seventh-floor office and told me she wanted me to take over as the State Department's Coordinator for Counterterrorism, but she was getting resistance from some on her senior staff. As a relatively young former army colonel—I was forty-three at the time—I didn't fit the typical profile. This was an ambassador-rank post traditionally held by seasoned gray-haired diplomats with extensive Middle East experience, and there was strong support within the building to keep it that way. Secretary Albright, with the support of Jamie Rubin and Richard Clarke at the White House, persevered against the tide, and I began work in the fall of 1998. Since my appointment, the trend of appointing nondiplomats has been sustained, as my successors have been a retired Air Force general with an intelligence background, two career CIA officers, and a three-star Special Forces general.

The East African embassy bombings kicked up a flurry of interest in counterterrorism, and the former chairman of the Joint Chiefs of Staff, Admiral William Crowe, was appointed to examine what went wrong. Unfortunately, like previous and subsequent reports prior to 9/11, the response to these attacks was basically defensive. The U.S. government posed the question "How can we keep bombers away from our barracks or embassies?" instead of "How can we crush the terrorists' capability to organize these attacks?" Admiral Crowe recommended that the State Department invest $10 billion to harden our embassies against terrorist bomb attacks.[1] But over time the embassy bombings faded from public memory, and counterterrorism once again fell several notches on the government's agenda. America simply shook off the nightmare of August 7 and went back to sleep. It is important to understand the depth of our slumber, for it sheds light on the shocking awakening we experienced in the aftermath of 9/11.

To describe that slumber, let me take you forward to the fall of 2000, as the presidential election of that year was drawing to its conclusion. It was October 17, and Vice President Al Gore and Governor George W. Bush were about to begin their third and final debate. I had friends working on both campaigns and I was invited to attend "debate parties" by both Republicans and Democrats. But I was feeling tired and decided to watch at home, alone. I was eager to see what both candidates would say about al Qaeda and the threat of terrorism. Just five days earlier, a U.S. warship, the USS *Cole,* had been hit by a boat bomb in the port of Aden, Yemen. Seventeen sailors were killed and a billion-dollar warship was almost sunk. As Gore and Bush squared off at the debate, the *Cole* was still smoking in the harbor in Aden and the bodies of those young sailors weren't even buried yet.

The debate was held at Washington University in St. Louis, Missouri, and was moderated by the veteran correspondent Jim Lehrer. Lehrer opened the debate with a reference to the plane crash and death of Governor Mel Carnahan of Missouri the day before. Lehrer offered a moment of silence in Carnahan's honor. *Nothing on the seventeen sailors,* I thought with a twinge of dismay. Vice President Gore opened his prepared remarks by mentioning Governor Carnahan and "the families" of those sailors who were killed on the USS *Cole* five days earlier. *A little bit better,* I thought, *but what about al Qaeda?* Gore quickly shifted his attention to the issue of health care. When Governor Bush's turn to speak came, Bush said something like "God's blessing on the families whose lives were overturned . . . last night." He did not make a single mention of the *Cole.*[2]

The debate then shifted to questions from the audience. The first question referred to the Middle East. Bush answered first, asserting that we must have a "strong vision" and that Saddam Hussein was still a threat in the Middle East, that our "coalition must be strong," and that the man "may be developing weapons of mass destruction." Gore responded, touting his wartime service in Vietnam and sharing how he'd learned about nonproliferation and terrorism as a member of the Senate Intelligence Committee. Gore then reiterated his support for the first Persian Gulf War and reminded us of his eight years as a member of the National Security Council under President Clinton. Terrorism was mentioned in passing, but not a word was spoken about the *Cole,* not a word about al Qaeda, by either candidate.[3]

The next question pertained to our military. Gore spoke about his commitment to keep the military strong, celebrating the fact that we had not lost a soldier in Kosovo and pointing out that he'd be asking for a larger increase in the military budget than Governor Bush would. Governor Bush responded by saying that our military missions must be clear: "Soldiers must understand why we're going. The force must be strong enough so that the mission can be accomplished. And the exit strategy needs to be well defined. I'm concerned that we're overdeployed around the world. . . . I think the mission has somewhat become fuzzy. . . . There may be some moments when we use our troops as peacekeepers, but not often."[4] And that was the end of the discussion of foreign policy issues.

The audience then asked the candidates about handguns, family farms, taxes, Hollywood morality, Social Security, affirmative action, taxes, the death penalty, and political promises. But the closing statements, prepared and rehearsed, were still to come: another chance to address the attack that had occurred just five days before (not to mention the embassies that had been hit two years earlier). However, the debate ended without any discussion of the growing threat of terrorism. In contrast, it would be virtually impossible to quell the response today if one of our warships was almost sunk by a terrorist attack. But in October 2000, just eleven months before 9/11, terrorism wasn't an important issue to either candidate, nor to the press, nor to the public asking the questions.

Whenever I hear partisan rancor and see post-9/11 finger-pointing, I think back to this debate and remember that the entire country was asleep to the threat. You can search the record;

terrorism wasn't discussed by the mainstream press and policy analysts even *after* the debate, when they'd had time to reflect on its content. Terrorism was simply not part of the campaign discussion. During his last months in office President Clinton was focused on the ultimately unsuccessful Camp David peace process between the Israelis and the Palestinians. After the November 8 election, less than a month after the *Cole* attack, President-elect Bush began preparing for what he thought would be a domestic presidency.

The irony is, it wasn't necessary to have had a secret intelligence briefing in order to know about al Qaeda. All the relevant facts were in the public record. The news networks had covered the *Cole* attack extensively; it dominated the networks for about three days. A smoking, listing ship appeared on every news channel. Bin Laden's fatwas calling for attacks against America were also covered heavily. CNN's Peter Bergen and ABC's John Miller, two outstanding and brave journalists, personally interviewed bin Laden, in March 1997 and May 1998, respectively. I got to know both these individuals during my tenure at State, and I thought their interviews were illuminating. The East African bombings had been equally well reported, and by January 2001 it was very clear that the *Cole* was an al Qaeda attack. But nobody seemed to notice. These events were just too far away and easily forgotten, perhaps deemed a cost of doing business in a dangerous world.

September 11: The Rude Awakening

Terrorism remained off the public agenda during the transition from the Clinton presidency to the Gore campaign and during the first eight months of the Bush administration. We know that the Bush cabinet didn't meet on the issue until after the attack. Although they claimed to be moving on the Afghan-Taliban issue, nobody was contemplating an invasion and nothing significant was likely to come of any of these initiatives. I doubt that a Gore administration would have acted much differently. Prior to 9/11 there was simply no national will to attack Afghanistan, and even less inclination to invade the country and take it over. Even under the most dramatic scenario, had I remained ambassador for counterterrorism and been able to convince either president that we had to take down the Taliban in 2001, it probably wouldn't have prevented the Atta team from launching their attacks on September 11. Atta was already deployed and his team was self-sufficient. What might have made a difference was a higher FBI awareness and tighter airport security.

I've been over that horrible day thousands of times in my head. I was in New York City on 9/11, no longer actively working on a counterterrorism team, but rather at the United Nations as an assistant secretary general in the Department of Peacekeeping Operations. I first heard about the attack from my brother, who called to tell me he'd be delayed on his trip into New York City that morning because a small plane had crashed into the Trade Center. I didn't think much of it; I was busy preparing for my morning meeting. But when the second plane hit, I knew immediately that the worst nightmares of the counterterrorism community had been realized and al Qaeda fingerprints were all over the place. A family member (my mother's cousin) and a friend of mine (former FBI official John O'Neill) were killed on that terrible day. O'Neill died in the World Trade Center and my mother's cousin was one of the courageous civilians on board Flight 93—the first Americans to strike back at al Qaeda as they sacrificed their lives to bring that plane down in a field in Pennsylvania. I was stunned yet emboldened by the courage of those and other Americans that day. As news of the attacks spread across the nation, America was jolted from its slumber like a sleeping giant awakened by a wasp sting in the eye. In a rage filled with anger and fear, America leapt up from its state of denial, thrashing wildly at enemies real and imagined. For me, the fight against terrorism had become even more personal.

Most Americans had no knowledge of these people called "al Qaeda." If we'd known the name, we might have recognized 9/11 as part of a continuum. President Bush, New York City mayor Rudolph Giuliani, the press, and many members of Congress acted as if this were the first attack on the United States, not to mention New York City. They asserted that this was the beginning of the global war on terrorism. Of course it wasn't. But this was the first time that the terrorists had struck us at home and caused destruction on such a deadly scale. Quickly, pressing questions arose: Was this organization really different from the one that had been attacking us for the past three years? How good were they? Had they somehow become the equivalent of Nazi Germany and imperial Japan in the late 1930s? Or were they that same small, determined, and somewhat incompetent group of killers that had attacked us in East Africa and Yemen?

In seeking answers to those questions, I looked to my long association with Special Forces sergeants and NYPD detectives. Not surprisingly, these two groups have a lot in common. They're smart, dedicated professionals with some formal education and a whole lot of street smarts. They're both at the cutting edge of their professions. They're confident in their expertise, and like professional athletes at the top of their game, they have a certain swagger. They also share a great sense of humor and a quiet knowledge of their own limitations. They understand their foe, enemy guerrillas for the Special Forces troopers and the street criminal for the detectives. They learn to never underestimate the cunning and potential lethality of their enemy—but they also appreciate the limitations of their adversary in the same way they understand their own shortcomings. Both Special Forces sergeants and NYPD detectives live by the old maxim "Thank God our opponents are dumber than we are—or we'd be in real trouble."

Lessons from the Front

First, the bad news: terrorists, like criminals, can be cunning and lethal—and they occasionally show signs of brilliance. The good news is that most are not especially bright. They're not the "wise guys" depicted in movies such as *The Godfather,* nor are they evil masterminds like so many other Hollywood villains. They're most often of above-average intelligence, with a penchant for cunning and ruthlessness, but they're generally not geniuses.

I first learned of this dichotomy in El Salvador when I was deployed to Central America as an Army Special Forces captain in August of 1985. Only two months before, six Marines had been brutally gunned down in the streets of the capital, San Salvador. When I arrived there shortly after the shooting, everyone was on pins and needles. New rules restricted the movement of the soldiers in the city. Special Forces soldiers still went to restaurants, but we stayed away from the usual areas and sat with our backs to the wall, armed to the teeth. I, like my partner, Sergeant First Class Juan Gonzalez, carried a .45 caliber pistol locked and cocked inside a European-style man's purse. In the machismo culture of the Special Forces, carrying a purse was a cause for endless ribbing, but I figured it wasn't a matter of whether the gunmen would strike again, but when and where. There were plenty of guerrillas and they had plenty of capability. It seemed like an easy equation. But, in fact, it wasn't. Much to our surprise, the guerrillas never replicated that assault in the next six years of the war.

Six months after I returned from my one-year tour, though, the base where I'd been stationed was overrun by guerrillas in a nighttime raid. One of my replacements in the brigade compound where I served, Staff Sergeant Gregory "Red" Fronius, was killed in the attack. And then four years later, when many thought the war was winding down, the guerrillas mounted a massive counterattack that rocked the country, as well as America's confidence, that this resilient foe could be defeated.

El Salvador taught me a few enduring lessons. Although the guerrillas seemed largely incapable of picking off the easiest targets—American soldiers sitting in a few hotels in central San Salvador, for example—they remained lethal on other fronts. Guerrilla warfare, not unlike terrorist activity, may be intermittent and protracted. Defending against both requires a long-term commitment and concentrated focus.

Al Qaeda's Modus Operandi

Al Qaeda has a clear modus operandi (MO). Even as it evolves as an organization, its key methodology remains fairly consistent. Early in my tenure at NYPD, we embarked on an intensive study of al Qaeda, starting with the history of their operations and a detailed analysis of their MO. One of the first things I did was revamp the intelligence analysis shop. Commissioner Kelly had recommended that Dave Cohen and I hire civilian analysts from the best schools in the country and team them with our detectives. And so we hired some of the best young talent available. We then tracked the development of al Qaeda's ideology, operations, and recruiting patterns around the world, including, of course, in New York City. We worked very hard to understand both the consistency and adaptability of the organization, bringing our newfound knowledge to every policy and program we developed and implemented.

Al Qaeda's operational method wasn't a mystery to us. They generally used two types of bombs: big truck bombs against major buildings (such as those used on our embassies in East Africa) or smaller multiple backpack bombs used in enclosed areas (as in the train attacks in London and Spain). NYPD analysts studied years of terrorist MO to develop a clear assessment of what types of attacks we might anticipate. We prepared to respond to the types of attacks the terrorists had executed repeatedly for years, always keeping in mind that they might try something new and original.

One of the most effective ways to determine the strengths and weaknesses of a terrorist group such as al Qaeda is to closely examine their past attacks and plots. Al Qaeda has a long track record of successful and unsuccessful strikes against Western targets, and this history contains clues to their preferred modes of attack, their operational improvement or regression, their recruitment strategies, and, in the case of unsuccessful attacks, their undoing. Learn the history and maybe, just maybe, you'll figure out a way to prevent future attacks.

The First WTC Attack: An Ominous Foreshadowing

The first World Trade Center attack was conducted on February 26, 1993, by a group of men who were, in fact, precursors to the formal al Qaeda organization, which was still taking shape in Afghanistan. The architect of the plot was Ramzi Yousef, the nephew of Khalid Sheikh Mohammed, who would later plan and conduct the 9/11 attack. While neither Yousef nor Mohammed was formally tied to al Qaeda, they were both part of a growing ideological network, which included bin Laden and others in and out of Afghanistan. Fortunately, the first World Trade Center attack was another amateur operation. Yet, against a sleeping enemy, they were capable of delivering a deadly and devastating blow. The enormous blast of that attack cost six people their lives and wounded another thousand. But at the same time, the incompetence and downright idiocy of the attack's so-called masterminds demonstrated an organizational weakness and inability to sustain operations, deficiencies that later would come to characterize the mature al Qaeda.

The big blunder of the first attack on the World Trade Center is legendary: the renters of the Ryder truck that carried the explosives actually went back to the rental center to pick up their deposit, claiming the truck had been stolen. Their almost comical stupidity led to the full disclosure of the plot's origins, which allowed the prevention of a follow-up attack in New York City that year, and eventually contributed to the arrest of Yousef in 1995.

Yousef, a Pakistani raised in Kuwait, had partnered with a Palestinian from Jordan in his plan to terrorize New York City. Filled with more political hatred than religious ideology, Yousef used timed fuse detonators (no suicide bomber here) and a thousand pounds of urea nitrate with nitroglycerin to boost the blast.[5] The attack was successful, but it fell far short of its desired effect. Yousef later complained that he didn't have enough money to buy more ammonium nitrate to make a bigger bomb, which could have threatened the integrity of the load-bearing columns of the north tower.[6] Yousef's whining is either a reflection of extremely poor planning or a cop-out, because another four thousand pounds of fertilizer would only cost about $10,000, and although it isn't clear what that size bomb would have done to the tower, it could have been devastating. A few years later, Timothy McVeigh, no genius himself, was able to put together a five-thousand-pound bomb made of fertilizer to attack the Murrah Federal Building in Oklahoma City. If Yousef had been equally equipped, the north tower might have come down in 1993.

Al Qaeda Comes Out: The East African Bombings

The attacks al Qaeda launched against our embassies in East Africa demonstrated strengths and weaknesses that still characterize the organization today. The embassy plot was a major success for al Qaeda. It was their first attack since they openly declared war against the United States earlier in the year in their February 1998 fatwa.[7] Two American embassies were hit virtually simultaneously, killing 224 people and injuring almost 5,000. The coordination of the two attacks by an organization isolated in the mountains of Afghanistan demonstrated a strategic reach previously unforeseen. Al Qaeda showed patience, for it's clear today that planning for this attack began prior to 1995, during the U.S. intervention in Somalia. But the perpetrators were bunglers nonetheless. My first understanding of their limitations came shortly after the attack as reports of the plot passed through FBI channels. The attackers, although successful, had made glaring mistakes before, during, and after the attack. These errors warrant close scrutiny.

In Nairobi, the attack plan was to force the embassy guards to lower the gate, at which point the bomb truck would be driven down to the basement parking area of the embassy. An underground detonation would likely cause a catastrophic collapse of the building—or "pancaking" of the floors—as the load-bearing columns were shattered. This type of collapse had been achieved by Hezbollah bombers in Beirut in 1983, when a determined truck bomber crashed through the gate of the barracks while under fire, penetrating the underside of the building. The collapse of that building resulted in the death of more than two hundred Marines. But the al Qaeda attackers in Nairobi weren't of the same caliber as the Beirut bombers.

On the morning of August 7, 1998, Mohamed Rashed Daoud al-Owhali, a Saudi also known as Khalid Salim, put a pistol into his jacket and hopped into the bomb truck with Mohammed Saddiq Odeh (aka Abdull Bast Awadh), also from Saudi Arabia. Owhali's job was to get out of the truck and force the sentry at the American embassy to raise the gate, but Owhali bungled it when he jumped out and left his weapon on the front seat. When the guard didn't lower the gate, Owhali didn't have a weapon to force him to do so, nor was he capable of killing the guard and lowering the gate himself. Instead, he threw a stun grenade, similar to a large firecracker, on the ground and ran off. Unfortunately, the bang attracted some attention, and when the driver detonated the truck, some of those who'd gathered were killed in the blast. The truck exploded outside of the embassy and took the face off one side of the building, causing much damage to adjacent buildings. But the embassy building itself didn't collapse, sparing the life of the ambassador and dozens of others. Although destructive, the attack didn't go off as planned. It was bungled by the would-be suicide bomber who ran away from the truck at the last minute with no money, no passport, and no plan for escaping Kenya.

In Dar es Salaam, the attackers ran into even more problems. Here, the truck wasn't able to get past a wall surrounding the embassy and the blast was detonated outside of the grounds, again causing significant damage to one side of the embassy, but failing to destroy the building. In that attack, surprisingly, no Americans were killed and only seventeen Africans died. After the attacks, al Qaeda's incompetence continued. Odeh was arrested attempting to get into Pakistan. Under interrogation at the airport he quickly admitted his involvement. Perhaps he was naive and thought his questioner, who was also Islamic, would be sympathetic. In any case, his arrest led to the quick unraveling of the entire cell and the arrest of many others.[8]

The East African attacks represented the international "coming out" of al Qaeda, six months after bin Laden's fatwa condemning the United States. The attacks demonstrated al Qaeda's brutal lethality and ability to project two simultaneous attacks across continents. Again, despite poor tradecraft, the teams were largely successful with their attacks (although they failed to get inside the compounds or underneath the parking garages, as originally intended). In this plot, al Qaeda demonstrated a preference for official targets and a penchant for long-term planning. (The concept had been in the works for at least four to five years, and the operational planners had spent several months preparing the final details.) Lesson learned—but, unfortunately, too late to thwart that attack. Even though American intelligence had received a foreshadowing of the plot from an embassy walk-in source, once again we were asleep when the bombers struck.

Bungler at the Border: Ressam and the Millennium Plot

In late 1999, as the world approached the beginning of a new millennium, computer experts were concerned that we might have a global computer failure as the machines' internal clocks reached the date of January 1, 2000—or "passing 00-00-00" in numeric code. This code and the coming of the new millennium were labeled "Y2K" (year 2000) by the computer security community. The counterterrorism community was also picking up unusual chatter associated with the major events marking the millennium. This time, I thought, the chatter might actually have some correlation to an increase in terrorist activity.

In mid-December 1999, just a few weeks before the celebration was to begin, an Algerian-born militant associated with several radical cells in Montreal, Canada, attempted to smuggle explosives into the United States. Ahmed Ressam had trained in Afghanistan, was in contact with al Qaeda, and was connected to the Algerian-based Salafist Group for Preaching and Combat (GSPC). Ressam seemed like a pretty well-connected terrorist, but he too was a bungler. With big plans to strike the United States, Ressam packed the trunk of his rental car with several hundred pounds of explosive materials and drove it to Victoria, Canada. Officers with the United States Immigration and Naturalization Service allowed him and his vehicle to board a ferry to Port Angeles, Washington, a major point of entry to the United States. He arrived on American soil on December 14, 1999.

Unfortunately for Ressam, the Port Angeles border crossing is relatively quiet during the winter months compared to the bustling summer tourist season. He was also unlucky to run into alert customs inspector Diana Dean, who thought Ressam seemed nervous and sent him to a secondary inspection location. When the secondary inspection began, Ressam panicked, ran, and was apprehended by customs agents. Although the identity of Ressam's target was initially unclear, it was later discovered that he'd been on his way to California to bomb Los Angeles International Airport. Had he been a better planner, he might have carried the explosives across the border on foot at a remote area, crossed the border with a clean vehicle, and circled around to pick up his payload. Driving through the checkpoints was unnecessary, although he probably would have made it through undetected if he'd been a bit cooler under pressure.

Deadly Bunglers in a Boston Whaler: The USS Cole *Attack*

On October 12, 2000, the USS *Cole* was attacked by al Qaeda in the port of Aden, Yemen. The plan was hatched by a Saudi al Qaeda operative and longtime associate of bin Laden, Abd al Rahim al Nashiri. He was successful only because he struck a sleeping giant—in this case, the U.S. Navy. But al Qaeda demonstrated a startling degree of incompetence before, during, and after the attack. For starters, the plot was originally set to strike the USS *The Sullivans* on January 3, 2000. (This could have been part of the millennium chatter, but even now I'm not sure.) However, as the boat-bomb was launched into the port of Aden to attack *The Sullivans,* it sank under the weight of the explosives it carried. The next day the disappointed terrorists sheepishly fished their Boston Whaler out of the water with a winch, rebalanced their load, and waited until another U.S. ship sailed into the harbor, nine months later.

On the morning of October 12, 2000, the USS *Cole* entered the port of Aden for a routine fuel stop. While the *Cole* was refueling at about 11:00 A.M., a small boat with two men aboard floated into the harbor and slowly approached the American warship. A few sailors casually noted their approach, assuming they were local boatmen checking out the enormous ship. Even if the crew on watch had suspected that the little boat was a hazard, Navy rules of engagement dictated that the *Cole* not fire unless first fired upon. As the boat-bomb pulled up alongside the ship, one of its passengers stood up as if to salute the ship, detonated the bomb, and blasted an enormous forty-by-forty-foot hole in the *Cole*'s hull.[9] Either by pure luck, great ship design, or the grace of God, the ship's massive weapons magazine and its fuel storage didn't ignite or explode. Nevertheless, seventeen members of the crew were killed and thirty-nine more were injured, and the rest worked furiously well into the evening to prevent the ship from sinking. The *Cole* had to be towed across the Atlantic, finally reaching a Navy shipyard in Mississippi on Christmas Eve of 2000.

A billion-dollar warship had been crippled by two men in a Boston Whaler, but the al Qaeda operative who was assigned the job of videotaping the blast, capturing images that would be of huge value in advancing the attack's psychological damage, dozed off and missed the moment.

To sum up, despite al Qaeda's successes, every time a cell launches a strike it reminds us of who they really are. Al Qaeda can be very effective killers, as they demonstrated with three attacks in a three-year period between 1998 and 2001. But, at the same time, they've exposed themselves as a loosely bound assembly of incompetent bunglers. It is important to see the organization from both angles, because understanding their strengths and weaknesses is the key to defeating them in detail.

Post-9/11 Attacks: Al Qaeda Under Pressure

After September 11, al Qaeda was thrown off balance by the rapid success of the U.S. invasion of Afghanistan, particularly by the powerful collaboration of tribal militias and U.S. Special Forces teams. Al Qaeda's central leadership "went to ground"—a term used by intelligence operatives to indicate that a target isn't only hiding but also curtailing any activity that might give up their position. Many midlevel leaders were also killed or captured. Nevertheless, al Qaeda operations actually picked up pace for about two years after 9/11, almost exclusively in the Islamic world, executed by a variety of affiliate cells with varying degrees of connectivity to the central leadership.

The first of these attacks was conducted by Riduan Isamuddin, an al Qaeda commander in Indonesia who went by the nom de guerre Hambali. He'd been sent by Osama bin Laden to Indonesia to build the organization and carry out operations from cells based there. Hambali linked up with locals of similar ideology, mainly centered on the radical cleric Abu Bakar Bashir. The organization, Jemaah Islamiyah, became an al Qaeda subsidiary. On October 12, 2002, a little over one year after 9/11, al Qaeda struck in Bali, Indonesia. This attack would show al Qaeda's continued strength, but it also demonstrated some of the post-9/11 weaknesses that would plague the organization for the next five years. In Bali, as in most attacks overseas, most of the people killed were locals, many of them Muslims.

In the West, al Qaeda also tried to keep up the momentum of their attacks. And they were able to do so, but only twice in the six years after 9/11: in Madrid on March 11, 2004, and in London on July 7, 2005. In both cases, terrorist operatives hit countries that were asleep to the al Qaeda threat, thinking it was "an American problem."

Interestingly, both Spain and the United Kingdom had built a robust counterterrorism capability, but they were largely focused on the Basque separatists and the Irish Republican Army, respectively.

The Spanish and British terrorists had a few key traits in common. Unlike the imported hit men of 9/11, these terrorists were homegrown residents of their target countries. In the case of the United Kingdom, the plotters were born and raised as citizens of England. They also used backpack bombs built in urban labs, which they detonated in crowded passenger trains. Both operations had links to the central al Qaeda operation (although in Spain the link isn't as clear or direct). In both cases an energized national security service began to round up residual capability. To date there hasn't been a repeat in Spain or in Great Britain, although there were a few close calls in both countries right after the attacks.

Sleeping Giants Make Good Targets

So how do these bunglers wreak so much havoc? Quite simply, they're deadly killers when they're able to operate in areas where nobody is paying attention. If you are asleep, you are an easy target. We know they've been fairly active in the Islamic world, particularly in areas of raging insurgency such as Iraq and Afghanistan. But almost without exception, they've had difficulty sustaining operations in countries that turn the full force of their intelligence apparatus against them. Most countries, including the United States, think they're immune from terrorism until an attack actually happens to them. Then they wake up to the presence of extremists within their communities, crack down, and generally put them out of business—for a while, at least.

Although al Qaeda has expressed interest in obtaining a weapon of mass destruction, they've not been able to do so. Almost all of their attacks have been carried out with improvised explosives, either truck bombs or backpack bombs. Periodically, a cell will turn to the reliable AK-47, the weapon used in a deadly attack in the tourist town of Luxor, Egypt, in November 1997 that killed sixty-two people, and also in a foiled 2007 plot to attack U.S. military personnel at New Jersey's Fort Dix Army installation. In insurgent areas kidnappings and beheadings are also common methods of attack. But improvised high explosives are still the weapon of choice. The terrorists use truck bombs when they can, because of the devastating power of the blast. If they can't make that big a bomb, they'll use backpack bombs and position them in enclosed areas such as trains or subways to maximize damage and terrorize users of public transportation.

Although al Qaeda has been relatively quiet in the West, we must never rest in our resolve to crush them. Al Qaeda is different from most other terrorist organizations of the past fifty years. Osama bin Laden has created an organization with a coherent ideology, a global reach, and a unified desire to maximize civilian casualties. Members show no compunction about killing innocents in large numbers. They seek to acquire weapons of mass destruction—and if they get them, they'll use them. The organization is small, but it springs from a much broader movement with deep roots in Sunni extremist movements around the world. Al Qaeda and other groups associated with this movement will pose a significant strategic threat to the United States for at least another generation. We must stay awake and keep watch for this threat for a period of decades, even if they only attack us intermittently.

Chapter 2

Know Your Enemies

New York City has had a long history of people plotting and conducting terrorist attacks within the city limits, before and after 9/11. As head of the counterterrorism office at NYPD, I knew that if we were to effectively protect the city, we'd need to know who these people were and what motivated them. We'd need to identify ideological themes that could tip us off to a predilection toward this kind of violence. To this end, we set out to gain a detailed understanding of radical Islamic movements, including their antecedents and current variants. Rather than fulfilling some lofty academic objective, we followed a basic tenet of any military or police work: *know your enemies.* This makes perfect sense to a good soldier or cop. And the detectives in counterterrorism were among NYPD's finest cops. They came from a cross section of investigative squads, including those dealing with narcotics, gangs, organized crime, homicide, vice, robbery, and every other form of mayhem. These guys knew the criminal element on the street as well as they knew their own partners. We tried to adapt this mind-set to our understanding of modern terrorism as we set some of the world's greatest detectives on the trail of the world's most notorious terrorists.

Who Are the Terrorists?

During the early morning rush hour on July 7, 2005, Mohammad Sidique Khan (known as MSK by the counterterrorism community) led a group of suicide bombers into the subway system in London, England. The four killers were British citizens from Leeds, an industrial city about 180 miles north of London. They'd traveled down to London from Leeds that morning by train and transferred into the subway system on the outskirts of the city. Three of the men were second-generation Pakistanis, born and raised in the United Kingdom. The fourth bomber was a Jamaican British convert with an African American father and a Jamaican mother. Each carried a backpack of improvised explosives that had been processed in their makeshift lab in an apartment in Leeds. At 8:50 in the morning, three of the bombs exploded in three different trains within fifty seconds of one another. The fourth bomb, due to unforeseen difficulties, exploded on a bus almost an hour later. Unlike the Madrid bombings a year earlier, this was a suicide mission. The killers brought fifty-two Londoners to their deaths alongside them. Seven hundred more were wounded.

MSK and his homegrown crews of suicide bombers caused much speculation about the origins, motivations, and methods of the next wave of radical Islamic terrorists. About a year after the attack, I sat on a panel gathered to discuss the new al Qaeda threat of homegrown terrorists. The event was hosted by the New York University Center for Law and Security. The homegrown phenomenon was the subject of many terrorist conferences around the world in the wake of the Madrid and London train bombings. Both attacks were conducted by local citizens, in contrast to the September 11 attacks, where Mohamed Atta and his crew, in a very real sense, invaded the United States and conducted a mission that effectively declared war on a foreign nation. The Madrid and London terrorists, however, were either native-born or long-term, seemingly normal residents of their respective countries. This fundamental difference sparked great concern and speculation in academia and throughout the CT community.

As is often the case in these conferences, many "experts" blamed the attack on social ills and lamented the failure of second-generation immigrants to become fully integrated into their societies. Especially in Europe, but to a certain degree in the United States, some academics assumed that these young-men-turned-killers were disenfranchised from their societies, making them easy prey for jihadi ideologues preaching hate. This explanation may have been true in other scenarios, but it simply didn't track with my understanding of the London and Madrid bombers.

I listened patiently to these well-meaning critiques as my fellow panelists outlined the many failings of Western society. After all, why else would these people attack us? Something must be wrong—with us! The academic consensus was that these terrorists were a product of European class structure and racism, and that their afflictions were further aggravated by horrific American foreign policies in Iraq and the Middle East. The approach of this panel was very familiar terrain for me, as American foreign policy has been the punching bag of universities around the world for at least as long as I can remember. But the longer I listened, the more I realized that most of these "experts" had only a superficial knowledge of the actual people who perpetrated the attacks. They'd studied the latest polling numbers on dissatisfaction with American policy in Iraq and knew of the relative poverty among immigrants in Europe, and from this knowledge base they formed conclusions about why terrorists kill. Although I'm no social scientist and no apologist for American foreign policy, and I concur that Europe—and to a lesser extent the United States—should do a lot more in terms of reaching out to their new populations, as I listened to my fellow panelists' arguments I became increasingly aware that all of this had very little to do with the current case. My temper simmered at a low boil until it was my time to speak. Throwing away my prepared remarks, I launched into a bit of a rant.

"Mohammad Sidique Khan wasn't disenfranchised," I began. "MSK was born and raised in one of the finest democracies in the world, the United Kingdom. He was happily married, he had a young child, and his wife was pregnant with their second child. He worked in a public school as a teaching assistant for the children of new immigrants, a program designed to help promote their healthy assimilation. Although this wasn't a very high-paying job, it was one in which a society gives its highest level of trust. Regardless, the same thirty-one-year-old man who took part in the massacre of fifty-two British citizens had bounced five-year-old schoolchildren on his knee the day before he attacked. In the grand scheme of social oppression, do you consider this man truly disenfranchised?" I asked. "If so, by *this* standard, how many young men growing up in this world are *not* disenfranchised?"

But most angry young men don't blow themselves up on a crowded subway train.

"What about his principal accomplice, Shehzad Tanweer?" I continued. "Tanweer was the twenty-year-old son of a successful Leeds businessman. Tanweer's father had come to the United Kingdom from Pakistan to build a better life for himself and his children. And he succeeded. Tanweer grew up in a middle-class family and his friends described him as politically moderate. His best friend through most of his life was a fair-skinned local Leeds boy who lived across the street. Tanweer graduated from Wortley High School and worked in his father's restaurant while attending a local college. He was an excellent athlete who competed in cricket, triple jump, long-distance running, football, and jujitsu. He drove around town in a Mercedes provided for him by his father." I added a few chuckles to my rant when I told the panel, "I drive a Toyota Corolla. I hope I can be disenfranchised enough to get *me* a Mercedes someday."

Now, this isn't to say that minorities, especially those who are black- or brown-skinned, don't face serious racial and ethnic issues in the United States and Europe. And yes, the London bombers were likely enraged by American foreign policy in Iraq. But these young men had other options if they had felt truly disenfranchised. They could have resettled in Pakistan, for they had passports and travel money. Instead, they sought out al Qaeda and received further training and indoctrination in order to return to the United Kingdom and kill civilians for their cause. On MSK's last trip to Pakistan, he plotted an attack, made a suicide tape, and built the bombs that would be used to kill his crew and their fellow citizens. MSK and Tanweer had become terrorists via a methodical and steady radicalization over a period of seveal years. They were motivated by a powerful ideology with a religious underpinning and fierce political agenda, not by a sense of disenfranchisement.

Al Qaeda's Leadership: A Historic Union

We must look at al Qaeda's leadership—Osama bin Laden and his deputy Ayman al-Zawahiri—to understand the organization's religious and political justification. Bin Laden and Zawahiri are a historic combination. These two men, each quite limited on his own, joined in a political and personal partnership that spawned the terrorist organization al Qaeda. Without the two of them, there'd be no al Qaeda, no 9/11. Yet even today the importance of these two men is downplayed. U.S. policy toward bin Laden and Zawahiri has changed from a posture of "wanted dead or alive" immediately following 9/11 to vague statements that diminish the importance of these two mass murderers. Some terrorism experts downplay their significance by instead concentrating their attention on the local cells that have filled the void since the Afghanistan invasion forced the top al Qaeda leadership underground. Indeed, bin Laden and Zawahiri face serious operational limitations in the post-9/11 climate, but they're still out there motivating their adherents, supporting camps, and trying to piece together a global operational capability. We should know better than to ever underestimate them again.

The debate over the importance of bin Laden isn't new. I arrived at the State Department's Office of Counterterrorism in the fall of

1998 in the wake of the attack on our embassies in East Africa. One of the first controversies to hit my desk was a wanted poster created by the State Department's Office of Diplomatic Security calling for the arrest of bin Laden. It featured a large photo of bin Laden dressed in long white robes and carrying an AK-47. It was a flattering portrait of the terrorist, and some said it looked like a recruiting poster for al Qaeda. Others argued that the counterterrorism community was "hyping" bin Laden—and that the U.S. government was actually empowering bin Laden by acknowledging him. There'd been a chorus of criticism regarding the missile strikes launched against suspected al Qaeda sites in Sudan in response to the attacks on two U.S. embassies in Africa. Some went so far as to claim that it was those missed missile strikes, not the destruction of the embassies, that made bin Laden a folk hero in the Islamic world.

At the State Department, we took this criticism under consideration and changed the image on bin Laden's wanted poster to show a photo of the damaged U.S. embassy taken right after the explosion. I recognized then that although we didn't want to make him a movie star, we had to keep talking about bin Laden and al Qaeda to convince the American people that this man and his followers constituted a serious threat. I wasn't trying to inflame the situation—the last thing I wanted to do was self-terrorize our population. However, I became increasingly dismayed as I watched the initial outrage regarding the embassy attacks quickly fade within the administration, on Capitol Hill, and in the media.

The stories of Osama bin Laden and Ayman al-Zawahiri are well known. Perhaps the best writing on the subject to date is found in the book *The Looming Tower* by *New Yorker* journalist Lawrence Wright. I met Wright—like me, a fellow at the New York University Center for Law and Security—at a luncheon where he briefed us on the findings in his forthcoming book. I was impressed by the depth of his understanding of al Qaeda; he's clearly a great researcher and a gifted writer. In *The Looming Tower,* Wright describes how bin Laden and Zawahiri complemented each other perfectly, building a team from hell in pursuit of global terror against the enemies of Islam, primarily the United States.

Bin Laden and Zawahiri were both pious youths from elite families. Osama bin Laden is the only son of the tenth wife of Mohammed bin Laden, a self-made billionaire builder in Saudi Arabia who constructed some of the most important infrastructure in the country, including the national mosque in Mecca. Osama was an athletic young man who became increasingly radical as he sought his purpose in the Afghan jihad against the Soviet Union during the 1980s. Initially a supporter of the Afghan and Arab fighters, bin Laden later shifted gears and became the leader of a ragtag band of Arab fighters that weren't really taken seriously by their Afghan partners. The Afghans were focused on fighting for the future of Afghanistan; bin Laden's purpose was always grander.

Despite his rather questionable leadership on the battlefield, which is well documented by Wright, bin Laden built a reputation for himself during the Afghan war as a brave and stoic man. By turning away from the comfortable life of a billionaire and providing financial support to his early organization, bin Laden developed a loyal cadre of adherents to his nascent al Qaeda organization in the early 1990s.

Ayman al-Zawahiri, an Egyptian who was trained as a medical doctor, also came from a distinguished family. Zawahiri's career as a militant began in the radical Egyptian movements that opposed President Anwar Sadat, particularly the peace he made with Israel in 1979. When Sadat was assassinated in 1981, Zawahiri's fluency in English made him famous as the informal spokesman for a group of more than three hundred radicals who were rounded up and tried for their association with Sadat's killers. Zawahiri was imprisoned from 1981 to 1984 and was allegedly tortured mercilessly; he came out further radicalized by the experience. His mission to foment revolution and establish *sharia* law in Egypt led him to form the radical group Egyptian Islamic Jihad (EIJ). But Egyptian president Hosni Mubarak was taking no chances with the Islamic radicals that killed his predecessor, especially after several attacks were conducted in Egypt and an assassination attempt against him during his visit to Addis Ababa, Ethiopia, was thwarted in 1995. Mubarak cracked down brutally on the EIJ and the related group

Gama'at al-Islamiyya. Many of these groups' leaders were killed, jailed, or exiled. Zawahiri fled Egypt and eventually ended up in Afghanistan. There he became increasingly linked to the wealthy and quietly charismatic Osama bin Laden.

Another founding member of the movement was Omar Abdel Rahman, known as the "Blind Sheik." Like Zawahiri, he was also kicked out of Egypt, but instead of going to Afghanistan, he landed in the United States in 1990. He preached at a radical mosque in Brooklyn, New York, with ties to bin Laden and other radical mujahideen, and was at the center of the emerging al Qaeda in the United States. American officials naively thought these characters were still "political refugees from autocratic Arab states" or stray mujahideen whom we'd supported against the Soviets. But in reality, the Blind Sheik was building al Qaeda's religious foundation and promoting jihad through his anti-American radical sermons.

Bin Laden and Zawahiri were part of a growing radical fundamentalism that had been developing since the early 1980s, parallel to but separate from the Shia fundamentalist movement led by the revolutionary government of Iran. Bin Laden and Zawahiri took this radical and violent movement in a new and bolder direction—directly against the United States. Bin Laden's antipathy toward the United States was of long standing but grew incrementally in the early 1990s after George H. W. Bush launched the Gulf War to evict Saddam Hussein from Kuwait. Bin Laden's offer to the Saudi leadership to personally conduct a jihad against Saddam, rather than allow American infidels into the holy lands of Mecca and Medina, was rejected by the Saudis. His relationship with the ruling family deteriorated rapidly after this slap in the face, until he was finally cut off and stripped of his Saudi citizenship in 1995.

Upon returning to Afghanistan from Sudan, bin Laden again partnered with Zawahiri. Both were at low points in their careers, but still young and ambitious. Bin Laden had just been thrown out of Sudan, had lost most of his personal fortune, and was persona non grata in his own country, Saudi Arabia. Zawahiri was also effectively exiled from Egypt and the EIJ was in tatters. It seemed as if the two radicals had lost their grip on their respective Mideast revolutions. Together, however, they were able to rebuild a new venture to directly confront the American government. This was a great leap forward in the jihadi movement, bringing new focus to an old fight. Until then, most of the Sunni brand of Islamic radicalism was directed against the secular regimes in the Arab world, such as Egypt, or was focused on defensive jihad against outside incursions into Muslim lands, such as the Soviet invasion of Afghanistan. Taking it to America and targeting civilians there was a major new direction for these movements, completing their transition from insurgent groups to a new brand of international terrorism. By setting their sights on the United States, al Qaeda took jihad to the "far enemy," a phrase lifted from the Koran. In creating a religious justification for their mission, bin Laden and Zawahiri further stretched the tenets of Islam to include killing as part of a Muslim's duty.

But the desperate alliance of these two men and the preaching of a radical sheik wasn't enough to create the special circumstances that enabled al Qaeda to become a strategic threat to the United States. Their movement lacked a home base, a sanctuary from which to conduct their global operations. Both bin Laden and Zawahiri had been chased around the world and were under increasing pressure from various intelligence agencies, primarily Saudi, Egyptian, and American. But another person was about to enter the scene and become the final piece that completed the al Qaeda puzzle: Mullah Mohammed Omar.

Mullah Omar's Taliban: An Alliance of Convenience

The Soviet Union pulled its troops out of Afghanistan in 1989, but the puppet regime established by Moscow before they left showed surprising resiliency. They were still around five years later, fighting off a residual jihadi resistance made up of warlords vying for power in post-Soviet Afghanistan. This postwar chaos left Afghanistan in a state of ongoing poverty and violence with warlords tearing the country apart. Enter Mullah Mohammed Omar and the Taliban.

Mullah Omar was a veteran of the anti-Soviet jihad, in which he had lost an eye. In 1994, Omar organized a small group of *talibs* (students) from the radical Islamic *madrassas* (schools) that were in the Afghan refugee communities along the Afghanistan-Pakistan border. The Taliban, as they became known, promised a return to a strict interpretation of Islam, which appealed to many in this war-torn country that had been exhausted by the violence and debauchery of warlords. Afghanistan has two primary ethnicities in its population: the Pashtuns (about 42 percent) and the Tajiks (about 27 percent). Other important groups include the Hazaras (9 percent) and the Uzbeks (9 percent).[1] The Taliban are predominantly Pashtun, a tribe that extends across the border of Afghanistan and Pakistan and whom the Pakistanis had traditionally dominated in the multiethnic Afghan power struggle.

By 1994, both the Americans and Russians were long gone. The Taliban quickly consolidated control in their Pashtun stronghold in the southeast corner of the country and began moving north toward Kabul, the country's multiethnic capital. Bin Laden arrived in Afghanistan just as the Taliban were taking control of Kabul and extending their reach into bin Laden's new hometown, Jalalabad. Neither bin Laden nor Zawahiri knew Mullah Omar from their previous years in Afghanistan. However, they all shared a similar radical fundamentalism through which bin Laden quickly forged a relationship with the mullah.

Although little is known about Mullah Omar, and his personal relationship with bin Laden isn't well understood, these two men clearly became increasingly bound to each other's destiny. Bin Laden helped Omar in his goal of establishing full control of the country. Omar's remarkable march to power was assisted to some degree by the Pakistani army's intelligence service, the ISI. They supported him mostly because they saw him as the eventual winner and they wanted to back, and later influence, whoever was going to take charge of Afghanistan. To the great surprise of virtually everybody following the scene, including the Pakistanis (and perhaps even the Taliban themselves), Omar quickly consolidated control over most of Afghanistan. By 1997, the only remaining resistance to complete Taliban control of Afghanistan was the Northern Alliance, a band of Tajik warlords led by Ahmad Shah Massoud. Massoud, one of the most proficient of the Afghan military fighters in the campaign against the Soviets, was known as the "Lion of Panjshir," after the rugged mountainous terrain in northeast Afghanistan where he and his band of fighters maintained control of a small corner of the country. The Uzbek tribes, led by Abdul Rashid Dostum, were virtually chased out of Afghanistan (although you wouldn't get that impression from Dostum, who has returned to Afghanistan post-9/11 to reestablish himself as the predominant Uzbek warlord).

Though Massoud controlled only his small mountain redoubt in Panjshir, he did provide the only viable opposition to the Taliban and thus prevented the student radicals from gaining international recognition as the authorized government of Afghanistan. He received support from many sources, including the Russians and Americans, who kept his coffers filled and helped him ward off the Taliban in the north. Although nobody thought Massoud could ever seriously threaten the Taliban without massive assistance, he was certainly instrumental in preventing full Taliban control of Afghanistan. Dostum did little to resist the Taliban or help the Northern Alliance until the Americans showed up with massive Special Forces and CIA support.

Bin Laden used the ongoing civil war in Afghanistan to further develop his own jihadi forces. He provided money, vehicles, weapons, and Arab fighters to support the Taliban. In return, Omar afforded sanctuary to bin Laden and al Qaeda. Zawahiri, for his part, provided a core of fairly well-trained and disciplined Egyptians who formed a circle of lieutenants around bin Laden. These men helped organize, train, and deploy the increasing stream of Arab fighters coming into the region.

All of the pieces of al Qaeda as we know it were in place by early 1998. Along with a newly focused ideology, a strategic goal was formed: attack America. The leadership was in place: bin Laden and Zawahiri. Money and new recruits began to flow from bin Laden's contacts in the Gulf, and training camps were established in Afghanistan with a dual purpose: to defeat the Northern Alliance and to train a small cadre of international suicide terrorists. The Afghan camps became the primary world destination for a growing number of radical and violent young men who wanted to join in jihad against an array of opponents, including the Taliban's Afghan opposition, the secular Pakistani government, India, Russia, Israel, and, increasingly, the United States of America.

The Taliban welcomed these foreign fighters as extra soldiers in their war to consolidate control of Afghanistan and, to a certain extent, they shared al Qaeda's radical Islamic worldview. Although the Taliban never expressed much interest in the outside world, they were aware of bin Laden's ambitions and continued to provide him sanctuary as his record of terrorist attacks grew. This complex alliance and my failed attempts to break it up hold historic significance in the context of 9/11, as I discuss in detail in Chapter 7. Without the sanctuary provided to al Qaeda by the Taliban and the constant flow of fighters to the region, al Qaeda wouldn't have developed into the global terror force it became.

Regional Leaders Step Up: Hambali in Indonesia

Since the loss of the Afghan sanctuary following the American defeat of the Taliban in 2001, bin Laden and Zawahiri have been holed up in the mountain border regions of Pakistan and Afghanistan. Although seemingly out of the reach of American and Pakistani military operations, they've remained under constant pressure. This situation has caused a significant increase in the importance of regional al Qaeda leaders, who've become central to the organization's viability. Within this new leadership structure, al Qaeda has sought to establish connections with local groups with local agendas and integrate them into their more international agenda.

However, in contrast to the period prior to 9/11, it's very difficult these days for al Qaeda's top brass to communicate with their subordinate leaders, and the camps that were so instrumental in recruiting, training, vetting, and networking operatives are smaller and transient. As a result, regional leaders have become increasingly important in the planning and execution of attacks. The most important al Qaeda leader to emerge immediately after 9/11 was Hambali. A native Indonesian who was exiled to Malaysia during the Suharto regime, Hambali was dispatched to Indonesia by al Qaeda in 2000 and quickly made contact with a group of radicals at a religious school founded by the radical cleric Abu Bakar Bashir.[2] While with this group of radicals, known as Jemaah Islamiyah, Hambali plotted a car bomb attack against a popular club frequented by Westerners in the resort town of Bali. The attack killed 202 people, 164 of whom were foreign nationals (including 88 Australians), in addition to 38 Indonesian citizens.[3] The attack took place about a year after 9/11 and seemed to indicate that al Qaeda had effectively spread its operational capability to East Asia.

Jemaah Islamiyah followed with another suicide attack against the Marriott hotel in Jakarta on August 5, 2003. A car bomb exploded outside the lobby, killing 11 Indonesians and 1 Dutch businessman and injuring 150.[4] In the past this particular hotel had been used by the U.S. embassy and so had acquired a connection with things Western. Fortunately, Hambali was tracked down and arrested in Thailand, and the spiritual leader Bashir was arrested in Indonesia. Hambali is currently in U.S. custody at the American detention facility at Guantánamo Bay, Cuba; the cleric was tried in Indonesia and received a short sentence, which he has completed.[5] Terrorist violence in Indonesia has dropped off dramatically since these arrests. It appears that the al Qaeda infrastructure has been severely disrupted, and as of 2007 no equal leadership has emerged to take the place of Hambali. Although still a very problematic area, seething with small pockets of radicalism, Indonesia has been spared any major terrorist attacks in recent years.

The Importance of Tactical Leadership

Clearly, the senior leadership of bin Laden and Zawahiri was central to al Qaeda's first attacks. Subsequently, regional leaders such as Hambali were the key to their ability to expand their regional franchises. However, at NYPD, I insisted that our intelligence analysts engage in case studies and not rely on broad-stroke analysis in their research. The NYPD counterterrorism team became immersed in the details surrounding attacks, organizations, and individuals. We called in a small group of Harvard graduate students to do some work for us on the profiles of terrorist leaders. Again, our purpose was to better understand the organization and its leaders and use that knowledge to root al Qaeda out of New York City before they could attack again. I was particularly concerned about tactical leaders, including Ramzi Yousef and Mohamed Atta.

What did we find out about these tactical leaders? How can we find the next one before he attacks? By looking at each case and analyzing its origin, development, and execution, we can learn a lot about key leaders and the individual threats they pose, in the process gaining a better understanding of the larger global threat of Islamic terrorism. In each case, we recognized the absolute indispensability of the tactical leader on the ground. Radical hotheads are easy to find, and plots to attack the United States are even more plentiful. But it takes a special person—with the right measure of ideological fervor, discipline, and leadership ability—to organize a small group to assemble a bomb and conduct an attack.

Khalid Sheikh Mohammed was the mastermind of the 9/11 attack. He took his nephew Ramzi Yousef's plan to blow up multiple airplanes over the Pacific Ocean and adjusted the plot to convert the planes to weapons that could be directed at one of Yousef's previous targets, the World Trade Center. This was evil genius. And without Mohamed Atta, it would have been just another al Qaeda scheme never to be implemented (there've been plenty of those over the years). Bin Laden recognized that of all the youths circulating through his camps in the late 1990s, Atta was the ideal person to lead this attack cell. Although not a great innovator or thinker, Atta was single-minded and disciplined in his leadership and decision making. His graduate-level education and familiarity with the West equipped him with the expertise to micromanage every detail of the plot. Most important, he was able to recruit the core of pilots and organize the "muscle hijackers" into four coherent cells.

Thankfully, not all of al Qaeda's leaders are as effective as Atta. As a case in point, look at Abu Issa al-Hindi, the operative who conducted reconnaissance on the New York Stock Exchange, the Citigroup building in New York City, and two other buildings in Newark, New Jersey, and Washington, D.C. Hindi began his work in 2000 and briefed a plan of attack to al Qaeda leadership in early 2003.[6] Hindi was an articulate and careful planner and he had plenty of ideas about how to attack civilian targets. A veteran of the jihad in Kashmir, he had access to the best al Qaeda training. Hindi had the experience and commitment, but he was never able to advance his planning beyond the conceptual phase. When he was arrested in mid-2003, he hadn't advanced a real plan either in the United Kingdom or in the United States. Radical dreamers such as Hindi are a dime a dozen in al Qaeda. A tactical leader such as Atta is their single most important asset.

Aktas and the Turkish Attacks

In November 2003, Turkey came under attack by al Qaeda. First, on November 15, a pair of truck bombs destroyed two synagogues in the Old City of Istanbul. Five days later, on the twentieth, two more truck bombs struck, this time against the British consulate and the London-based bank HSBC. The leader of the second attack was Habib Aktas. Although not a traditional member of al Qaeda's central apparatus, Aktas and some of his crew were veterans of an al Qaeda camp in Khaldun, Afghanistan, where they were further trained and radicalized. It appears Aktas was in Pakistan on September 11, 2001.[7] Rather than "go to ground" and hide out, as many al Qaeda operatives did after 9/11, Aktas was inspired to return to Turkey to organize attacks on behalf of al Qaeda, specifically bin Laden's chief of operations, Mohammed Atef. Bin Laden instructed Aktas to attack American or Israeli interests there, preferably the U.S. military base at Incirlik. However, the American targets were well protected, so Aktas adjusted his plans and directed the attacks against Jewish and then British targets. He was successful and escaped to Iraq, where he was later killed in combat.

Again, in the case of Aktas, we find a well-motivated and disciplined operative able to pull off a very sophisticated operation. And there are some other very important lessons to be learned here. The terrorists were ready for an operation, but the American target (an air base) was too hard to attack. The operatives didn't wait (for waiting increases their exposure time and vulnerability to penetration); instead they attacked the next best thing, a British diplomatic and financial target. The lesson is that good defenses do help protect targets, but if you don't crush the cell, the terrorists will find another target.

Al Qaeda in America: Homegrown Terrorists

The conception and propagation of terrorist cells from within the U.S. population presents a huge concern for counterterrorism professionals. We must look closely at this distinct breed of terrorist lest they enter international terrorist networks.

The case of the Lackawanna Six is an interesting one. To some, these were just some suburban boys who were wanna-be jihadists—certainly not terrorists. But let's take a closer look. Six young men who grew up in Lackawanna, New York, a small town outside of Buffalo, were inspired to form an al Qaeda cell by a man named Kamal Derwish in the spring of 2001. Derwish was born in the United States but lived much of his life in Yemen and Saudi Arabia. He was the most radical of the group, and impressed his friends with his war stories. He did more than just talk, unlike so many other young hotheads in their group; he'd been to Bosnia and the Afghan camps. His radical fervor inspired his friends, and he was able to convince them that they too had a duty to join in the jihad. All six went to Afghanistan and attended the al Qaeda camps, where they met with bin Laden and were very much aware of his responsibility for the East African bombings and that of the USS *Cole*.

Derwish, a proven fighter and recruiter, was meanwhile sent on to advanced training. While he was gone, it appears that the others' enthusiasm waned. They returned to the United States, while Derwish, upon completion of his higher training, went back to Yemen. In Yemen, Derwish found himself in the wrong place at the wrong time. Riding in a vehicle with a known al Qaeda operative, he was killed when a Hellfire missile from an unmanned CIA Predator aircraft struck the convoy. Without his leadership, the cell lost its focus and determination. The Lackawanna Six were arrested in September 2002 and pled guilty to terror charges to avoid being sent to a military camp. No one knows what that cell might have become if Derwish had returned to the United States to organize them. But these were not the innocent travelers that they've been portrayed by some to be. They knew about al Qaeda, its history of killing Americans (in Africa), and its determination to attack and kill more Americans. They willingly went to the camps. Although not active after they returned, the fact that not one offered any assistance to the U.S. government or any counterterrorism officials in the fight against terrorism indicates where their true loyalty was.

Another potentially dangerous al Qaeda operative in the United States was Iyman Faris. He was well known to NYPD because he was instructed by al Qaeda to attempt an attack against the Brooklyn Bridge. Some pooh-poohed the idea of a terrorist taking down the Brooklyn Bridge, but we at NYPD became convinced that we'd dodged a bullet when we looked closely at the story. For security reasons, I still can't get into the details of the vulnerabilities of the bridge to the type of attack he contemplated, but I can tell you this: Faris was the real deal. Like Derwish, he was a veteran of both Bosnia and the Afghan camps. Faris met bin Laden on multiple occasions and was one of al Qaeda's great hopes for leading another American operation. Fortunately, Faris wasn't an Atta-like leader. He didn't seem to have the leadership talent to organize a cell, nor was he linked with a charismatic leader. But he was a truck driver and had a license to carry hazardous materials. Given the proper leadership, Faris could have been a key component of a massive terrorist attack.

According to NYPD, Faris informed his handlers that "it was too hot" in New York City in 2003, an obvious reference to the city's heavy counterterrorism presence. And although he claimed he really had no intention of attacking, we'll never know, for he was arrested as part of a roundup of personnel identified as al Qaeda members in an overseas investigation (according to some sources, the National Security Agency's wiretap programs helped uncover the cell that led to his arrest). In this case, everything came together for the United States (unlike prior to 9/11). An overseas investigation was coordinated with domestic intelligence and a potential operative was found. Faris also clearly felt the heat of our domestic operations post-9/11 and seemed to be trying to keep a low profile. Our programs were effective in this case.

Al Qaeda in the United Kingdom: Small-Unit Leadership Proves Deadly

As indicated earlier in this chapter, Mohammad Sidique Khan was the perfect local terrorist cell leader for the post-9/11 era. Born and raised in the United Kingdom, Khan opted for the radical cause well before 9/11 and the Iraq war. He traveled to Pakistan before and after the Persian Gulf War and increased his radicalism on each trip. Before departing Pakistan on his last trip, MSK and his partner Tanweer made suicide tapes produced by al Sahab, al Qaeda's propaganda arm. MSK had sufficient charisma to recruit and train a dedicated cell of British citizens to carry suicide bombs into the trains in London on the seventh of July, 2005. It was his small-unit leadership ability that made him an invaluable asset to al Qaeda.

I often describe the pivotal role of central al Qaeda operations in the successful outcomes of local cells in terms of the difference between the two July 2005 attacks in London. On July 21 a cell tried to pull off a copycat operation two weeks after the July 7 attack.

Clearly, this band of radicals was contemplating action prior to the first attack, although there's no evidence whatsoever that there was any connection between the two. Fortunately for the British, the bombs didn't go off on July 21 as planned, though, according to British police, they very well could have. It was perhaps just a little bit of luck that either the detonator didn't work or the mix or temperature of the chemicals was incorrect. Or perhaps the difficulty the perpetrators of the failed second bombing in London faced in connecting with al Qaeda's central leadership placed significant strain on their operation.

The trial of the July 21 bombers revealed that, like MSK, the failed plot's mastermind, Muktar Said Ibrahim, had traveled to Pakistan to attend camps.[8] His bomb design has al Qaeda's fingerprints all over it, but perhaps we will never know the actual extent of al Qaeda's role. Again, though, we see the importance of the local cell leader in assembling the team and constructing the bomb—and the importance of his connection to the central al Qaeda operation. Perhaps if the July 21 attackers had been able to go to Pakistan for more bomb-making training, their attack may have succeeded. The lesson? For a cell to succeed, the central organization still matters, the ability to travel is critical, and real live explosives training in camps is also very important.

Fakhet and the Madrid Train Attack: An al Qaeda Link?

For me, perhaps the most puzzling of the regional attacks, in terms of the links to al Qaeda, is the Madrid attack. The Spanish government downplays the al Qaeda link, but there are others within Spanish police and intelligence who think the link is quite substantive. What we know is that a local homegrown cell was organized by a group of about four operatives, and the leader was probably Sarhane ben Abdelmajid Fakhet. Fakhet had links to the Syrian cleric Imad Yarkas. The Yarkas cell had known links to al Qaeda, and Yarkas was arrested for his involvement in the 9/11 conspiracy for arranging a meeting between Mohamed Atta and two known al-Qaeda operatives and 9/11 conspirators in July 2001.[9] Fakhet was also involved with people associated with a 2003 al Qaeda attack in Casablanca through his brother-in-law Mustapha Maimouni. We also know that Fakhet sought support from al Qaeda but wasn't able to get it, so he had his people trade drugs for explosives on the black market. It's still unclear who the bomb maker was for the Madrid plot. Ten of the thirteen backpack bombs exploded, killing 191 people and wounding more than 1,600. So although the debate continues in Spain, in my mind the Madrid attack also had clear links to al Qaeda, and I hope that someday we'll find out who made the bombs and where the bomb makers were trained. It's my best guess that they were trained in one of the jihadi camps in Pakistan or North Africa. This homegrown cell, like the British group, was undoubtedly connected to al Qaeda's central leadership.

Al Qaeda's Leadership: A Three-Tiered Tower

It's useful to look at three levels of al Qaeda's leadership. At the top are bin Laden and Zawahiri. Although initially they were the strategic and operational planners of al Qaeda, their current role is to be more the ideological center of a broad radical Islamic movement. However, I insist on reminding people that they're more than cheerleaders. As we saw in the London attacks, there is a strong correlation between a plot's success and its connection to al Qaeda's upper leadership. Next in line in this informal network are regional leaders cut from the mold of Hambali in Indonesia or Zarqawi in Iraq. These second-tier leaders can also manage and direct local cells while conducting operations on behalf of al Qaeda's central leadership. At the bottom, but critically important to terrorist operations, are the field or tactical commanders. These individuals (such as Atta, MSK, and Ramzi Yousef) arrange logistics, train operatives, assemble weapons, and carry out attacks. Each of the three tiers is crucial to the ability of al Qaeda to sustain operations at the strategic level.

We need to know who the terrorists really are by name, not as an abstraction created in some broad-stroke analysis of global Islamic trends. We must remember that they're generally not disenfranchised poor men, but rather educated and middle- to upper-middle-class men who subscribe to a specific ideology. Jon Benjamin, the deputy consul general of the United Kingdom in New York, captures it perfectly. He says (and I paraphrase): "Al Qaeda terrorists are driven primarily by global issues and grievances only the educated and fairly well-off have the luxury to think about. The local poor and disenfranchised are more focused on their daily survival. If the lower classes turn violent, it is normally in a local insurgency, not a global terrorist movement." The better we get at differentiating between these two types of violence, the closer we will come to cornering al Qaeda's leaders.

A study of the facts and case studies (not idle speculation about what motivates terrorists) confirms Benjamin's observation. International terrorists are determined killers, motivated by a range of relatively complex and sophisticated grievances; we need to know them by name. Only when the killers are clearly identified can we begin to decode and understand the threat they pose and, just as important, know their limitations.

Chapter 3

Al Qaeda's Ideology: Why They Kill

THE UNITED STATES IS engaged not in a "war against terror," according to the 9/11 Commission, but in a war with "a radical ideological movement which has spawned terrorist groups across the globe."[1] To better understand and eventually quell this movement, we must familiarize ourselves with its core ideology. Most serious terrorist organizations throughout history have had a few common traits: a strong ideology, extreme hatred of their foes, and a sense of military inferiority that leads them to attack a stronger enemy outside the rules of war recognized by regular armies. Terrorist organizations tend to emerge when fringe members of popular movements become frustrated or humiliated. Unable to achieve their goals by conventional armed force, they turn to terrorist tactics to punish and intimidate their enemies. Although attacking civilians is usually rejected by the mainstream citizenry, if the root of the terrorists' complaints resonates among the general populace, they may receive a pass on their methods from some. Al Qaeda fits this generalization.

The key to cracking the al Qaeda code lies in its ideology, for this is what fuels their galvanizing hatred and explains their murderous ways. Understanding what makes terrorists tick—and what ticks them off—is useful on a practical level as well. As I laid out in the previous chapter, we must know our enemies if we're to find them before they attack. And we must know our enemies to effectively set priorities and not waste precious resources on activities that don't really diminish their capabilities.

Ideology Matters: What They Are Thinking

Bin Laden's ideology is often misinterpreted by Americans. He's been repeatedly accused of "hating freedom," but stamping out freedom has never been primary to his agenda. Although full of hate and bluster, bin Laden's message is founded upon several themes of populist resentment, and his violence is justified by a twisted but compelling ideology. Similarly, some reduce al Qaeda's motivations to the promise of seventy-two virgins in paradise for suicide bombers, and portray Islam in a cartoonish light. But those who choose to end their lives in a murderous blast aren't simply following an eternal lust. Their motivations are based on a more complex set of circumstances and beliefs. As we confront bin Laden and like-minded terrorist leaders, we need to avoid oversimplified, unsophisticated interpretations of their ideologies and gain a real handle on exactly what they embrace and promote. We can do so accurately only if we examine their words and actions in the historical and cultural context of radical militant Islam.

Religious extremism should not be confused with terrorism, as they're not one and the same. Fundamentalism isn't necessarily a militant movement, but like terrorism, it is linked to a very deep sense of frustration and humiliation within the Islamic world. The current radical movement within Islam, characterized by a strong revival of religious fundamentalism, was born out of a broader crisis within the Islamic world. Religious fundamentalists blame current leaders in Islamic countries and Western influence, specifically that of the United States, for weakening and desecrating Islam. Although most Muslims don't share the extremist doctrines of religious fundamentalists, many do relate to the fundamentalists' frustrations, feeling on a visceral level that Islam has lost its way in a Westernized world. Support for fundamentalist doctrines isn't easily gauged, but there's clear evidence of widespread satisfaction when militant extremists are able to score some sort of vengeance against the West. And in a related trend, the electoral gains of Islamic parties that feed off of these same frustrations can be seen in Turkey, Jordan, Egypt, and Pakistan.

The terrorism associated with al Qaeda is actually a violent offshoot of a long-term movement of Sunni fundamentalism. The audacious destruction and penchant for killing that characterizes this radical wing has brought the movement great attention, and so for them it can be said that in some ways terrorism has worked. However, the same bloody tactics that capture headlines do simultaneously limit the broader appeal of the movement among peaceful, nonmilitant Muslims, almost ensuring that this movement will remain on the fringe and ultimately burn out. Unfortunately, that will take time, and in the interim, militant fundamentalist Islam remains a deadly threat to the West and a very destabilizing force in much of the Islamic world.

Where does this ideology come from? At NYPD we grappled with this question not as social scientists but as pragmatists. We needed to develop a working expertise in a movement that was developing in New York City and being imported from other parts of the world. Every other Thursday, I met with the senior counterterrorism officials in each of NYPD bureaus and major commands. When I arrived at NYPD in June 2003 these officers were fairly well versed on al Qaeda and the events of 9/11. However, I wanted them to know the lessons of the first World Trade Center attack as well as many case studies from around the world in great detail. Then they could apply true expertise to their operations in the streets of Brooklyn, Queens, and the Bronx. To that end, I had my intelligence detectives research and prepare briefs on a series of terrorist attacks. Inspector Hugh O'Rourke, a reserve Air Force major with an intelligence background and a top-secret clearance, led the briefing team. O'Rourke has a keen analytical mind and an understated briefing style. We started with the 1993 attack against the World Trade Center, a local case and a textbook example of a bungled investigation both before and after the attack.

Let's begin in 1990, when the Blind Sheik Omar Abdel Rahman arrived at JFK International Airport from Pakistan. His connection with terrorist groups in Egypt went back many years, including his involvement with the jihadists who murdered Egyptian president Anwar Sadat in 1981. (In the eyes of militant Egyptians, Sadat was guilty of making peace with Israel, a crime for which he'd pay with his life.) When Abdel Rahman arrived in the United States, his movement's ideology was undergoing a significant shift, turning its bitterness toward Abdel Rahman's newly chosen home, America. In fact, at the time of his arrival in the United States, Rahman was on the State Department's terrorist watch list, a fact we should remember when we're quick to condemn the Bush administration's decisions to prevent some firebrand clerics from entering the United States. Abdel Rahman began preaching hate at several mosques in and around the New York area almost as soon as he got off the plane. He was later named as a conspirator in the 1993 attack on the World Trade Center and convicted in a subsequent plot against New York City landmarks, including the federal building in Manhattan and the Lincoln and Holland tunnels. And although Abdel Rahman currently alternates residences between a federal penitentiary and a hospital ward, others with his same ideology still continue to meet and plot within the city limits.

I always reminded my detectives at NYPD that, in a way, al Qaeda was born in New York City, not Afghanistan. In many ways, the 1993 Trade Center bombers showed the way forward to al Qaeda in Afghanistan. They acted on their growing hatred for America with a terrorist attack in New York City five years before bin Laden's famous fatwas and embassy attacks of 1998. I pounded home my point: we could never again afford to have a terrorist movement spawned under our radar and over the dead bodies of innocent New Yorkers. We'd have to find these movements before they attacked, know them as they developed in our streets, and not wait for the State Department, CIA, or FBI to tell us who was a threat. The feds had missed before and could miss again.

In the spring of 2004, I got an e-mail from former Navy secretary John Lehman, who was one of the more active, informed, and impassioned members of the 9/11 Commission. I knew Lehman from his active work in the counterterrorism world before, and although I didn't know him well at the time, I'd admired him for many years. He asked me to interview a young Columbia University graduate named Daniel Rudder, who'd recently returned from a year of living in the Middle East. After a short conversation with Rudder, I asked one of my assistants to hire him immediately as a consultant to NYPD. Shortly afterward, I put him to work on my Muslim ideology project. I sat him in my outer office next to two burly NYPD detectives, Anthony Amorese and Jimmy Fogarty. Both these guys towered over the rather slight Ivy Leaguer and made sure he felt at home by relentlessly teasing him, to the great amusement of the whole office. This was Rudder's initiation to the Department. He learned to hold his own against the never-ending barrage of insults, and eventually was accepted by the cops and respected as an instructor. Rudder has a degree in religion and anthropology from Columbia, had lived in Lebanon for a time, and speaks Arabic fairly well. He put together a course for our detectives dealing with the radical Islamic threat and rehearsed his lessons with Deputy Commissioner David Cohen and me after our normal workday ended. We helped focus his work to keep it relevant to the streets of New York City—and learned a lot about radical Islam in the process.

Radical Salafism: Al Qaeda's Ideological Roots

As is true for most modern movements, the key to understanding radical Islam lies in a nuanced understanding of its history. Al Qaeda's ideology has its roots in radical Salafism, which is a branch of Islamic ideology that is based on an extremely conservative interpretation of the Koran. It's a broad movement whose name is derived from the Arabic *al-salf al-salih,* meaning "the venerable forefathers."[2] The Salafists believe that during the time of the Prophet Muhammad and immediately after his death, Muslims enjoyed a strong, almost utopian society. However, that perfection was lost in the eighth century, after the third generation of Muhammad's followers died. Salafists desperately want to restore that righteous and glorious society, and believe that the only way to achieve their goal is to adhere to the true faith as guided by a literal interpretation of the Koran. A central tenet of this belief is that all Muslims should be subject to *sharia,* or Islamic law. Radical Salafists reject national or civic structures and believe that the global Muslim community, known as the *umma,* should unify around their identification with pure Islamic faith and culture.

Not all Salafists are alike. For our purposes at NYPD, and at the risk of oversimplifying a complex movement, Rudder divided the Salafists into three broad categories: the purists, who focus on religion only and don't engage in politics; the political Salafists, who believe that understanding local and global politics is essential to advancing their belief system; and the violent Salafists, who agree with political aspects of the movement but also believe that militancy is a religious requirement. These distinctions were useful, for they clarified that we weren't concerned with the first two groups of Salafists, who are peaceful and pious people. It was the radical and violent fringe that concerned us. According to Rudder, the militants believe that the only way to recapture the purity of the early Islamic period is to wage war against governments that resist implementing *sharia.* They consider martial jihad a fundamental requirement of the Islamic faith and believe that those who don't participate in the militancy are shirking their responsibilities as Muslims.

The next history lesson Rudder walked us through pertained to the period from about A.D. 900 to 1500. Again, during this period, Islam was strong and the Muslim caliphate (religious kingdom) dominated much of the known world. Although conquered by the Mongols in the mid-thirteenth century, the Muslims successfully converted their East Asian conquerors to the faith en masse in the year 1295. It was during this period that an important Islamic scholar, Ibn Taymiyya, developed the religious justification for violent overthrow of a government—even if that government was purportedly run by "good Muslims." Ibn Taymiyya argued in a fatwa in 1303 that the Mongol leaders, although Muslims in name, were actually apostates. This not only gave "true" Muslims the right to overthrow them but also conferred on them the duty to do so. Ibn Taymiyya was a revered Islamic scholar whose writings have been taken out of the context of fourteenth-century Islam and used as a source of twenty-first-century militant dogma. His justifications of violence in the name of the faith remain the basis of al Qaeda's warped religiosity. Although this ancient doctrine may seem irrelevant to us, it's very much alive in the teachings of the modern al Qaeda.

Radical Salafism is an old, pan-Islamic movement that has taken various shapes and forms over the years. The most important of the Salafist movements is the one that evolved in the birthplace of Muhammad, Saudi Arabia. There, the royal family has had an alliance with very conservative clerics since the mid-1800s. These clerics adhere to a brand of Salafism known as Wahhabism, a doctrine named after Muhammad ibn Abd al-Wahhab, the Islamic cleric who reintroduced *sharia* to the Arabic peninsula in the nineteenth century. The Wahhabist sect was fairly well contained to Saudi Arabia until the 1950s and 1960s, when the Saudis began competing with Egyptian president Gamal Abdel Nasser's pan-Arabic movement and other clumsy attempts to unify the Arab world. And it was during this time that the Saudis also gained the great oil wealth that enabled them to export their religious beliefs.

As the House of Saud grew richer and the freewheeling habits of the princes became more unruly, the clerics began to voice their objections and challenge the Saudi leadership. They shamed the royal family into establishing and maintaining a strict interpretation of *sharia* (which seemingly only applied to the rich princes when they were in Saudi Arabia, not when they were partying in London or the south of France). To placate the clerics and to establish their religious credentials, some members of the regime began to support more radical brands of Wahhabism, at home and abroad. They began funding the construction of mosques and financed the missions of radical clerics who traveled abroad to preach their doctrines. This activity continues today. When I was at the State Department, one of the old Arab hands who was a bit of a cynic described it this way:

> A young prince spends a two-week vacation in London (or on the French Riviera) chasing loose women, driving fast cars and drinking twelve-year-old scotch. When he returns, through either guilt, pressure, or a combination of both, he sends a check to the local radical cleric—to keep him off his back and burnish his "Islamic" commitment. All too often, some of those funds find their way into the hands of the wrong people.

At the same time, other radical and fundamentalist movements were being spawned in Pakistan and Egypt. In Pakistan, the fundamentalist Deobandi movement developed in response to British colonialism in India, which was believed to be a corrupting force. In 1985, the terrorist group Sipah-i-Sahaba (SSP) was created in Pakistan to counter growing Shia activism that had been inspired in part by the success of the Iranians. In 1977, General Zia ul-Haq overthrew the popularly elected government of Zulfikar Bhutto. Zia became prime minister of Pakistan and began to implement fundamentalist doctrines and *sharia* in the country. Overlaid on top of this conservative movement, two issues kept the flame of radicalism alive in Pakistan: the internal strife between the Sunni and Shia sects of Islam, and the struggle with India over Kashmir. Kashmir in particular generates great passion among most Pakistanis, and a small but significant percentage of the population is further radicalized in their hatred of the Pakistani Shia. Al Qaeda in Pakistan grew out of these fundamentalist movements and remains intertwined with them, greatly complicating the equation there for both the United States and Pakistani president Pervez Musharraf.

The Muslim Brotherhood is considered the father of many militant Sunni organizations around the world. Founded in Egypt in 1928 by a primary-school teacher named Hassan al-Banna, the Brotherhood isn't really related to the Salafists, for it is a much more politically based movement. But its fundamentalist doctrines have melded well with those of the classic Salafists in many regions. After its beginnings in Egypt, the group expanded into Syria and Jordan, and by the late 1940s it was formidable enough to participate in the 1948 war against the nascent Israeli state. After the end of that war, the Brotherhood blamed the secular Egyptian government for the failure to destroy Israel and were highly critical of the regime. As their activism grew, they were banned from Egypt, and Banna was killed the next year, 1949, by the Egyptian secret police. But the Brotherhood survived.

In the 1950s, the Muslim Brotherhood began to reemerge in strength within Egypt and throughout the Middle East. During this period, Sayyid Qutb, a militant member of the Muslim Brotherhood, was imprisoned during a government crackdown. While in prison, Qutb authored *Milestones,* an outline of his vision for a radical reform of the Muslim world. Published after his release in 1964, *Milestones* remains one of the most influential manifestos of militant Islamic thought around the world. In it, Qutb argues forcefully that the truly faithful are required to wage war against what are considered apostate regimes. Qutb was executed by the Egyptian government in 1966 along with other senior members of the Muslim Brotherhood, but his teachings, summarized in *Milestones,* continue to have significant influence on the thinking of radical terrorists, including bin Laden and Zawahiri.

The Brotherhood was set back but not eliminated in the late 1960s. Ironically, it was the peace deal of 1979 signed by Egyptian president Anwar Sadat and Israeli prime minister Menachem Begin that revitalized the organization. Two years later, Saddat met his death at the hands of former Muslim Brotherhood members who had joined the group known as Egyptian Islamic Jihad. As I mentioned earlier, a young Ayman al-Zawahiri, who would go on to be Osama bin Laden's deputy, was among those arrested and charged as a member of the broader plot. Zawahiri became the de facto leader and spokesman of the EIJ from his jail cell, and would later reorganize the group and take it to Afghanistan in the late 1980s to join up with bin Laden. Also arrested in the plot was the

Blind Sheik, Omar Abdel Rahman, who was to become linked with the evolution of militant Islam in New York City.

In examining the history of radical militant Islam, the key players and central themes relating to al Qaeda come to the surface over and over. As early as 1990, you can see the strands of this global radical movement come together. Its ideological origins were a direct spin-off of the fundamentalist Salafist movement, yet the principles of the movement have broader popular appeal than one might think at a glance. Saudi Wahhabism exported its radical Islamic ideology around the world, where it resonated with the fundamentalist Pakistani and Afghan Pashtuns who were congregating in refugee camps along the mountainous border area and would later form the Taliban. The Egyptians provided radical clerics from their most prestigious religious schools, who often became the chief clerics of the movement (like the Blind Sheik). The Egyptians, veterans of their own jihad at home, also provided a cadre of experienced leaders for the fledgling al Qaeda. The mixture of radical Salafist doctrines (Saudi, Pakistani, Afghan, and Egyptian) and seasoned Egyptian operatives all contributed to the lethal brew being cooked up in the camps of Afghanistan.

The Fatwas

In the 1990s, at the intersection of religious fundamentalism, political activism, and violence in the mountains of Afghanistan, a newly organized and focused organization called al Qaeda was being transformed from a local jihadi group to a global terrorist organization. Osama bin Laden's road to the creation of al Qaeda had been a long and winding one. By 1996, he was increasingly isolated from the world: kicked out of Sudan, banned from returning home to Saudi Arabia, and not really interested in the local Afghan war beyond exploiting the situation to sustain his own sanctuary. Bin Laden devoted much of the 1980s and early 1990s to developing his half-baked religious justification for terrorist attacks against the West and rallying support for his cause.

Although a fatwa is technically defined as a religious ruling or interpretation put forth by a recognized religious authority, bin Laden had no such credentials within Islam. Nevertheless, he has repeatedly used this religious forum as a declaration of war. Two key fatwas established bin Laden's primary agenda, which hasn't changed dramatically in the past ten years. In 1996, he released a long and rambling fatwa that didn't attract much attention at the time. Upon closer study, it reveals al Qaeda's ideological and religious justification for jihad against the United States. In it, bin Laden was highly critical of the Saudi government's secularism and their support for the American intervention in Iraq. But as in all of his subsequent pronouncements, he reserved most of his polemic for the Americans. Bin Laden again invokes the fourteenth-century cleric Ibn Taymiyya to justify his targeting of the "far enemy." He then provides a religious justification for martyrdom, or suicide bombing, by quoting the following *hadith,* which is a saying or action attributed to the Prophet Muhammad: "A martyr's privileges are guaranteed by Allah; forgiveness with the first gush of blood."[3] Bin Laden also makes reference to the famous seventy-two virgins in this fatwa. Actually, they're described as houris, the beautiful maidens of paradise. This is often mocked by Americans as a sexual image tempting pious Muslims, but in doing so we miss the far more important motivator of suicide bombing in another Koranic reference that promises a martyr the power of intercession on behalf of seventy relatives.[4] For a true believer and his family, this is extremely powerful. By becoming a "martyr," a hopeless young man can help open the gates of paradise for seventy of his family members.

The second fatwa, issued in February 1998, was a more precise prelude to the opening of bin Laden's terrorist campaign against the United States. In the 1998 fatwa, bin Laden portrays America as the abject enemy of Islam. First, he outlines three specific issues regarding U.S. behavior in the Middle East, each with resonance throughout the Islamic world. Then he paints these transgressions as a direct attack against Islam. And finally, he concludes that it is the duty of Muslims to defend the faith against the American attacks.

Regarding the continued U.S. military involvement in Saudi Arabia following the first Gulf War's mission to Kuwait, bin Laden states "the United States has been occupying the lands of Islam . . . plundering its riches . . . turning its bases into a spearhead through which to fight neighboring Muslim peoples."[5] He then turns to Iraq for evidence of the American intent to destroy Islam: "Despite the devastation inflicted upon the Iraqi people by the crusader-Zionist alliance, and despite the huge number of those killed, which has exceeded one million . . . despite all of this, the Americans are once again trying to repeat horrific massacres . . . [They] are not content with the protracted blockade [against Iraq] . . . so here they come to annihilate what is left of this people and to humiliate their Muslim neighbors."[6] Bin Laden presents the sanctions against Iraq and the enforcement of the no-fly zones after the Gulf War as salt in the wound, rubbed in to demoralize all Muslims.

Finally, bin Laden broadens his appeal to the greater Muslim world by linking all American activity in Muslim countries with the Arab-Israeli conflict. By stating that the "aim behind these wars are religious and economic, the aim is also to serve the Jew's petty state and divert attention from its occupation of Jerusalem and murder of Muslims there," bin Laden effectively sounds the battle cry to all of Islam.[7] Once he establishes that Islam is under attack, he calls upon all Muslims to defend the faith in a defensive jihad—which is an obligation for pious Muslims.

This remains the fundamental doctrine of al Qaeda, and although it now includes the American occupation of Iraq, it hasn't changed much at all. The basis of his argument is that American soldiers (and the United States' foreign policies) are crushing Muslims around the world. American support for Israel against the Palestinians has also been very prominent since the beginning and remains so. Bin Laden concludes that it is the duty of all pious Muslims to defend the *umma* with jihad. Let me be clear: there is very little or no mention of Western freedoms, the spread of democracy, or the socioeconomic conditions of poor Muslims around the world. This is largely a political argument that purports to be responding to a Western attack on Islam, followed by a religious justification for a violent defense that includes the use of terror.

The Basis of bin Laden's Deadly Doctrine

Too many people around the world who haven't studied who and what bin Laden is jump straight to unfounded conclusions—which sometimes conveniently support other tangential agendas. I served at the United Nations in the period immediately after September 11, when terrorism dominated the formal and informal discussions of the organization. One popular notion I heard often at the UN was "as long as the Israeli-Palestinian issue festers, the terrorists will keep attacking." It's easy to blame the chronic instability and violence between the Israelis and Palestinians for all of the region's woes, but this argument withers under close scrutiny. In fact, one of the antecedents of al Qaeda—Ayman al-Zawahiri's Egyptian Islamic Jihad—was actually boosted by peace efforts in the Middle East: the EIJ was bolstered by those who rallied against Anwar Sadat's signing of the 1979 Israel-Egypt peace treaty. Furthermore, if a peace accord were forged today between Israel and Palestine that included the existence of the State of Israel and some compromise on Jerusalem, the terrorists and nations that ally with them would surely reject it and redouble their efforts to attack the United States and Israel. Of course, the process should be pursued until peace is achieved. Over the very long term, the increased stability will indeed help let the air out of the radical movements. But in the short term, there should be no illusion: peace between Israel and Palestine would have little or no impact on the terrorists with whom I've been concerned for the past ten years. The same is true in Kashmir and Chechnya. The most radical groups would reject any compromise in those regions short of complete control by Pakistan (for Kashmir) and a separate Islamic state (for Chechnya). Terrorists are simply not interested in bargaining.

The Making of a Terrorist

Al Qaeda was founded on an ideology that won't go away anytime soon—nor will it go quietly. The radical fundamentalist Salafist ideologues cling tightly to the notion that by returning to the purity of the golden Islamic age of Muhammad, the *umma* will regain its past glory. This utopian dream has broad resonance in the Islamic world, particularly in those areas plagued by long-term humiliations. Economic duress is a factor, but it holds much less power than grief over political-religious defeat (for example, Palestine, Chechnya, Kashmir, and Iraq) and disappointment with failing or underperforming secular regimes (as in Egypt, Indonesia, and North Africa). There is no quick fix to this problem. As long as these humiliations endure, the "sacred rage" will continue.

In three separate places we see the tangled web of issues that make this problem difficult to resolve. In Saudi Arabia, a pact with fundamentalist clerics prevents the royal family from clamping down on those who threaten it with the spread of virulent hatred. In Pakistan, the Sunni fundamentalist movement has broad support in its efforts to win back Kashmir from the Indians, and to purify the faith by attacking the heretical Shia. These movements too easily cross paths with al Qaeda jihadists in Pakistan, creating a dangerous knot that President Musharraf will have great difficulty unraveling. And in Egypt, the political and ideological center of Arabic philosophy, the radical spin-offs of the Muslim Brotherhood continue to thrive and are being exported around the world. Until the Saudis, Pakistanis, and Egyptians get a handle on their radical populations, militant groups will continue to breed and suicide bombers will continue to terrorize innocent citizens.

Most suicide terrorists are not crazy. In fact, most are very thoughtful and deliberate about their decision to conduct an operation. Nevertheless, it isn't natural to kill oneself in a fiery blast, no matter how committed one may be to a particular objective. There is clearly something more going on here. It appears, on the surface, that most terrorists follow a certain progression of emotion. It begins with a deep personal frustration, compounded by local or global grievances of an ethnic and/or religious dimension. Many seek religion for the solace it offers—a perfectly normal and legitimate response to the frustrations they face. However, some of these seekers make contact with religious radicals who distort the tenets of Islam and couple religion with a political agenda to form a compelling and violent ideology. Feelings of frustration are gradually elevated to a sense of humiliation seething with hatred, which leads down a slippery slope to an acceptance of jihadist ideology.

U.S. policy has indeed caused widespread frustration in the Islamic world, but no matter how misguided our policies may be, this does not explain why a healthy human being would commit suicide in an attack against innocent civilians. Again, we must resist the temptation to oversimplify the issues in the interest of explaining away the problem of terrorism. Something much more complex than aggravated frustration is at work here. Bin Laden's twisted political-religious justifications for terrorist tactics do not ring true with many Muslims, yet a small but steady stream of recruits will continue to be generated around the world for at least another generation. And worse yet, some of those will be born or raised right here in the United States.

Chapter 4

Iran and Hezbollah: Bloody but Restrained Terrorists

When I arrived at NYPD in 2003, my initial focus was on al Qaeda and its associated groups. However, Hezbollah, long a killer of Americans, was never far from my mind. During my first days on the job, I was briefed by our Hezbollah team. The Hezbollah unit dated back to the 1980s, and its members were legends in the New York Joint Terrorism Task Force. They had many arrests under their belt, had received awards from both CIA and FBI for their exploits, and had developed an extensive network of informants in the city. While their briefing was impressive, I was a bit wary; I wasn't nearly as comfortable as they were that we had a handle on the Hezbollah threat in New York City.

My first impression was that we'd conducted investigations and tried cases against Hezbollah supporters with clear sympathies to Hezbollah's political organization, not its militant wing. Of course, these individuals had broken the law and we were taking appropriate action. However, I wasn't sure that these people would be associated with a serious Hezbollah attack if it was conducted in New York City. Instead, I thought real Hezbollah terrorists would avoid these people like the plague.

My questions to the Hezbollah unit started from a more fundamental basis. First, what is the real Hezbollah threat to the United States? Are these people you're investigating going to attack us, or are they primarily interested in making money and sending some of it home to support the militants in their war against Israel? If Iran was threatened by the United States, would it use Hezbollah as a surrogate to attack the United States at home? Or would the Iranians use their own national intelligence operatives unilaterally? If teams were deployed from Iran, would they seek local support from sympathizers or would they stay far away from them on the assumption that the locals had been penetrated by U.S. and/or Israeli intelligence? I never got a good answer to these questions from my NYPD detectives, nor from FBI or CIA. We simply don't know for sure.

In 2005, the long-simmering tensions with Iran began to heat up again. Iranian meddling in the Iraq war, coupled with their refusal to curtail their nuclear program, put Iran front and center with the Bush administration. When the Iranians initially refused to comply with demands to inspect their nuclear program back in September 2003, the UN's nuclear watchdog organization, the International Atomic Energy Agency, began applying pressure. By 2005, the Iranians were still moving forward on their uranium enrichment program, and the Bush administration began rattling its sabers. The press began to speculate that the administration might conduct a preemptive strike on Iranian nuclear facilities in an effort to knock out Iran's uranium enrichment program.[1]

At NYPD headquarters, Commissioner Raymond Kelly, Dave Cohen, and I assessed the likely impact on New York City. If Iranian nuclear facilities were attacked by the United States or Israel, how might the Iranians react? We wondered if they might even try to beat the United States to the punch by conducting a preemptive terrorist attack of their own against U.S. interests. If Iran conducted a preemptive strike, we suspected that it probably would be conducted abroad. But if they were responding to an American strike, they'd likely strike within the United States. Regardless, we needed to be prepared. If an attack were to come to the United States, New York was a likely target.

Iran and Hezbollah were no strangers to us. We knew them well from our previous assignments in Washington, and we were familiar with their recent activities in New York City. I knew from my experience at the UN how problematic the Iranian mission there was. In fact, within the previous years, several Iranians had been kicked out of New York City for conducting intelligence operations.[2]

In the "subway spy case," an NYPD transit cop observed some suspicious activities by several men who were videotaping the subway tracks on the number 7 line in Queens at one-thirty in the morning. As he'd been trained to do, the transit cop approached the men to see what they were up to. Like many officers from NYPD's recent recruit classes, this cop was a multilingual son of immigrant parents and spoke Farsi and Urdu. So he addressed the suspects casually in their native tongue. This got the men flustered, and with a few more questions, the cop knew he was on to something. And he was right: they were Iranian operatives who'd been in the United States for less than a month, and they were clearly conducting reconnaissance missions. They were on temporary duty from Iran as "embassy security personnel"—but what they were engaged in had nothing to do with their embassy. They were intelligence operatives. To this day I am not sure whether they were conducting training for their operatives or conducting a real assessment of our subways. In either case, it was unacceptable; we reported the incident to FBI and U.S. Department of State, and the men were kicked out of the country.[3]

We also knew about Hezbollah's local activities. In fact, NYPD and FBI had been monitoring Hezbollah in New York City for many years. Most of the activity we detected had to do with funneling support to Hezbollah back in Lebanon. In 2002, FBI broke up a cigarette smuggling ring that reached from North Carolina to Michigan. The selling of contraband cigarettes is relatively easy and extremely lucrative because the tax structure varies from state to state. According to the *Washington Post,* a cigarette smuggler can make $2 million in profit from a single truckload of cigarettes.[4] Mohamad Hammoud, a twenty-eight-year-old native of Lebanon, was sentenced to 155 years in prison for his involvement in the smuggling of $7.9 million worth of cigarettes. His sentence was so steep because he was caught on wiretaps communicating with some of Hezbollah's military leadership back in Lebanon, which confirmed the charge that the smuggling ring was providing support for terrorism. The seriousness of this operation, although a bit overblown by some in the press and FBI, serves as an indicator that Hezbollah has a support structure within the United States, at least for monetary support.

At NYPD, we knew full well that Hezbollah supporters and Iranian espionage operatives were in the city, but rather than thrashing about looking for them under every rock, we developed a strategy that asked the question "How would they attack us in New York, and who would the operatives reach out to for support within the city?" There seemed to be several possible scenarios. The attack could be directed by the Iranians using agents from, or managed by, their intelligence service or the Republican Guards, or they could deploy Hezbollah operatives. In each scenario, Iranian agents or Hezbollah surrogates, we faced two other considerations: Would they send in shooters from the outside or activate internal assets? If the assets came from outside, would they likely contact their support structure here—or behave more like Mohamed Atta and stay away from anyone who might be under surveillance by local or federal authorities? To anticipate Iran's and Hezbollah's response here, we needed to review our understanding of who our enemy was, historically and globally.

Iran and the Radical Shia Revolution

The Iranian revolution was a critical point in the revival of Shia radicalism throughout the Middle East. Shias represent between 10 and 15 percent of the entire Muslim world, but they're dominant in Iran and have large populations in Iraq and Lebanon as well.[5] The religious split dates back to the seventh century and the tumultuous years immediately following the death of Muhammad, when a bloody struggle for control of the faith ensued. In the Shia sect, the succession of Muslim leadership follows the bloodline of Ali, the cousin of Muhammad who married the Prophet's daughter Fatima. The Sunnis follow another line dominated by the Umayyads, another clan from Muhammad's tribe. They believe that the caliphs should be chosen by a form of community consensus called *shura,* as endorsed by the Koran, rather than by following the bloodline of Ali.

In many parts of the world, Sunnis and Shia get along without incident. But their history is also marked with spasms of terrible violence between the two, commonly referred to as "sectarian violence" in the press. In countries such as Iraq, Lebanon, Pakistan, and Afghanistan, the Shia-Sunni conflict is constantly erupting into violence. The Iranian revolution of 1979 energized the global Shia population and, because of its fundamentalism, also stirred Sunni radicals such as Ayman al-Zawahiri who were inspired by their revolutionary zeal. Hezbollah was created as a fundamentalist Shia movement to aid the Lebanese resistance against the Israeli occupation of southern Lebanon in 1982. Iran was the principal patron of this new organization. However, the Syrians are the key power brokers in Lebanon and play an important intermediary role between Hezbollah, who are fellow Arabs, and the Iranian Shia, who are Persians. If this seems hopelessly complicated, that's because it is. But allow me to walk through some of it as it pertains to U.S. counterterrorism.

My relationship with Iran began in 1979, the same year I volunteered to join the Special Forces. Just two years out of West Point, I was deployed to Fort Bragg, North Carolina, where I was to earn the coveted Green Beret. In November, during the final phase of the course, I was on a three-week training mission in the mountains of North Carolina. My team was trying to organize, train, and direct a band of guerrillas operating behind enemy lines. The "guerrillas," who were actually Special Forces sergeants and some local recruits, were being as difficult as could be expected. Indeed, they were behaving like a real group of resistance fighters, exhibiting agendas and operating styles that were often at variance with the instructions being radioed in to us from our headquarters. While camped out in the middle of nowhere, we were told by the Special Forces instructors who rotated in and out of the field exercise that the American embassy in Tehran had been taken over by an unruly mob of Iranian students. None of us thought too much about it. Iran had been in chaos for the better part of the year, ever since the shah had left in exile in February. It was expected that the issue would be resolved quickly, so we turned our focus back to the exercises.

Of course, the hostages were not released for another 444 days, on the last day of President Carter's term and the inauguration of Ronald Reagan, leading into a protracted standoff with Iran. Little did I know as I trained in the mountains that my first assignment as a Green Beret would be in Panama, where I would be assigned to the hostage rescue team of a counterterrorism unit (aka "door kickers"). When the shah was shipped to Panama to get treatment for cancer, our team was alerted and deployed as part of the protection program.

The hostage crisis served as an effective wake-up call to America regarding the threat posed by Iran. All of the hostages were released, and although they were visibly weakened by the experience, none appeared to be seriously harmed. One of those hostages, a Foreign Service officer named John Limbert, would become my deputy at the State Department's Office of the Coordinator for Counterterrorism eighteen years later. John is a unique individual. Although quite young at the time of the hostage crisis, he'd already earned a Harvard doctorate in history and Middle Eastern studies and spoke Farsi fluently. He's a true expert on the region, and as a former hostage, he has firsthand knowledge of Middle Eastern terrorism. At State, John would rarely talk about his experiences as a hostage, but he was quietly determined that I understand the complexity and lethality of Iran and Hezbollah.

In April 1979, Iran became the first fundamentalist state in modern history. Ayatollah Ruhollah Khomeini had returned to Iran in early 1979, as the shah's rule was beginning to collapse. By April, the shah was out, and Iran declared itself an Islamic republic. The ayatollah, who is so closely associated with the hostage crisis, actually had nothing to do with the plan to take down the U.S. embassy. He and his cronies were, however, intensely involved in whipping up the anti-American hysteria that was sweeping through Tehran after President Carter's humanitarian decision to give refuge to the shah when he was diagnosed with cancer. Khomeini used the popular jubilation surrounding the hostage crisis to surge into power and isolate the ruling coalition that had been loosely governing Iran since the shah's departure. Khomeini exacerbated and prolonged the crisis to strengthen his grip on the country, a technique that Iranian rulers have used repeatedly. They try to foment hysteria and violence in the streets as a means of rallying their domestic base, and Israel and the United States are their favorite enemies to invoke.

The ayatollah and subsequent leaders of the Iranian revolution fancied themselves the leaders of all Shia Muslims around the world, and as such, they have maintained strong ties to the Shia in Lebanon. The Iranian Shia are of Middle Eastern ethnicity and have historically had a very tense relationship with their Arab neighbors. Most of the Arab states in the region have Sunni majorities, with the exception of Iraq and Bahrain. When the Shia radicals gained control of Iran it was a boost to fundamentalist Muslims around the world, including some Sunnis—even those who thought the Shia were an apostate splinter of true Islam. But the revolution was even more important to fundamentalist Shia minority populations in the Arab world, particularly in southern Lebanon. And it is in that part of the world that Hezbollah was created and then cultivated by the active patronage of Iranian mullahs.

Although the Arab Shia and Persian Shia were not always a match made in heaven, they shared a common fundamentalist ideology and an intense hatred of Israel. For Iran, courting the Lebanese Shia was a huge opportunity to expand their power base. The Lebanese Shia were a poor minority group residing largely in southern Lebanon along the border of Israel, where they were discriminated against by the Sunni majority. Lebanon had been wracked by civil war since 1975, and the country was in a shambles. The Shia's poverty and alienation from the powerful Sunni and Christian power centers made them easy targets for fundamentalists importing violent dogma from Tehran.

In the early 1980s, Iran began to increase its presence in southern Lebanon within the radical Shia communities. The Israeli invasion of Lebanon that occurred in 1982 was a watershed event. Although some people in southern Lebanon initially welcomed the Israeli intervention into the ongoing civil war, the Israeli presence quickly became a rallying point for radical Shia groups and accelerated Iranian support for the fledgling Hezbollah movement. Iranian trainers and funds flowed into the Bekaa Valley camps, and Hezbollah began to thrive as the only significant resistance to the Israeli occupation.

Hezbollah and the Invention of Suicide Terrorism

Hezbollah, which means "party of God" in Arabic, was officially founded in 1982. It was designed to be a more religious and fundamentalist alternative to the militant Amal organization of southern Lebanese Shia that had begun in 1975. Like Amal, Hezbollah soon became swept up in the multisided conflict in Lebanon between Sunnis, Shia, Druze, Palestinians, Israelis, and international peacekeepers. It was hard to keep track of the shifting alliances, but expelling the Israel Defense Forces from southern Lebanon became the central organizing purpose of Hezbollah until 2000, when the Israelis finally withdrew. Today, Hezbollah is headed by its secretary general, Hassan Nasrallah, and over the past ten years has put more emphasis on the development of its party structure and political power, keeping the revolutionary zeal strong by occasionally confronting Israel. Although it remains the minority, it has growing representation in the Lebanese Parliament and the begrudging support of most Lebanese, Shia and Sunni alike, for its defiance of Israel.

Hezbollah is considered by many to be the world's premier terrorist organization. It's especially threatening because it has the support of the state apparatus of Iran, including its intelligence service and the elite army units known as the Revolutionary Guards. It was in the chaos of Beirut in the 1980s that Hezbollah, with the support of its Iranian patrons, invented the modern concept of Islamic suicide terrorism. Hezbollah had employed truck bombs with devastating effectiveness and mastered the art of brutal hostage taking and killing. But most shocking was the new and profound commitment among fighters who were willing to follow their cause to their death as suicide bombers.

The most famous of the early suicide attacks was in Beirut against a U.S. Marine barracks. On October 23, 1983, at about 6:20 A.M., a large truck rumbled through a checkpoint at the Beirut National Airport, where the U.S. Marine Corps had set up its local headquarters. The guards were alert and fired on the vehicle, attempting to disable it. But the driver was determined. He plowed through a barbed-wire fence, crashed through the gate, careened into the lobby of the headquarters, and detonated more than twelve thousand pounds of explosives. The blast rocked Beirut. Because of the size of the vehicle and its explosive charge, and the penetration of the truck into the building, the blast caused the collapse of the load-bearing columns of the building, crushing its inhabitants. Images of young Marines being dragged out of the rubble filled the airwaves. Some 241 American servicemen were killed and 60 more Americans were injured. America was shocked, for the Marines had been in Lebanon as part of an international peacekeeping mission. Along with French and Italian peacekeepers, they were there to help alleviate the misery inflicted by the brutal civil war. We'd thought we were the good guys.

Two days later, President Ronald Reagan, in a remarkable strategic pivot, invaded the tiny island of Grenada and threw out the Marxist regime that was planning to build a military-grade airport with the help of Cuban engineers. In the Cold War context of the day, this battle was seen not only as a punch in Fidel Castro's nose but as an important victory over Communism. The successful Grenada operation drew public attention away from Beirut while the Marines were quietly withdrawn and Lebanon continued its slide into chaos. With the barracks bombing and subsequent operations, Hezbollah achieved its strategic goal of driving the United States out of Lebanon by means of a relatively inexpensive, crude, but audacious weapon—the suicide bomber. The lesson was noted by others who'd later adopt the same terrible tactic.

My friend, mentor, and predecessor at the State Department counterterrorism office, Ambassador Robert Oakley, who held official posts under President Reagan and in the George H. W.

Bush administration, later summarized the impact of Iranian and Hezbollah terror:

> It was a concerted effort, which succeeded in pushing the United States out of Lebanon, and it also produced a big change in our policy towards the Middle East. We'd been pursuing a very positive, active policy towards the Middle East as a whole, encouraging further agreements between the Arab governments and Israel. This put a stop to it. We really went into a period of paralysis so far as Middle East diplomatic policy was concerned. We were very much on the defensive.[6]

Hezbollah was quiet for a short time after the 1980s, but emerged back on the terrorist scene with a series of attacks on more unusual targets. On March 17, 1992, a suicide bombing of the Israeli embassy in Argentina killed 29 and injured more than 250. Two years later, on July 18, 1994, a suicide bombing of a Jewish center in Argentina killed 87 and wounded 300. The Argentinean authorities finally concluded more than ten years later, in November 2005, that the perpetrator of the attack was a twenty-one-year-old Hezbollah operative who was probably able to infiltrate the country through Paraguay or Brazil (where there are large Lebanese populations). They also concluded that the operation was probably orchestrated by Iranian intelligence, but the details are sketchy and under wraps in Argentinean intelligence files. Better late and partial than never, I suppose.

The next attack, also conducted outside of Hezbollah's traditional area of operation, took place in Saudi Arabia in 1996. On June 25, members of Saudi Hezbollah, a branch of Hezbollah composed primarily of Saudi nationals from the Shia minority, converted a sewage truck into a bomb containing more than ten thousand pounds of TNT and detonated it at an Air Force housing complex for airmen stationed in Saudi Arabia called Khobar Towers. The massive bomb killed nineteen U.S. servicemen and one Saudi, and injured another 372 people of various nationalities. With this attack the statement these terrorists made was as loud as the blast: foreign influence, especially American, wasn't welcome in Saudi Arabia. One Lebanese was tried in connection to this attack, but it is clear that the Khobar cell also had direct links to senior level officials in Iranian intelligence, a point that several Clinton administration people made to Congress. But the Khobar bombing faded into memory within weeks of the attack, just as the USS *Cole* bombing would four years later.

These enormously successful attacks demonstrated Hezbollah's worldwide capabilities. So why did Hezbollah suddenly stop conducting suicide missions after enjoying such success? Why did they refrain from using such an effective tactic? The answer lies in the evolution of Hezbollah as an organization and the limits of terrorism in achieving strategic goals for serious organizations or countries.

At about the same time that Hezbollah was brandishing its international terrorism prowess, it was also beginning to mature into a political party in Lebanon and, as such, began polishing its image with Europeans and citizens of other regions. By emphasizing their political activities (even winning seats in Parliament) and their social service activity in the most impoverished and neglected Shia neighborhoods, Hezbollah was beginning to enjoy a certain degree of legitimacy in Europe as well as Asian and Latin American capitals.

What accounts for Hezbollah's altered strategy? As the evidence poured in of Hezbollah's links to terrorist attacks in Argentina and Saudi Arabia, international pressure began to build. In my estimation, Hezbollah's leaders knew that if they continued to conduct these types of attacks overseas, they'd suffer the consequences of international condemnation. So they pulled in the reins on the suicide bombers. Simultaneously, they realized that they could get away with a certain degree of indirect support for Palestinian terrorist groups as long as it was discreet and limited to Israel and the occupied territories.

What are the lessons of these attacks? First, Hezbollah, with Iranian support and direction, has an extensive global reach in its terrorist operations. Second, the power and presence of the state apparatus of Iran gives Hezbollah a certain advantage over an organization such as al Qaeda, which has no state links. However, that same advantage also puts a brake on Hezbollah. We can see that after the Europeans and Saudis put political pressure on Iran and its Hezbollah surrogates, they stopped the killing. Hezbollah got away with all of that mayhem, but then quietly responded to diplomatic pressure to knock it off. The Europeans and Saudis basically said (although not in these words): "Okay, we know you killed those Jews and Americans. But stop it now, or else when you get caught red-handed again, we'll join those crazy Americans and hammer you with sanctions." And by the way, another unspoken message was: "It's okay to support Palestinian terrorism as long as you keep it in Israel and the occupied territories; if you do that, we won't brand you as a terrorist organization and lump you in with the likes of al Qaeda." It's a very cynical equation.

As the ambassador at large for counterterrorism at the U.S. State Department, one of my duties was to formally and legally designate terrorist organizations for the U.S. government. Hezbollah was always one of those organizations, both for its past deeds directed against Americans and for its more recent support in training Palestinian terrorist groups. In that post, I got to see the results of terrorism up close. Early on in my tour at State, I had the privilege of meeting Patricia Stethem, the mother of the American naval diver Robert Dean Stethem, who was murdered by Hezbollah terrorists. Petty Officer Stethem was on board TWA Flight 847 when it was hijacked in 1985. Even though he was flying in civilian clothes, the terrorists singled him out for being a soldier, beat him severely, shot him, and dumped his body onto the tarmac at Beirut International Airport. Stethem's mother is a wonderful, dignified lady who is committed to the cause of bringing to justice the men who killed her son and held an airplane full of people hostage for seventeen days. I would meet with Mrs. Stethem occasionally and give her updates on the State Department's efforts to keep the pressure on Hezbollah and Iran. Unfortunately, Mohammed Ali Hamadi, the only Flight 847 hijacker to be detained, was found and tried in Germany, where he served eighteen years of his life sentence before being paroled, possibly as part of a questionable prisoner swap for a forty-three-year-old woman who'd been taken hostage in Iraq. Hamadi was on a plane back to Lebanon on the day of his release. Once again, Hezbollah managed to evade international censure while good people such as the Stethem family must continue to wait for justice to prevail.

Meeting the families of those most directly affected by terrorist murders gave me a personal perspective on these crimes. Their faces are indelibly etched on my mind. I felt a personal kinship with the late Lieutenant Colonel William R. Higgins, an Army colonel like myself who served with the United Nations while on active duty. While heading a peacekeeping mission in Lebanon in 1988, Higgins was kidnapped, tortured, and murdered by Hezbollah terrorists in Beirut. Calling themselves the "Organization of the Oppressed on Earth," the killers released a videotape of a man they claimed to be Higgins hanging from a gallows. (So much for their assertions that the United States shouldn't attempt to rescue him before he could face trial.) Higgins's wife, Robin, a Marine Corps lieutenant colonel, is another woman of great dignity who's been active in Washington, pushing for justice to finally catch up with Hezbollah. Although the perpetrators of William Higgins's death remain at large, she's kept the memory of her husband alive in a city that sometimes forgets its heroes too quickly.

Hezbollah has come a long way since the 1980s and 1990s. In 2000, they achieved their primary strategic victory when Israel pulled out of southern Lebanon, virtually ceding full control of that area to Hezbollah. At the same time, they somehow morphed from terror-mongers into a quasi-legitimate political party while more discreetly supporting radical Palestinian terrorist organizations with training and other support. In just over two decades, they went from initiating the use of suicide tactics to holding 14 of the 128 seats in the Lebanese Parliament after the 2005 election. So who are these guys? Are they the Iran-backed A-team of terrorism, as they're sometimes referred to by American counterterrorism officials? Or are they a political party that's trying to find its way in the violent and byzantine world of Lebanon and the rest of the Middle East?

I have had the opportunity to observe Hezbollah up close on their home turf. In May 2000, Israel completed its withdrawal from southern Lebanon after more than twenty years of occupation. Hezbollah declared victory and moved south to occupy the checkpoints along the border. In the summer of 2002, when I was an assistant secretary general with the United Nations' Department of Peacekeeping Operations, I took a trip to the Middle East to visit our operations there. One unit known as UNIFIL, an acronym for United Nations Interim Force in Lebanon, was stationed along the southern border of Lebanon with Israel. An Indian two-star general named Lalit Mohan Tewari took me on a guided tour of the border. Major General Tewari was a veteran of the Indian mountain troops that had fought wars and skirmishes with the Pakistanis, often at elevations of over fourteen thousand feet in the Himalayas. Tewari was a smart professional with a very astute military and political mind, and we'd come to be good friends during our service at the UN.

The UN peacekeeping unit in Lebanon was never intended to dictate peace on the border; it was a stabilizing force, no more and no less. Tewari's troops were disciplined and motivated. A detachment from Ghana manned one outpost overlooking the heavily militarized border, part of an alliance of thirty separate nations under the UN umbrella. Many of these troops had received training and equipment from the U.S. Army's Third Special Forces Group, which had been quietly training African peacekeepers for the past several years. They were a proud and well-organized unit.

Tewari was in a difficult situation. His predecessor had been part of an embarrassing UN scandal in which it appeared that UN soldiers had watched passively as Israeli soldiers were kidnapped by Hezbollah paramilitaries not far from the front of their border observation posts. This was bad enough, but it was the cover-up of the incident that caused quite a stir at the UN and further validated the notion that the peacekeepers were useless at best, and even harmful because of their clear anti-Israeli bias. Tewari was determined to restore credibility to the unit—a tough task, especially for skeptical Americans. He knew I was one of those skeptics, even if I was working with the UN at the time.

I stood at the front edge of a heavily sandbagged guard post that looked as though its design had been borrowed from a Vietnam War–era U.S. Army firebase. I looked across the border into the lush green Israeli valleys that contrasted so starkly with the brown, dusty ground and ramshackle towns on the Lebanese side. The contrast reminded me of Korea. On my trip across the DMZ en route to North Korea two years earlier when I was working for the State Department, I witnessed the same stark disparity. On the same terrain, separated only by a fence, one side looked like a thriving first-world economy full of hope and promise, while the other was clearly wracked with third-world poverty and despair.

The Lebanese-Israeli border had three flags flying: those of the UN, Israel, and Hezbollah. I knew the Hezbollah colors very well from a captured flag I'd been given by the Israelis when I was at the State Department. (That flag now hangs on the wall at NYPD's counterterrorism office in Brooklyn.) The flags represented three entities at odds with one another. They engaged in a twenty-four-hour stare-down, with mutual mistrust all around. On the southern side of the border, the Israelis sat well armed and trained. On the northern side was the UN force, stretched thinly along the "green line" with a weak mandate to observe and report, and not do much more. On the northern side, not too far from the UN positions, Hezbollah set up its own guard towers, very similar to the Israeli and UN compounds.

By this point Tewari knew me fairly well and was aware that I'd spent many years with third-world soldiers around the globe, both in the Special Forces and with UN peacekeeping. He took me on an up-close and personal tour of Hezbollah, beyond the normal boundaries of an official visit from headquarters. Tewari and I both wanted to get a good look at Hezbollah and share our thoughts about the nature of their organization. The Hezbollah troops were generally very alert. They were in quasi-uniform; although they sported a variety of different fatigues, they were generally similar in appearance. They wore their equipment at all times and either carried their arms or kept them within easy reach. In short, they appeared to be better disciplined than most third-world armies I had been around, and much more organized than I expected. They were clearly developing into a regular army.

Like a precocious teenager who knows how to evade curfews and break the house rules without getting caught, Hezbollah functions as a political party but uses terrorist tactics to threaten, intimidate, and coerce when it can do so without international outrage. They know the limits of what they can get away with outside of Israel and the occupied territories. This explains why Israel regards Hezbollah and its backer, Iran, as a far greater security threat than does the rest of the world. Because the two are, relatively speaking, rational and restrained terrorists, they're able to push the envelope of acceptable international behavior.

Iran and Hezbollah are very different from al Qaeda. Iran is a member of the international community, and although it consistently provokes both the United States and Israel, it does, in fact, nurture its relationships with most other parts of the world and has been traditionally responsive to international pressures and concerns. The Iranians recognize that they can take their bellicose behavior only so far. Working in concert with Hezbollah, they clearly support terrorism, but they keep their unsavory alliances tightly managed and focused on Israel, and conduct operations only in Israel and the immediate surrounding areas (including southern Lebanon and the occupied territories). Whenever possible, action is directed against the Israeli military—although Iran supports some Palestinian terrorist organizations directly and through Hezbollah. With the U.S. presence in Iraq, they have also stepped up their activities to resist American efforts in that country and to pursue their broader agenda to support Shia revivalism in Iraq.

Regarding their nuclear program, like the North Koreans and Pakistanis, the Iranians are aware that they need equal parts of technological development and political capital to acquire a bomb. But they also know that if they're patient and persistent they can probably get one, and the rest of the world (with the exception of the United States) will do very little to stop them. Again, like the North Koreans and Pakistanis, they'll eventually make a rational decision regarding the cost-benefit ratio of acquiring a nuclear weapon. At this point it's clear to me that Iran is pursuing that capability, despite the costs.

Iran's heated rhetoric calling for the annihilation of Israel and rants against the United States notwithstanding, most countries consider Iran to be a rational actor and thereby much less of a threat to international peace and security than Americans and Israelis do. And to the extent that Iran does represent a threat to peace and security, the rest of the world knows that the threat will be focused on the United States and Israel, not on their territories or interests. The Iranians are acutely aware of these sentiments and work carefully, underneath their violent anti-American spasms, to keep economic and diplomatic relationships with other nations intact while splitting the Americans away from the rest of the world.

As the war in Iraq continued to deteriorate in 2005 and 2006, the Bush administration increasingly shifted much of its most heated rhetoric to Iran. Iran warranted concern based on several factors. The first was that the relatively moderate mullahs had been in control of Iran for several years when a new firebrand, Mahmoud Ahmadinejad, was elected in 2005. His anti-Israeli rhetoric is several notches above the usual rantings of Iranian radicals. Three months after taking office he gave a speech at "The World Without Zionism" student conference in which he suggested that Israel should be "wiped off the map."[7] A few weeks later in a speech to thousands in the Iranian town of Zahedan, he called the Holocaust a "myth" and suggested that if such atrocities actually did occur, then Israel should relocate to Europe as reparation for Germany's crimes against the Jews.[8] These positions are really nothing new from the most radical Iranian mullahs. However, the Iranian leader's comments were more inflammatory, more direct, and tied to a troubling record of increasing mischief. Iran's support for Hezbollah and other Palestinian terrorist groups, their meddling in the Iraq war, and their insistence on developing a nuclear program provide major challenges for future American administrations.

Hezbollah Returns in the Summer of 2006

Hezbollah burst back onto the scene in the summer of 2006 when it kidnapped three Israeli soldiers along the Syrian border, touching off a confrontation with Israel that has been generally described as a disaster for the Israeli army. The criticism has perhaps been most vehement in Israel itself. Israel responded to the kidnappings with ferocity, bombing Hezbollah positions and other targets in Lebanon, and Hezbollah countered by firing hundreds of Katyusha rockets deep into Israel. The violence on both sides continued to escalate, leaving hundreds dead on both sides and considerable collateral damage. All in all, it was a frustrating episode for the Israelis and has caused them to rethink their military strategy vis-à-vis Hezbollah.

Questions of Hezbollah's legitimacy aside, at NYPD we intentionally looked at these characters from a very parochial point of view. We knew they were the fierce enemy of our Israeli allies, and we knew they had the blood of many Americans on their hands, but our concerns were more immediate: Who exactly are Hezbollah? What sort of presence do they have in the United States and New York City? Do they have the capability and/or intention to strike within the United States? Would they act as surrogates of Iran if the United States attacked Iranian nuclear capability? Unfortunately, we never obtained very clear answers to those questions. However, in considering our next steps, it is critical to know Hezbollah and Iran—their history, motivations, and capabilities. Their history is soaked in the blood of Americans (in the 1980s and 1990s), but they have been restrained in their terrorist activity outside of Israel since 1996.

Chapter 5

Lone Wolves, Cults, and Radical Movements

SINCE 9/11, WHEN AMERICANS talk about "the terrorists" they mean al Qaeda, but bin Laden and his confederates are not the only players in terrorism. As we examine the full implications of terrorism in our day and consider our responses to it, it's also important to understand other terrorist attacks and the movements, organizations, and individuals that perpetrate them. Prior to 9/11 there were many attacks on our soil launched by a host of different terrorists with national and international issues spanning the entire political spectrum. Right- and left-wing extremists (including militias), anti-abortion and anti-gay movements, animal rights groups, ecoterrorists, and others have vented their anger in countless killings. Religious cults (and other people on the fringe, such as the Unabomber, Ted Kaczynski, who struck out against science and technology) can have a grievance about any conceivable issue. By training our eyes not only on 9/11 but also on the many attacks that occurred before and since, we can glean important lessons and develop a more complete understanding of what we're up against.

American terrorists come in all shapes, sizes, and colors. Oklahoma City bomber Timothy McVeigh was a twenty-five-year-old white male who grew up in rural America. Nothing about him resembled the profile of the typical terrorist. I often used him as an example in reminding my team at NYPD that terrorists don't always *look* like terrorists. Most of the al Qaeda operatives we studied fit a clear profile: twenty to thirty-year-old males of Middle Eastern or South Asian descent. However, we couldn't limit our counterterrorism efforts to this profile alone. At NYPD we denied ourselves the temptation of conducting racial profiling, not in the interest of being politically or legally correct, but primarily because that approach wouldn't sufficiently protect us against all of our potential enemies.

Over the past twenty years, most of the terrorists who've attacked America have been lone wolves—that is, independent agents who aren't part of a larger organization. However, a deeper investigation of each case usually reveals a connection to a broader movement. Today there are many radical organizations and movements in the United States, and although they often don't appear to pose an immediate threat, it's from those ranks that we typically see someone emerge who is contemplating a one-off terrorist attack. Historically, of all the "lone wolves," the ones who may have come the closest to having a strategic effect were the Beltway Sniper team of John Allen Muhammad and Lee Boyd Malvo when they terrorized and virtually paralyzed the Washington, D.C., metropolitan area between September 5 and October 24, 2002. But because they weren't part of an organized group, once they were captured their impact was short-lived.

The real threat of these national fringe groups, as with al Qaeda, lies in their potential to acquire a chemical, biological, radiological, or nuclear (CBRN) weapon. A CBRN weapon would give them the potential to create the sort of havoc that would have a true strategic effect on our country. For that reason, although these groups don't preoccupy the national consciousness as does al Qaeda, FBI and local law enforcement organizations must always take them seriously. They can be just as deadly.

Every other Thursday morning while I was with NYPD, I met with the inspectors who were responsible for counterterrorism programs and policies in the precincts of New York. NYPD has eight regional precincts and several other functional commands such as transit (for the subways), housing (for the particular needs of public housing projects), and schools. It also has separate commands for the Detective Bureau (which handles major investigations) and narcotics. We began each of those meetings with a PowerPoint briefing that analyzed a current or past terrorism event. We covered all events in the United States and many around the world, knowing that every borough of New York City had a slice of the entire planet in it somewhere. Not only does the city have a population of more than eight million people but in Brooklyn and Queens over 40 percent of the population is foreign-born. New York is a real melting pot of the world's populations, which accounts for much of the city's energy and vitality. But it also leaves open the possibility that the world's most complex and heated issues may boil up on its streets. A new radical movement in a far-flung corner of the world could be just one e-mail away from showing up in one of New York's five boroughs.

My Thursday morning sessions with the counterterrorism inspectors set the tone for the rest of our week. Rather than sit around and speculate about how terrorists might attack us, my intelligence analysts developed a thorough understanding of dozens of past operations and acquired a true and deeply nuanced expertise in terrorist tradecraft. They knew how a terrorist might organize a cell, establish a safe house, procure finances and bomb-making materials, construct a weapon, and conduct an attack. To augment the analytical process, we actually built two replicas of bomb-making safe houses so as to have a more complete understanding of exactly what it takes to organize a plot. "Operation Kaboom," as we called it, was a very illuminating exercise for my cops and detectives, the details of which I'll discuss in Chapter 10.

Terror in the United States

Terrorism has historically been part of life in the United States in general, and New York City in particular. On September 16, 1920, one of the first truck bombs (actually a horse-drawn wagon) exploded on Wall Street opposite the House of Morgan in downtown Manhattan. Forty people were killed and hundreds more were injured. Bolshevik or anarchist terrorists were blamed, but the crime was never solved.[1] Fifty-five years later, at noontime on Friday, January 24, 1975, in the same Wall Street neighborhood, a bomb was set off in a doorway of the historic Fraunces Tavern, killing four and injuring another forty. A radical, pro-independence Puerto Rican nationalist group called FALN claimed responsibility for that attack, but no one was ever prosecuted. FBI responded by creating the first Joint Terrorism Task Force in 1980.[2] FALN continued to terrorize New York into the 1980s, including four separate bombings on New Year's Eve 1982, which targeted three federal courthouses and police headquarters.[3]

In March 1977, a group of Salafist Muslims known as the Hanafis stormed three buildings in Washington, D.C., including the B'nai B'rith headquarters, in part as an act of protest toward a film about the Prophet Muhammad that they considered sacrilegious. Two people were killed and 149 were held hostage for thirty-nine hours. The episode caught the local police and FBI completely off guard. By all accounts, this event showed the counterterrorism response capability of the U.S. government to be dismal. For example, when a fire ladder was hoisted up the side of the building, it was noted by the press and subsequently communicated to the Hanafis inside. The media was soundly criticized for its sympathetic reporting and contribution to the botched operation, but the entire episode was a fiasco and left many in the U.S. government, in both foreign and domestic policy, contemplating our lack of counterterrorism capability.[4] As a result, the U.S. government started to develop a national counterterrorism capability in FBI and the U.S. military.

The 1970s was a decade of wide-ranging terrorist activity around the world. The most notorious of those international terrorists were the Palestinians. The era of modern terrorism and its relationship to the media can be traced to the 1972 Olympics in Munich. Palestinian members of Black September, a terrorist group connected with Yasser Arafat's Fatah, stormed the dormitory rooms of the Israeli athletes, held eleven young men hostage for two days, and then killed them during a siege by German police at a Munich air base. The massive media presence that was on hand for the Olympics made this terrorist massacre a worldwide media event, a bonus that wasn't lost on future terrorist organizations.

In addition to the Palestinian terrorists wreaking havoc during that period, there emerged a new group of radical leftist European organizations, including the Italian Red Brigades and the German Baader-Meinhof Group. And other supernationalist groups from Croatia and Puerto Rico sprang up to touch off violence in New York City and elsewhere. But the Vietnam War, the civil rights movement, campus unrest, and the overhanging Cold War deflected media attention from these terrorist incidents. As a result, terrorism didn't really penetrate the American consciousness during this period (with the possible exception of the Munich attacks). Compared to those other issues, leftist terrorists were not a top story. At the close of the decade, these movements quickly faded. Far before the end of the Cold War, even the politically motivated leftist movements had mostly burned out in the United States and the rest of the West. And so for most of the 1980s our terrorism problems were clustered in places such as Lebanon and Libya. That changed on April 19, 1995, in Oklahoma City.

Timothy McVeigh: Anti-Government Terrorism

Timothy McVeigh was a lone wolf, but his story is actually more complex than that moniker implies. McVeigh was on the fringe of the militia movement in March 1993 when he began planning his attack. He was motivated by two controversial incidents with federal law enforcement agencies: Ruby Ridge and Waco.

The incident on Ruby Ridge was less publicized than the Waco disaster, but it did quite a bit to aggravate already agitated American separatist groups. On August 21, 1992, FBI agents surrounded the home of Randy and Vicki Weaver, suspected militia radicals who'd fled what they perceived to be the evils of American civilization to raise their four children on a secluded ridge in northern Idaho. Before they reached the house, the agents encountered the Weavers' fourteen-year-old son Samuel, who was purportedly hunting with his dog. They shot the dog, sparking a scuffle that left Samuel and a federal agent dead. A ten-day standoff ended in the wounding of Randy Weaver and his friend Kevin Harris by an FBI sniper. The same sniper also inadvertently shot and killed Vicki Weaver during the firefight as she hid behind a door, holding her ten-month-old daughter in her arms. Randy Weaver and his friend surrendered and were acquitted of the charges filed against them, but the damage had been done. FBI's reputation for competence and good judgment was severely damaged on Ruby Ridge and, for the radical fringe militia movement, the incident simply bolstered their worldview of an American government run amok.

Six months later, the Bureau of Alcohol, Tobacco, and Firearms (ATF) raided Mount Carmel, a compound of religious radicals known as the Branch Davidians who congregated near Waco, Texas. The Davidians were armed and ready when the agents arrived, thanks to a news reporter who tipped them off by asking a mailman who happened to be related to the sect's leader for directions to the compound. ATF (with FBI) pursued the raid anyway and ended up laying siege to the Branch Davidian compound for fifty-one eventful days. After a violent standoff, FBI (taking the lead for the response away from ATF) initiated an assault on the complex, using increasing amounts of tear gas to try to flush the Davidians out. Finally, with the building in ruins, the remaining Davidians started several large fires and went to their deaths in an apocalyptic blaze. Some accuse the assaulting federal units of igniting the blaze, but evidence indicates that the fire was primarily a result of those inside torching their buildings. Seventy-nine people died, including twenty-one children and the group's leader, David Koresh.

Timothy McVeigh was a racist loser who became involved in the militia movement just prior to enlisting in the U.S. Army at twenty years of age.[5] During the Waco standoff, McVeigh drove from Arizona to Texas to protest the siege on the Branch Davidians. He witnessed the final day of the standoff and, among other protesters, was photographed on-site by FBI agents. McVeigh was a veteran of the Gulf War but otherwise had a less than noteworthy Army career. While on active duty, he sought entry into the U.S. Army Special Forces but was rejected. At the time of his military discharge, he had no special training to equip him as a terrorist. After leaving the military, he joined the Ku Klux Klan and began frequenting conferences and gun shows associated with extreme right-wing movements.

McVeigh was influenced by a novel called *The Turner Diaries,* written in 1978 by William Pierce under the pseudonym Andrew MacDonald. This book, a favorite at gun shows, is a violent, racist manifesto that calls for an uprising of "the white revolution" to overthrow the U.S. government. The hero of the book, Earl Turner, responds to gun-control legislation by making a truck bomb and blowing up the Washington FBI building. This seems to have been the motivation for McVeigh's attack on the Murrah Federal Building in Oklahoma City. In his twisted mind, McVeigh thought that his attack would precipitate a broader, violent movement against the U.S. government. But in reality, he would always be a lone wolf.

McVeigh planned and conducted a massive terrorist attack with only limited support from his primary accomplice, Terry Nichols. His weapon of choice, the truck bomb, was very similar to those used by IRA and Islamic terrorists around the world. Unfortunately, it wasn't hard for McVeigh to figure out how to build the bomb; information on bomb making was readily available in the anarchist literature that McVeigh was exposed to at the gun shows he frequented. The basic material to build the main charge of the bomb, ammonium-nitrate-based fertilizer, was readily available in rural settings. To detonate the explosives, McVeigh stole commercial-grade dynamite and blasting caps from a quarry in Marion, Kansas.[6]

McVeigh and Nichols built the bomb the day before the attack in a remote area of Geary Lake, Kansas. They loaded a mixture of ammonium nitrate and fuel oil into barrels in a truck rented from Ryder (the same truck rental company that Ramzi Yousef had used in the first World Trade Center bombing). McVeigh then drove the truck down to Oklahoma City and parked it in front of the Murrah Building a little before 9:00 A.M. on April 19, 1995—the second anniversary of the end of the Waco siege. While seated in the front seat of the truck, he ignited the time fuse with a pull-cord detonator, which ignited a backup fuse at the same time. He then climbed out of the truck and calmly walked to a yellow 1977 Mercury Marquis that he had previously parked around the corner.

McVeigh's bomb worked perfectly. The explosion was clean, detonating the entire five-thousand-pound charge. The entire face of the building came off, with significant collapse of floors. One hundred and sixty-eight people were confirmed dead, including nineteen children and infants at a day care center, plus the unborn children of at least three pregnant women, and more than eight hundred people were injured; if the building had fully collapsed, many more would have died.

In his getaway, McVeigh made a series of blunders. He'd positioned his getaway car around the corner three days before the attack. Concerned that it might get towed, he took off the license plates and left a note on the windshield that said the car had an engine problem and shouldn't be moved. McVeigh thought of everything before he ignited his time fuse, but after the fact, he was nervous and made several major errors. When he jumped into the yellow Mercury to make his escape, he failed to put the license plates back on the car, a surefire way to get pulled over. His second big mistake was having an unregistered handgun in his possession, which led to his immediate arrest. His third and final strike was that he was speeding north on Interstate 35. Speeding, no plates, and an illegal firearm landed McVeigh in jail—where, after a few days, an alert investigator connected the dots and identified McVeigh as a suspect in the bomb attack. He was tried, convicted on all counts, and sentenced to death by lethal injection.

As this case clearly illustrates, domestic movements can spawn deadly terrorists. The Oklahoma City bombing was the most successful terrorist attack against the homeland prior to 9/11. This example demonstrates how a very small cell can plan and execute a major attack. The operation was essentially McVeigh's one-man show, with some assistance from a secondary player. Although McVeigh had a basic military background, he was essentially self-taught in explosives. He obtained his materials by burglarizing a construction company's storage facility for explosives as well as through regular, legal purchases. McVeigh serves as a constant reminder that evil can live next door and major devastation can be accomplished by a pair of disgruntled citizens.

The Beltway Snipers: Paralyzing a City

In October 2002, a little over one year after the 9/11 attacks, two men held the Washington, D.C., metro area in fear for several weeks. Forty-one-year-old John Allen Muhammad and seventeen-year-old Lee Boyd Malvo, known as the Beltway Snipers, began their Washington-area killing spree on October 2 with a series of six shootings in two days. In the next sixteen days they engaged in at least another thirteen shootings in which ten people were killed and three were severely wounded.

Muhammad and Malvo had designed a simple and effective killing machine: a sniper platform in the back of a nondescript car. This is the type of ingenious little operation that many have expected al Qaeda to conduct since 9/11. It didn't require sophisticated equipment; in fact, the rifles and ammunition the duo used are readily available in many Wal-Mart stores around the country. The required training was also minimal. Although Muhammad had had military weapons training, he hadn't been trained as a sniper. The youngster and primary shooter, Malvo, had very little training, and what little he had was provided by Muhammad himself.

Although somewhat reckless in their targeting, they were able to get off well-aimed and deadly shots and then disappear into the road networks of Virginia and Maryland with relative ease. It was the simplicity of the operation that made it difficult to stop. That and the fact that the cell was a self-contained unit of two people kept the intelligence leads to a minimum. Like McVeigh's, this was a small operation, and the snipers didn't talk about it outside of their tight circle, making it very difficult for law enforcement to track them.

It's interesting to compare these operations with some of the foiled terrorist plots in the United States and the United Kingdom. In many of these cases, groups of Islamic radicals discussed and plotted their attacks with like-minded radicals, and as the plots became more elaborate, they became vulnerable to penetration. In the case of Muhammad and Malvo, there was no support structure and no ideological group, just two determined killers. They were finally betrayed by their own greed and growing egos.

Puffed up by the sick satisfaction of serial killing, the snipers started leaving tarot cards at the scenes of their crimes and later left plastic bags with convoluted messages in them, including a note that demanded $10 million and alluded to targeting children next. In an attempt to burnish their credentials as killers, they took credit for the killing of a liquor store clerk that had transpired the month before in Alabama. Their boasting inadvertently yielded information that allowed police to identify the car they used. Then it was only a matter of time before they were caught sleeping in their car at a truck stop and arrested. Again, even these two shrewd and elusive killers were revealed as bunglers when it came to staying abreast of developments in their own case. Had they been aware that authorities had a description of their car, they might have switched vehicles and eluded capture.

The Beltway attacks show the vulnerability of our society to a determined and fairly disciplined killer. Weapons are easily attained and targets are plentiful. Terror can be engineered through a period of sustained attacks. But what other lessons can be drawn from this incident? Small cells are less likely to be compromised, and lone wolves who keep their mouths closed are very difficult to capture. However, an organization such as al Qaeda, by its very nature, tends to expand and expose its contacts to a wider group of adherents. The Beltway case also showed that the public response to an isolated event or series of events can be contained. When attackers are not part of a broader organization or strategy, their capture leads to a quick return to normalcy. The wave of fear inspired by the Beltway Snipers didn't spread out of the Washington, D.C., region because they were not seen as part of a wider plot.

Olympic Park Bomber Eric Rudolph: Anti-Government Sociopath

Eric Rudolph, also known as the Olympic Park Bomber, was another notorious American terrorist. In addition to the Atlanta Olympic bombing in 1996, Rudolph also confessed to three other bombings: at an abortion clinic outside of Atlanta in January 1996, at a gay-lesbian nightclub in Atlanta in February 1997, and at another abortion clinic in Birmingham, Alabama, in January 1998. The last attack was notable because it was a double bombing. The first bomb was set off in a Dumpster near the clinic, injuring no one. However, Rudolph set a second explosive device that exploded shortly afterward with the clear intention of killing responders to the first event. In the second blast he succeeded in killing off-duty police officer Robert Sanderson and seriously injuring a nurse.

Like McVeigh, Rudolph was a militant racist. His ideology was rather tangled and his goal was to spark a guerrilla campaign against the U.S. government because of its support for abortion and the "homosexual agenda." Because Rudolph attacked abortion clinics and gay nightclubs, he got some support from the radical conservative fringe. The Christian Identity movement, for example, wrote two songs about him, and a very popular T-shirt with the words "Run Rudolph Run" was sold.[7] Deluded terrorists such as Rudolph believe their action will spur others with like-minded grievances. The fact is, however, that although they may be successful in their attacks, these bumblers rarely inspire others. Rudolph's case illustrates a few familiar themes of the terrorist phenomenon. First, a small disciplined cell or lone wolf can avoid detection for many years if he remains disciplined. Second, without a propaganda arm and without being part of a bigger organization, those terrorists typically have minimal long-term impact. And although they may have some sympathizers for their cause, their methods (killing innocents) ultimately alienate all but the most radical adherents to the movement.

"Unabomber" Ted Kaczynski: The Nerd Who Hated Technology

Ted Kaczynski was the prototypical lone wolf. The Unabomber, so called because of the FBI code name UNABOM, initially given to him for his bombing of universities and airline offices, was responsible for a string of mail bombings over a period of eighteen years. His first attack was conducted in 1978, in the form of a bomb sent to a professor at Northwestern University. He then sent bombs to airline executives' offices. He also sent letter bombs to computer stores, to another professor, and to an astronaut selectee. His attacks followed a vague theme related to the pursuit of science and his perception of the evils of industrial technology.

The most troubling of Kaczynski's attacks occurred in 1979 when he put a bomb in the cargo hold on American Airlines Flight 444 from Chicago to Washington, D.C. Thankfully, a timing mechanism misfired or the blast could have been devastating, for there were clearly enough explosives to take down the aircraft. We were lucky in this case, which foreshadowed the interest today's terrorists have in commercial aviation. If Kaczynski had been successful, he would have been considered a mass murderer of major proportions. For unknown reasons, he didn't try to take down any more planes after this, nor did he try to improve the lethality of his bombs. But he was a prolific terrorist nonetheless, setting off sixteen bombs in all and exacting a terrible toll: three dead and twenty-nine wounded between 1978 and 1995.

The Unabomber baffled FBI investigators for twenty-six years. And although his attacks were accompanied by the moniker "FC," which is the initials of the Freedom Club, this didn't provide much of a clue to investigators because he was the club's only member.

Like the Beltway Snipers, Kaczynski was done in by his own ego. In 1995, when he succeeded in having published in the *New York Times* and the *Washington Post* a manifesto in which he rambled on about his complaints about "industrial society and its future," his brother identified the rantings. Kaczynski's brother turned him in to FBI under the condition that his own identity not be revealed, but ironically, that information was quickly leaked. The very release of the manifesto was controversial in FBI; it was against general policy to publish the demands of terrorists. However, in this case, FBI flexibility paid off and led to the Unabomber's arrest, ending his killing spree and giving him a life sentence with no parole.

The Rajneeshee Cult: Hippies Gone Bad

The first serious biological terrorist event in the United States was conducted by a cult organized around an Indian guru, Bhagwan Shree Rajneesh, who celebrated beauty, love, and guiltless sex.[8] In 1981 the Rajneeshee cult bought land in rural Oregon and quickly began expanding, much to the consternation of some locals who suspected the cult was an excuse for drug use, free sex, and the growing wealth of its founder and leader. In September 1984, the cult members retaliated against local enemies by poisoning a salad bar in a nearby restaurant with salmonella, a biological toxin. Hundreds were sickened. Some suspected the Rajneeshees, but local law enforcement was naive and hamstrung by their own procedures. They finally dismissed the case as food poisoning spread by food handlers who failed to wash their hands.

However, after some internal machinations in the cult, the investigation was reopened in 1985 and it was found that members of the cult had established a rather sophisticated biological weapons program on the grounds of the compound. The investigation found that one of the cult members who'd developed an array of biological capabilities had seized on the idea of making the entire region (other than themselves) sick during an election so that their members could dominate the polls. She ordered the pathogens from a Seattle-based company and cooked them up in her lab on the compound.

The Rajneeshee cell teaches us that violent cults need to be closely monitored, for they can be very dangerous. Fortunately, even for an organization with extensive resources and fairly sophisticated scientific knowledge, it's difficult to create viable chemical or biological weapons. Nevertheless, as science continues to advance and the capabilities of makeshift labs improve, it becomes increasingly necessary to keep a sharp eye on these types of cults. When they begin to talk of using violence against innocent civilians, it's imperative for law enforcement to get an immediate handle on the organization.

Ecological and Animal Rights Terrorism

The Earth Liberation Front (ELF) and the Animal Liberation Front (ALF) joined forces in 1993, declaring solidarity.[9] These groups have a radical and violent agenda to protect animals and the ecology from what they consider egregious abuses by individuals, corporations, and the government. Most of their actions are sabotage in various forms, occasionally including arson, as was conducted against the Vail, Colorado, ski resort by ELF. A separate group, the Coalition to Save the Preserves (CSP), conducted a series of arson attacks on new home construction in Arizona.

These groups don't really constitute a serious terrorist threat, but we need to watch them. In particular, we should monitor whether they or any radical spin-offs try something more dramatic. Their radical and violent leanings deserve close scrutiny, even if their goals do have some political support.

Pre-9/11 Islamic Terrorism

After 9/11, many pundits erroneously referred to the attack as the "first attack on American soil" by this organization. Not only had al

Qaeda been attacking us overseas for the previous three years, but New York City was also subject to several deadly attacks by Islamic terrorists prior to 9/11, in addition to a few others that were foiled. People such as Ramzi Yousef—chief plotter of the 1993 World Trade Center attack—were engaged in terrorist activity against America before al Qaeda turned its attention to the west. Yousef himself was the point man and trailblazer for the organization as it evolved into a global terror network. Indeed, al Qaeda was in the terror business long before 9/11.

For an insightful exposé of the failings of our counterterrorism efforts prior to 9/11, I recommend *The Cell*, coauthored by John Miller. As I mentioned previously, Miller, like CNN journalist Peter Bergen, traveled to Afghanistan in mid-1998 to meet with bin Laden, a few months prior to the embassy bombing. Now the spokesman for FBI director Bob Mueller, Miller is one of a handful of journalists who before 9/11 understood the nature of the threat perhaps as much or more than the intelligence community.

The Cell tells a frightening story of incompetence on the part of FBI, where Miller now works. His account begins with the assassination of the head of the Jewish Defense League (JDL), Meir Kahane. Kahane was a firebrand who'd been previously linked to bomb plots of his own. Kahane's killer was El Sayyid Nosair, an Egyptian radical who was involved with the Alkifah Refugee Center in Brooklyn. Alkifah was an early al Qaeda front organization that helped recruit money and fighters for the jihad against the Soviets. After the Afghan war, as al Qaeda shifted its target more toward the United States, Alkifah also shifted its focus to the enemy at home. Nosair was in contact with a range of al Qaeda figures, including Abdullah Azzam, who was Osama bin Laden's mentor in Afghanistan, and the Blind Sheik, who was the spiritual leader of Gama'at al-Islamiyya, the EIJ, and the nascent al Qaeda.

Nosair gunned down Kahane in the Marriott Hotel in Manhattan at a speaking engagement for the Zionist Emergency Evacuation Rescue Organization. Nosair was defended by the radical lawyer William Kunstler and was convicted and jailed for life for the shooting of a postal worker and another man as he fled the room, and for commandeering a taxi at gunpoint. Astonishingly, he wasn't convicted for shooting Kahane. Apparently the jury bought Kunstler's argument that Nosair was charged with the crime for being the only Arab in the room at the time of the killing but Kahane was actually killed by other members of JDL.

Interestingly, NYPD detectives found in Nosair's personal library bomb-making manuals and maps of the Statue of Liberty, Times Square, Rockefeller Center, and the World Trade Center. Along with the manuals there were many documents written in Arabic, one of which was a manifesto written by Nosair that called on his fellow jihadis to "topple the tall buildings of which the Americans are so proud."[10] Unfortunately, FBI put the case to bed and didn't follow up on the group of violent people surrounding Nosair, who were subsequently found to be directly linked to the 1993 World Trade Center plot. These people communicated with Nosair from prison and continued plotting against New York City with the so-called landmark targets.

The Landmark Plot: Undone by Intelligence

The landmark plot spun directly out of the first World Trade Center bombing. The leader of this cell, Siddig Ibrahim Siddig Ali, was linked to Nosair's group, who were inspired by the Blind Sheik, Omar Abdel Rahman. Fortunately, after the first World Trade Center attack, FBI reactivated their informant, Emad Salem, a former Egyptian army officer. The plan was made with the collusion of Nosair from his jail cell, with Salem knowing everything.

The plot was very ambitious and included the murder of government officials and the bombings of several locations including the United Nations, the Lincoln Tunnel, and the Holland Tunnel. In an FBI tape of the plotters, they're seen driving through one of the New York tunnels discussing the potential attack. The plot was moving forward in a serious way when it was disrupted. Three of the plotters had tested the timing devices for the bombs in Connecticut at the end of May. The group also bought large amounts of fertilizer and began mixing the fuel and fertilizer into the bomb on June 23, 1993. FBI had the safe house under taped surveillance and raided it as the plotters were making the explosive brew in fifty-five-gallon drums. Thanks to excellent intelligence work, this plot was broken up before it was launched.

Palestinians Attack in New York City

On July 31, 1997, two individuals were arrested in a plot to attack the Atlantic Avenue subway station in Brooklyn with pipe bombs. Gazi Ibrahim Abu Mezer and Lafi Khalil were both Palestinians. Abu Mezer came to the United States under a false Jordanian passport and quickly set his plot in motion. Khalil was here a little longer as a visa overstay. They were linked together by Amin Awad, who was associated with the Al-Farooq mosque—whose spiritual advisor was, again, the Blind Sheik.

The two went to North Carolina for work together and it was there that they built their bombs. Then they came back to New York City to attack the subway station. The only reason the plot failed was because an Egyptian roommate in their house in Brooklyn reported the plot to police. NYPD then raided the apartment, and there was a brief struggle during which both Abu Mezer and Khalil were shot and injured. At the end of Abu Mezer's trial, when he was sentenced to thirty years in prison, he shouted that Palestinian children do not deserve to die. Khalil, described as Abu Mezer's stooge, got only thirty-six months and was deported to Jordan after his sentence was finished in March 2000. In a letter sent two days before the arrest, Abu Mezer had demanded the release of the Blind Sheik and Ramzi Yousef, along with Palestinian leaders serving time in an Israeli jail.

There's been two other previous killings, both by distraught Palestinians. In the first, which occurred on February 23, 1997, a man went to the Empire State Building and shot a couple of innocent tourists. In another, which occurred on March 1, 1994, a group of Palestinians pulled up alongside a car full of Orthodox Jews in a van and fired at them, killing Ari Halberstam. Although not the work of an organized group, these attacks were indicators of the rage that was building within a small but radical community within New York City prior to the actual establishment of al Qaeda.

Lessons Learned on the Local Level

The United States, like virtually all other modern countries, has a history of domestic and international terrorism. Although some attacks have been tragic, the organizations mounting them have not posed a serious threat to our stability or livelihood. However, as Timothy McVeigh demonstrated, it is fairly easy to make large truck bombs. And although the Rajneeshee cult wasn't able to develop effective chemical, biological, or radiological weapons, that goal may be attainable by another group somewhere down the road (as shown by Aum Shinrikyo, which I will discuss in Chapter 10). As ever, intelligence will be the key to containing that threat. We must look not only for imminent threats but for future threats as well. For example, Ramzi Yousef's 1993 World Trade Center attack has been improperly labeled as a solitary event. It wasn't. In fact, that attack and the plots surrounding it were direct precursors to the 9/11 attack.

Certainly we must heed the warning signs when the evidence is screaming in our faces. Unless our view of a given event is clear and accurate, our subsequent counterterrorism policy will be equally distorted, leaving us perpetually vulnerable to a range of violent groups.

PART 2

Inside Counterterrorism:

From Green Beret to NYPD Blue

Chapter 6

The U.S. Army Special Forces: Shooters and Advisors

I'VE HAD MANY DIFFERENT roles in the counterterrorism field, including serving as a diplomat, police official, United Nations bureaucrat, writer, researcher, and lecturer. But I started out as a "shooter" in the U.S. Army Special Forces. As a young first lieutenant, straight out of Special Forces training, I was assigned to a CT unit in the Panama Canal Zone in 1979. This unit was formed shortly after the national CT unit known as Delta Force was created at Fort Bragg, North Carolina. Delta was named after an elite Special Forces unit in the Vietnam War commanded by its founder, Colonel Charlie Beckwith. In Panama, my unit was prepared to augment Delta if they were deployed to Latin America as well as to conduct our own operations in the region if Delta was deployed on another mission.

Meanwhile, up north at Fort Bragg, Delta was being expanded and enhanced with an annual budget of about $10 million, at the time an extraordinary amount of money. (Now the units can burn up more than $10 million in a few hours.) Today, Delta is part of the military's Joint Special Operations Command, or JSOC, and they remain the most motivated, highly trained, and best-equipped soldiers in the world.

The heroism and fighting skill of the JSOC is unsurpassed, yet America's most-wanted men such as al Qaeda's Osama bin Laden,

Hezbollah's Imad Mugniyah, and the Bosnian war criminal Radovan Karadzic have eluded their grasp for years. Mugniyah avoided capture for over twenty years until he was finally killed in Syria in February 2008. Why can't we get these guys?

I wish I had a simple answer. The reasons are complex, but in my view the major problems lie in two areas: risk aversion by senior leaders (mostly in the Pentagon) and poor intelligence support from both CIA and military intelligence organizations. Most of the successful U.S. Special Operations missions over the years have been conducted in conjunction with local forces with the support of good human and signals intelligence. If we expect to succeed in nabbing the world's most-wanted fugitives, Delta must have that same support.

Although initially trained as a "shooter," I spent the later part of my Special Forces career as an advisor, training and assisting foreign forces involved in local wars, primarily in Latin America and including El Salvador, Honduras, Colombia, Ecuador, and the Dominican Republic. Our work was the continuation of a mandate issued by President Kennedy in the early 1960s to assist our allies in fighting a "new style" of guerrilla warfare that was spreading throughout the world. The Special Forces today still retain that vital training and advisory role around the world, with each Special Forces group focused on one geographical area.

As we look for an exit strategy in Iraq, the Army's Green Berets are always mentioned as a critical part of the equation. The Special Operations advisors will be tasked with staying behind to train Iraqi forces as our conventional forces start to be drawn down. The Special Operations "shooters" will have the job of attacking a terrorist stronghold as required when that is beyond the capability of local forces. U.S. Army Special Forces soldiers are both shooters and trainers, as we saw in Vietnam and then again in Afghanistan after 9/11. Both will be needed to keep the terrorists under pressure in Iraq so they're unable to extend their reach back to our shores. Sometimes U.S. special operators work alone, but they're most successful when they operate in partnership with local forces. To succeed in Iraq we must team them up with local forces and support them with ample intelligence.

Special Operations and Local Forces in Action

In the March 2007 edition of the *Atlantic,* Mark Bowden, most famous for his account of the Mogadishu operation gone wrong in *Black Hawk Down,* took his readers inside the secretive world of the U.S. Special Operations community. His article, which he titled "The Manhunt," reveals how a group of local operatives in the Philippines were able to penetrate a clandestine cell and eventually hunt down and kill its leadership, effectively neutralizing the organization. Bowden's story shows how this operation was conducted primarily by the local Filipino Marines, with the very active and important support of U.S. Special Operations Forces. In this case, the unit was the U.S. Navy SEALs, but this is certainly not the first time U.S. Special Operations partnered with locals to form a counterterrorism dream team.

The SEALs worked long and hard with their Filipino counterparts in tracking a group of terrorists responsible for several grisly kidnappings and murders. The organization in question was the Abu Saif group, a band of pirates and extortionists who claimed to have an affiliation with al Qaeda. Bowden describes how a human penetration of the group provided the key intelligence that was the basis for a successful combat operation. At the end of the story, the Philippine Marines intercept the terrorists at sea as the group tries to avoid being encircled by ground forces. The mission was a classic case of human intelligence and radio intercepts providing the key elements to a successful maritime special mission conducted by a local force aided by U.S. Special Operations units.

Two other successful examples of U.S. Special Forces operating with local forces are worth mentioning. They took place in the 1990s in my old area of operations, Latin America. Again in each example, the U.S. forces took a secondary role in helping the locals collect actionable intelligence and plan an effective operation. The first was in 1993, when the Colombian National Police tracked down and killed cocaine dealer and murderer Pablo Escobar.

(This operation is the subject of another outstanding book by Mark Bowden, *Killing Pablo.*) The apprehension of Escobar is tainted by allegations that U.S. Special Operations had been training and working closely with Colombian units that were using death squads to kill narcotics traffickers when the gringos weren't watching. Of course that's unacceptable if the allegations are true. However, the strength of this operation, which isn't often discussed, is the effectiveness of the teamwork between U.S. Special Operations Forces and Colombian National Police. An innovative and determined Colombian police officer triangulated Escobar's phone calls as he was trying to make arrangements to get his family out of Colombia. A violent assault was conducted on Escobar's safe house and he was killed while attempting to escape over a rooftop. While this final operation was conducted by Colombian troops only, with no Americans, Bowden shows how the long-term partnership with U.S. Special Operations imparted intelligence and advisory assistance that led to a successful outcome.

In another example set in Latin America, U.S. Special Operations Forces supported the Peruvian government in resolving a very difficult hostage situation. On December 17, 1996, a Peruvian leftist terrorist organization called the MRTA violently ambushed the Japanese ambassador's residence in Lima during a holiday party. The terrorists captured more than six hundred hostages. Within a few days many were released, but the situation turned into a prolonged standoff. On April 26, 1996, the 126th day of the hostages' captivity, Peruvian Special Forces stormed the residence. Only one hostage and two commandos were killed in the assault—a remarkable feat. The brilliance of the rescue mission, however, was also tainted by reports that the Peruvians killed some of the captured terrorists who tried to surrender.

It was widely reported that JSOC and CIA played a role in the planning and execution of the Peruvian raid. In my experience, the chances of an operation being successful are significantly higher if the locals take the lead. But here's the catch: when locals are involved it's not uncommon to witness practices that cross the line of what Americans find acceptable. By working closely with foreign units, we may be able to reduce human rights violations associated with these operations. But if we want to get things done, sometimes we *must* work in conjunction with tough organizations with spotty human rights records.

There are other examples of JSOC quietly working behind the scenes to resolve very difficult issues—but there's also a long history of missed opportunities. For this, I fault the Pentagon and ultimately the civilian leadership of the U.S. government for its failure to plan and approve an appropriate small, surgical operation in a timely fashion. My own personal experience in Special Ops, both as a policy maker and as an operative, was one of frustration when decisive action was called for. Of course, in Iraq and Afghanistan these units are extremely busy—but significant missions outside of major theaters of operations still remain very few and far between.

Panama, 1980

On February 27, 1980, seventeen guerrillas stormed the embassy of the Dominican Republic outside Bogotá, Colombia, taking dozens of diplomats hostage. Among the hostages were fourteen ambassadors from around the world, including the United States. Meanwhile, eight thousand miles away in Tehran, the three-month-old U.S. embassy crisis ground on. I was stationed in Panama as the executive officer for the assault team of the regional counterterrorism unit for Latin America. The newly formed Delta Force had the lead role for American missions worldwide, but since this operation was in Latin America, we were put on alert. Although we were not the "Tier-One" hostage rescue unit, my team was staffed with very experienced and professional soldiers.

The other teams handled sniper duty, intelligence, and support while my team was the assault element. We learned how to enter rooms behind an explosive blast, climb up the insides of buildings in their elevator shafts, and shoot a variety of pistols and machine guns with precise accuracy while differentiating between terrorists, hostages, and innocent bystanders. We were taught to focus on a person's hands, and if an individual was armed and dangerous, we fired a "double tap" of two rounds into the terrorist's "center of mass" (the chest). Although this team was poorly funded, it was a privilege to work with such an exceptional group of seasoned veterans. I was confident that this low-budget unit would be extremely capable when called to its mission.

I'd just turned twenty-five and was excited by the prospect of getting the call for the Colombian mission. I tried to show a cool exterior. I was surrounded by a team of combat veterans who went about their mission preparation with a calm seriousness, some gallows humor, and a gritty determination. They had volunteered to join the Army, then signed up for Airborne, Ranger, and Special Forces training and multiple tours in Vietnam, even when everyone else was going home. Then they volunteered for a hostage rescue team. They knew the risks, particularly for the first guy to kick down a door in a hostage situation. On the other side of the door could be a guy with a gun trained on your face, or worse yet, a booby trap with a massive explosive charge.

Ultimately, we didn't go to Colombia, and neither did the Army's Delta Force. The crisis was resolved the old-fashioned way, through painful negotiations. However, two months later, President Carter called upon Delta Force to conduct its first mission to rescue the American hostages being held in Tehran. They were primed and ready, but sadly, as fate would have it, their mission ended in disaster. At a rally point inside Iran, named Desert One, the commander, Colonel Charlie Beckwith, called off the mission due to the failure of several helicopters to reach the first staging area. In the evacuation, a C-130 airplane and helicopter collided in the desert dust, killing eight U.S. servicemen. The mission failure at Desert One not only helped bring down the presidency of Jimmy Carter but also kept Delta out of commission for about another decade. They weren't sent on any sensitive "out-of-area" missions by any president after that, as it was deemed too risky, both militarily and politically.

It soon became apparent to me that if Delta wasn't going to get a call, the chance of my second-tier team in Panama getting into the action was even more remote. Over time, our mission shifted from operational standby to training other Latin American nations to conduct special missions. Foreign units trained by my team and others like it around the world were more likely to be called in their home country. I was fortunate enough to be deployed with my A-team to assist another country to select, train, and deploy the national hostage rescue team. This is where I learned my first important lesson about the counterterrorism business: missions are usually conducted by local forces, not by commandos or secret agents from abroad.

Mogadishu, Somalia, 1993

In the aftermath of the failed Iran rescue mission, JSOC went back to their barracks at Fort Bragg and for about ten years trained relentlessly, becoming the finest fighting force the world has ever known. Americans would be very proud of this unit if only they knew a little more about it. These men are chosen for their physical strength and stamina in a vigorous selection process that lasts many months. But in addition to their military skills, they're also evaluated on their maturity and character. There are no cowboys in this group; they're trained professionals. During this period, JSOC deployed and participated in the major military interventions of that era, including Grenada (1983), Panama (1989), and the first Gulf War (1991). Like the regular Army, with each deployment they got better and better. By the end of the first Gulf War, JSOC had demonstrated its professionalism and effectiveness and earned its way into the good graces of the military. They would soon be tested again.

The U.S. involvement in Somalia began in the summer of 1992 with an airlift of humanitarian relief to four interior landing strips. As a member of the White House National Security Council (NSC) staff, I was brought into the planning of this operation. By Thanksgiving of that same year, President George H. W. Bush had decided to intervene with a U.S.-led peacekeeping force. Three months later, I was deployed to Somalia with Admiral Jonathan Howe, my former boss at NSC. Howe had asked my new boss and former college professor, UN ambassador Madeleine Albright, and me to accompany him to Mogadishu to help him get his office up and running. I was supposed to stay for only a few days, but when we got there we found no staff, no communications, and a U.S. peacekeeping force that was heading for the exits. It was a recipe for disaster, and Howe knew it. I wound up staying for two months, trying to help him piece together something resembling a real headquarters and shore up the flagging operation. But by April, Ambassador Albright was recalling me to New York, where I was to be her peacekeeping advisor at the UN. On June 6, two months after I left Somalia, I was with Ambassador Albright when we got word that twenty-five Pakistanis had been killed and ten were reported missing in an ambush in downtown Mogadishu organized by the Somali warlord Mohammed Farah Aidid.

The UN Security Council quickly passed a resolution granting the UN the authority to "take all necessary measures" against those responsible for the attacks and provide for their "arrest and detention." The UN, which was being humiliated in Bosnia at the time, wanted to flex some muscle against this Somali warlord. The resolution passed unanimously. Aidid was a wanted man, and it was now Howe's job to pick him up. Unfortunately, Howe didn't have the forces necessary to do the job.

In the middle of June, Admiral Howe asked (through back channels) for the Pentagon to deploy Delta Force to Somalia. Aidid was moving freely about the streets of Mogadishu with very little protection. He'd be a relatively easy mark for a small, well-trained unit such as Delta. But at the Pentagon Howe's request was viewed with great skepticism. By early July, the Pentagon hadn't responded. On July 4, I was back in Mogadishu with Ambassador Albright, on an official visit to the UN mission, and we reiterated Howe's request in a State Department cable we sent from Cambodia (the next leg of our trip).

Unfortunately, during the time elapsed between the original requests in early June, the internal machinations of Washington, D.C., and the arrival of the JSOC team in August, the conflict with Aidid had escalated and he was no longer an easy target. JSOC arrived not with a small team of guys in a few unmarked vehicles, as Howe had envisioned, but as Task Force Rangers, a force of several hundred heavily armed troops that set up a major operation at the Mogadishu airport. They would be ferried around Mogadishu by Black Hawk helicopter and carry out their mission in plain view. The window for a special operation had closed; JSOC was now involved in a much more conventional air assault operation, albeit with very highly trained and effective fighters. But in reality they'd lost their "special" nature.

Initially, JSOC had some success. They deployed around the capital, rounded up some midlevel operatives, and seemed to be closing the noose around Aidid. But on October 3, after a daytime raid netted some key individuals, two Black Hawk helicopters were shot down. The chaos that unfolded afterward cost the lives of eighteen U.S. soldiers from Delta and the Ranger unit deployed with them and injured seventy-three. Some say the training for the Somali militants had come from al Qaeda. I'm not certain if this assertion is true, but their shooters certainly were effective. It was yet another searing experience for Delta in their first major high-profile operation since the failed Iranian mission.

The impact of the Black Hawk incident and its impact on U.S. foreign policy with regard to Africa turned out to be immense. As a result of the beating America's image took, including grisly images of a U.S. serviceman's corpse being dragged through the streets of Mogadishu, U.S. forces pulled out of Somalia six months later, on March 31, 1994. Six days later, the crisis in Rwanda erupted. The United States, partly due to the political trauma of Mogadishu, was paralyzed. Rather than turn around the ships that were carrying our troops away from Africa and send them back to Rwanda, America opted to ignore the genocidal killing.

Learning the Wrong Lessons

When the military succeeds, it normally lavishes praise on its soldiers and commanders, while diplomats and intelligence operatives rarely get any credit. But the inverse is not consistent with this accountability line. When the military fails, its leadership is normally very quick to blame a "poor policy framework" (the State Department) or "bad intelligence" (CIA). But the Army also conducts its own internal reviews of its military failures. In the case of Mogadishu, the lessons were primarily that JSOC had insufficient airpower and not even enough combat power to overwhelm the Somali militia members who swarmed over the downed helicopters and pinned down America's most elite fighting force in brutal street-to-street combat. There were other lessons, to be sure, but the one that stuck most was that JSOC operatives wouldn't be hung out to dry again. The next time around they'd have proper air support and sufficient troop strength to deal with any contingency.

Unfortunately, this lesson takes the "special" out of Special Operations. Attack helicopters or fixed-wing gunships looming nearby make it impossible for Special Forces to conduct low-profile "snatch" operations. An alternative lesson that could have been construed from Somalia's disaster (but wasn't) is that Special Operations require a small, agile team to capture or kill wanted individuals. Small operations are risky in that they do not guarantee overwhelming force, but their effectiveness is in their stealth and agility. There are risks, but the men of JSOC are both willing and able to take those risks. That's what they volunteer for, train for, and hope to have the opportunity to do at some point in their career. Properly executed Special Ops missions could spare our nation from future disasters like 9/11 or avert another intervention like Iraq. When taken in this context, the risk seems manageable.

But instead of moving to smaller, lower-profile missions, the Pentagon enlarged JSOC missions, so as to never be outgunned again. In following that course, JSOC has virtually lost its ability to go small and early into an operation; instead, it ends up going in late and heavy. In my view, Somalia wasn't a force too light but a force too heavy and too late. But few Americans share my view of the lessons of this disaster. I guess the typical American response to a problem is to throw more resources at it, not less.

Bosnia, 1998: How Not to Catch a War Criminal

Shortly before I took over the counterterrorism duties at State in the summer of 1998, then Secretary of State Madeleine Albright asked me to go to Sarajevo and find out why we hadn't captured the Bosnian Serb war criminal Radovan Karadzic. At the time, I was working on the Balkans issue for the UN office of the State Department, but Secretary Albright knew of my Special Forces background and figured I might be able to give her some insights into this particular problem. Karadzic was known to be moving about in remote border areas of Bosnia-Herzegovina, an area dominated by more than forty thousand American-led NATO troops.

The United States had made an enormous commitment to get Karadzic, and JSOC and CIA assets were considerable. *U.S. News & World Report* noted that "the task force is so large for a Special Operations project—involving three hundred people or more—that one participant says its leaders 'are violating their own doctrine,' which is to keep operations as small as possible and do them quickly."[1] The cost was estimated to be $50 million, but clearly it went many times higher than that figure.

I came back to Secretary Albright and reported that we'd never get Karadzic unless he bumped his head and fell into the car of the American ambassador in Sarajevo. The problem wasn't that we were not expending resources or that we weren't trying hard enough—it was that our efforts were too big, too clumsy, and too risk-averse.

At one point in this long and painful process, I was privy to a plan cooked up by some operatives to insert an informant to meet with Karadzic. It was fairly well confirmed that this person had met with him before, and there was a decent chance he could pull it off again. The plan was simple: insert the contact, follow him, and take down Karadzic. But the operation never came to fruition for a variety of reasons. The source ultimately proved untrustworthy to the risk-averse U.S. government. (But what mole doesn't have a few skeletons in his closet?) Also, the details of the operation became bogged down in a stifling level of micromanagement from Washington.

Another part of the problem resembled the situation in Somalia. By the time we got serious and deployed hundreds of operatives, Karadizc was nowhere to be found. Once again we came in too late and with too many soldiers, just as in Somalia. It's always easier to get these people early on when they're off balance. By the time the American operation got into full swing, Karadzic and Aidid were hidden deep in their respective backyards. It was another classic case of too much too late. Unfortunately, it seems we have not yet learned our lesson, as evidenced by the search for bin Laden in Pakistan.

The Military and Special Intelligence

CIA and JSOC had been fighting fiercely in the year prior to my trip to Sarajevo, but when I got there I was told they were getting along much better. That was correct, but the problems ran much deeper than hard feelings. Although cordial, they were still physically separated. CIA agents and the Special Operations personnel lived and ate separately, meeting only to coordinate their plans. I sensed that this was just not acceptable in an operation that by its very nature was sensitive and high-risk.

The military, frustrated by CIA, had sent its own intelligence operatives to Bosnia. CIA, for its part, complained bitterly that the military was asking for too much information and opposed to taking risks. One CIA operative complained to me that JSOC wouldn't go through a door unless they knew the color of the socks worn by the people behind it. He'd given up on JSOC and was pursuing local options to lure the war criminal into the reach of some local thugs for hire. I sat down with military and CIA officials in separate meetings in separate buildings on opposite sides of Sarajevo. They both assured me that the feuding between the two had ended and cooperation was excellent. But I heard a refrain that became very familiar: the shooters complained that the intelligence was poor, and the intelligence collectors complained that the shooters had an insatiable appetite for detail, requiring an unrealistic degree of certainty prior to operating.

One of the Delta operators confided that this arrangement would probably never work. He believed that Delta needed its own intelligence collectors, ones who knew the organization and the shooters' requirements. But this is easier said than done. In fact, in the 1980s the Army decided to create its own capability to operate clandestinely abroad, thereby providing low-profile logistical support and intelligence to Special Operations Forces if they were called into a remote area. I was recruited into the supersecret unit in the summer of 1992, but when asked to return to the White House NSC staff, I took myself out of consideration.

One of the missions of these special units was to provide intelligence support to enable JSOC shooters to operate in remote, hostile, or denied areas. Support for infiltration, exfiltration, and site reconnaissance is critical to these missions. Ideally, that task would be provided by personnel within JSOC chain of command. In that way, the intelligence gatherers would be intimately familiar with the shooters' requirements and the shooters would know whom they could trust. For the operatives to have full trust and confidence in the information, its collection couldn't be outsourced to another organization.

The problem of who's in charge carried on from the field all the way back to the White House. I can remember many times sitting on the back bench of the White House situation room listening to cabinet members discuss these types of issues and potential operations. I often silently wished that the president would reach across the table and stick his finger in somebody's chest (either the secretary of defense or the director of central intelligence) and say: "I'm holding you accountable to get Karadzic. You have a huge organization with a massive budget; let me know if you need more to get it done. But I want options on my desk in ninety days—*realistic* options. And if you can't give me what I want, I'll find someone else who can. Any questions?"

But of course, it never happened; it never does in any administration. Instead, cabinet heads deftly shift responsibility to others and keep a long list of excuses handy: the intelligence is no good; we don't have authority to conduct assassinations; this is a local responsibility; it's somebody else's job. This attitude has plagued our government since President Carter ordered the Iranian hostage rescue attempt. The process has been dysfunctional, both in the field and in Washington. And as al Qaeda developed in the late 1990s and into 2001, this weakness in our national security apparatus became a major liability.

Khartoum, Sudan, 1999: Another Missed Opportunity

Shortly after I was appointed to the State Department as Coordinator for Counterterrorism, I was informed that CIA had identified a senior al Qaeda operative in Khartoum, Sudan. He was Mafouz Ould Walid, also known as Abu Hafs the Mauritanian, and was considered a major al Qaeda leader with close direct ties to bin Laden. I later found out that we knew exactly where he was staying in Khartoum: room 13 of the Dana Hotel. Confident of his anonymity in Sudan, he didn't seem to have much security at all. It seemed we had a golden opportunity. We needed to get this guy and we had a good shot. Abu Hafs might have had direct knowledge about future al Qaeda operations, such as the USS *Cole* or the 9/11 World Trade Center attack, both of which were being planned at that time without our knowledge. Even if he wasn't aware of these plans, his capture would have provided invaluable intelligence regarding the locations of bin Laden and other senior operatives in Afghanistan and elsewhere.

Over the next several days, a series of meetings were held, some in the Pentagon with only military personnel and some within the interagency community with representatives from across the government. The outcome was predictable: once again, the options put forth by the Pentagon were massive and cumbersome. The military complained that it lacked good intelligence. CIA said they were providing the best intelligence available. The political leadership, reluctant to challenge the professionals in either agency, sat idle in frustration. Outsiders (including me) were labeled cowboys if we suggested that we take some risks with small-scale snatch operations. The 9/11 Commission reported how General Hugh Shelton, former chairman of the Joint Chiefs of Staff, said that "such operations are not risk free," invoking the memory of the 1993 Black Hawk fiasco in Mogadishu.[2] As a result, the mission and Abu Hafs disappeared. We'll never know what could have come from his arrest.

But I did get an infuriating postscript to this aborted mission. Six months later, I was in the Philippines trying to justify $2 million in State Department funding for training the Filipino Special Forces to track down terrorists in the southern islands. I was at a cocktail party chatting with a Special Forces major, Joe Felter, who was on duty as an attaché at the embassy. He steered me into a corner to meet a fellow Special Forces officer who turned out to be a former JSOC operator.

After some small talk, we stumbled into a conversation about Sudan and the Dana Hotel. The officer had been a member of the planning team for the operation and shared with me some of the small, adroit, and feasible operations that the Delta operators had developed at Fort Bragg. He told me that those options, which I had never heard of before, had been shot down at the White House. I was stunned. He was under the false impression that the State Department (meaning myself) and the White House had spiked the mission. I went into a low boil of rage and informed him through clenched teeth that it was the Pentagon that had shot down his operation; it had never gotten to my desk as an option. In fact, State Department and White House officials had been lambasted by the Pentagon for pushing them on this mission. His story was exactly the opposite. He and his team at Fort Benning had been misled to believe that State Department "weenies" had shot them down again. In one of the more bitter ironies of my career, the Pentagon had shifted the blame for their inaction onto my boss and me when we had been the ones urging the Pentagon to move.

Intelligence Support to Delta

The effort to create intelligence capability within Delta was far more problematic than the creation of the original unit. The Intelligence Support Activity (ISA) was created in the aftermath of the failed Iranian hostage rescue attempt, when Delta found CIA's intelligence wanting. According to some reports, the unit had initial success running some small operations moving around sensitive people and assisting the Italian army in locating and freeing General James Dozier, who had been kidnapped by the Italian Red Brigades. They even had a small unit of shooters with the dexterity and speed that the much larger and more cumbersome Delta Force had lost. However, a series of scandals involving the abuse of travel vouchers doomed the unit. As a result, the unit was largely dismantled in the late 1980s.

What Delta really needs is well-placed non-official-cover personnel (NOCs, pronounced "knocks") who can support a complex operation in a remote area. NOCs, usually drawn from CIA and the Department of Defense (DOD), aren't assigned to the embassy as diplomatic personnel; not even the ambassador knows who they are. NOCs provide a deep undercover presence in foreign countries—and they may lie fallow for many years. The only action some may see over the course of time is small exercises or operations.

For Special Operations, NOCs and their networks provide eyes and ears on the target, help provide plausible cover for advance units that may need to infiltrate, and can help arrange clandestine transportation, communication, and safe houses. DOD's rebuilding of its human intelligence service since 9/11 had been a controversial issue for former secretary of defense Donald Rumsfeld. Some accuse DOD of selecting overly muscled military guys with obvious front organizations usually located within a few miles of the Pentagon. I'm not sure about these allegations, but I also understand fully why the Pentagon would want to establish its own NOC networks to support Special Operations.

In my view, if you want a unilateral capability to conduct operations, intelligence is the key—including human intelligence, black operations, and all the risks that come with the territory. But the U.S. government has not developed an extensive spy network because it doesn't want the associated baggage. In successive administrations, Congress and the press have come down hard on these units or operations when things go bad. Hearings such as those conducted by Senator Frank Church and his committee in the late 1970s still have an institutional impact on CIA and the Defense Intelligence Agency (DIA). The lessons to the intelligence community were clear: Don't take risks and you will survive even if things go bad. Nobody is ever fired for doing nothing. As a result, JSOC's record doesn't reflect their true potential.

Can It Be Fixed?

In spite of the bureaucratic and political haze surrounding them, the U.S. Army Special Forces are the most highly trained and capable military force in the world. Unfortunately, they've been constrained from action for many years in their most important job, defeating terrorism—and still are today. In my view, the problem is twofold. First, the higher-level commanders are too risk averse, and second, the military functions separately from the intelligence collectors whose information is key to their operations' success.

Can these problems be fixed? As one who has been involved in and repeatedly frustrated by Special Operations for nearly thirty years, I'm not optimistic. But if the situation is to be corrected, it must start with accountability. One organization, either CIA or JSOC, should be assigned the Special Operations mission and given both the military and intelligence tools to get the job done. If it's JSOC, they'll need their own intelligence operation; if it's CIA, they'll need their own military capability. Both scenarios are problematic, because either way an organization is forced to perform in an area of weakness. However, the current separation does not work, and endless commitments to coordinate better have repeatedly failed.

My recommendation is to support the Pentagon initiatives started after 9/11 to rebuild these capabilities within the military. That means forming an expansive and aggressive NOC program for JSOC that would need to be very closely integrated with CIA, but remain in direct support and under the control of JSOC leadership. And who should the command report to? Probably the secretary of defense, perhaps the CIA director, but it should be to one person only. Accountability to a single commander is key. Reporting directly to the White House would be a recipe for disaster, both operationally and politically—a solution that would unnecessarily expose the president and wouldn't work anyway.

Next Time at the Dana Hotel

Let's project forward, to Khartoum's Dana Hotel in the year 2015, where a situation similar to the one in 1999 exists. We're told that Mr. X is in the Dana Hotel, room 5. He and his organization are an immediate and grave threat to our national security; we need to get him out, and we cannot coordinate with the Sudanese. This time, we infiltrate with a five-man team to the edge of Khartoum. This same maneuver has already been practiced in a training exercise five years previously. The team is met by a local truck dealer who's been an agent for JSOC for eight years and has been tested to be trustworthy. He doesn't know the whole operation, only that he must deliver his assets to a predetermined location in downtown Khartoum. He would probably know nothing more about the operation.

As they approach the hotel, they're met by a sixth man, an NOC, who has been operating in and out of Khartoum for the past five years. He has stayed at the Dana Hotel and knows the lay of the land. They all blend into the streets of Khartoum; they look and smell like natives, and two of them speak Arabic fluently. They wait for the target to exit the hotel, when they'll steer him into a waiting van. If Mr. X doesn't come out, they'll enter the hotel, go up to the room, grab him and drag him into a truck. Deadly force has been authorized. Ideally, the team would wait until Mr. X leaves the hotel for a coffee, walk up behind him calmly, put him into a van, neutralize his bodyguards (with deadly force if necessary), and drive to the outskirts of the city, where an exfiltration plan is in place. He is then taken to the United States to stand trial. Mission accomplished. Of course, these are high-risk operations and are only rarely conducted, but if the opportunity presents itself, the U.S. government must be able to execute these types of missions with dexterity.

This type of operation is what it takes to nab the terrorists who are currently plotting attacks against the United States, but I'm still not sure the United States wants to go down this road. If someone else has a better idea, I'm all ears. But in the interim we'll continue to fail in our attempts to capture and eliminate the most wanted international fugitives if we insist on using large armies to invade countries. Somehow that has been deemed the easier route politically.

Counterinsurgency and Terrorism: Related but Distinct

Counterinsurgency and counterterrorism are related but very distinct forms of warfare, and both are the business of Special Operations Forces. They both fall under a broader subset of war that I prefer to categorize as "irregular warfare." General warfare is normally defined as fighting between uniformed professional armies. Irregular warfare normally entails nonprofessional combatants that tend to dress in civilian clothes and are organized in more informal ways. Irregular combatants include insurgents, militias, civil defense forces, and terrorists.

Understanding the difference is crucial to success in both forms of warfare. But first, one must understand the difference between insurgency and terrorism. An insurgency is a war conducted to overthrow government control, a tactic that is as old as warfare itself. Alexander the Great was followed by insurgent forces as he swept westward into Central Asia. In Spain, Napoleon was dogged by insurgents called "guerrillas"—from the Spanish word for war, *guerra.* Conventional war is normally defined as that conducted by armies representing separate nation states. Insurgency is a type of warfare that normally includes irregular forces, such as militias and other paramilitary organizations beyond the traditional, uniformed, professional army.

Examples of insurgencies abound in American history—in fact, the U.S. Army was born in an insurrection against the British Crown. The Confederacy was also an insurgency that included both regular units, such as Robert E. Lee's Army of Northern Virginia, and irregulars, such as Mosby's Raiders, who were part of the Confederate Army but were organized as "partisan rangers" who conducted guerrilla-style raids against the Union and then disappeared into the landscape. There is a long tradition of American involvement in these operations, from the Revolutionary War to the Civil War to World War II and beyond. In Vietnam, we engaged and fought in extensive irregular warfare, particularly through the Green Berets and their efforts to defeat the Viet Cong alongside Montagnard (Degar) tribesmen and other irregular fighters. During the 1980s, some of my Special Operations buddies who were training the contras in the Nicaraguan and Honduran border areas were, in fact, supporting an insurgent organization. The Special Forces operation in Afghanistan after 9/11 also exemplified irregular warfare, memorialized by a well-known photo of a bearded U.S. Special Forces soldier on horseback driving out the Taliban with local fighters and support from F-16 fighter jets.

While insurgencies have a legitimate place in the history of warfare, terrorism is considered an international crime. Terror attacks deliberately attack innocent civilians. Al Qaeda uses terrorism as a strategic weapon in an attempt to achieve its broader political goals. However, even strategic terrorists do not form units, do not try to gain and hold terrain, and are normally not involved in trying to overthrow a government and take control of a nation or region. Terrorists want to influence other governments, but they usually have no immediate or even midterm prospects of holding territory or taking power, whereas insurgents have a broader agenda to seize and hold territory, which normally will keep pure terrorist techniques in abeyance, for they hope to govern eventually and will need global recommendations for reliability and respect for the law.

The water gets muddy when terrorism and insurgency overlap. Perhaps the best place to examine this murky scenario is in Afghanistan. The Taliban are waging a deliberate insurgency campaign in the southern and eastern sectors of Afghanistan. They've formed units of militia fighters and have fought for and maintain some control over territory, although perhaps more in Pakistan than in Afghanistan. Their goal is to reestablish control of their traditional strongholds in the southeast and to eventually retake control of the country, much the way they did in the mid-1990s. But first they know that they have to drive out the Americans—and so they've recently been using the terrorist tactic of suicide bombers to augment their insurgency. The Taliban do not seem to have an agenda (like al Qaeda) to project their terrorist activity out of their area of operations. So, technically, they function as both insurgents and terrorists—but in the eyes of the U.S. government, they are just terrorists.

Al Qaeda, on the other hand, does not seek to gain and maintain terrain in the short term. Instead they seek refuge in remote areas where nobody is in control—or, better for them, in areas dominated by the Taliban, who have provided them sanctuary. A counterinsurgency strategy in Afghanistan or the tribal areas of Pakistan requires a long-term political and security plan to gain popular support. A counterterrorism strategy must be much more focused on the immediate goal of finding terrorist cells and crushing their ability to conduct attacks. Obviously, counterterrorism programs are supported by effective counterinsurgency programs that diminish areas where terrorists can hide. Counterterrorism programs also support counterinsurgency strategies by minimizing the enemy's ability to use terrorism to promote their strategy.

Insurgencies often breed terrorists, especially from among those on the losing side who become frustrated by their inability to succeed through traditional military means. But insurgents are covered under the Geneva Conventions if they remain within their guidelines. Terrorists, on the other hand, operate outside of the Geneva Conventions and are generally considered criminals and should be tried accordingly. Counterinsurgency is all about supporting and protecting the local population. It's about training the locals to provide their own security. It's about keeping a low profile, and it's best done by Special Operations Forces. Infantry brigades are good at providing short-term security umbrellas. But if they're not replaced very quickly by locals, over time they become part of the problem, not the solution, as they did in places such as Vietnam, Lebanon, and Somalia.

In El Salvador, we were lucky. We had a split government in Washington during the late 1980s: a Republican president who supported an intervention in Central America and a skeptical Democratic Congress. The Congress insisted on a fifty-five-man limit for El Salvador, which led to a favorable unintended consequence. By limiting our numbers, the Salvadorans were forced to fight their own war, with the gringos just a low-profile but important player in the countryside. You never saw Americans entering Salvadoran homes or killing Salvadorans on cable television. In this regard, despite our military and civilian aid programs (which were puny by today's standards of spending), we were successful.

In Iraq, we will need to employ both counterinsurgency and counterterrorism strategies simultaneously. Special Forces counterinsurgency trainers or advisors will be embedded with local forces, much the way I was in El Salvador, living with their counterparts and helping them conduct the campaign to win the support of the population while defeating armed insurgents. Other Special Forces shooters will work with CIA and local special units to find and crush terrorist cells when it is necessary to conduct a military-style raid. In a combat zone such as Iraq, the military will play a more active role than in normal conditions. As the war winds down, the plan is to decrease Iraq's dependence on Special Forces shooters, with the work being done instead by local intelligence and police forces. When we reach this destination, we'll know we are approaching some measure of success in the U.S.–Iraqi intervention. Unfortunately, that is a long time off. In the interim, Special Forces trainers and shooters will be very busy in Iraq, no matter who is inaugurated in January of 2009.

Chapter 7

Door Kickers, Diplomats, and Swamp Drainers

THE STAFF AT THE State Department Office of the Coordinator for Counterterrorism (S/CT) was an eclectic and spirited group. It comprised a mix of Foreign Service officers, civil servants, and a handful of military guys. Although the last group's mission was primarily to serve as a liaison to the Pentagon's elite CT units, the civilians in the office pegged them the "door kickers," in reference to the military techniques used when storming an enemy in urban warfare. The civilian staff kicked down doors as well, but in their daily battles those doors opened onto the offices of recalcitrant bureaucrats rather than the hideouts of armed terrorists. During my tenure at State from 1998 to 2000, I valued the door kickers in wing-tips or high heels just as much as those in combat boots.

My team at State was responsible for pushing the U.S. government and our allies to take tough measures to eliminate terrorist sanctuaries around the world. This was my primary mission at S/CT, a goal I often referred to as "draining the swamp." I tried to set the tone with an aggressive approach, and I was sometimes gently reminded that the language I used in the office was more suited for a Special Forces safe house. Other times I was faulted for being a "one-note Johnny" because I constantly focused on issues related to terrorism, and I was often accused of being obsessed with al Qaeda. I stand guilty as charged.

Steve Kashkent, a brilliant and irreverent young Foreign Service officer at S/CT, helped us not to take ourselves too seriously with custom T-shirts he had made for all of us. On the back was a bomb with a burning fuse with a red circle and slash across it, meaning "no bombs"—and under that the shirt read "S/CT: "Door Kickers, Diplomats, and Swamp Drainers." Kashkent made the shirts to poke fun at my mantra about draining the Afghan swamp and our continual focus on that mission. I still wear it proudly.

In the world of counterterrorism, it is far sexier to be a door kicker than a cookie-pushing diplomat. But as ambassador, I came to appreciate the fine art of diplomacy. Being a diplomat requires patience and vision. Diplomats are rarely involved in high-speed operations such as take-downs or assaults; that work is reserved for soldiers, cops, and spies. But my experience in counterterrorism over the long haul has convinced me that diplomacy plays an extremely important role, especially when employed against state sponsors of terrorism such as Iran and Libya. Diplomatic measures are also very effective in working with a terrorist organization that possesses a broad agenda, but they're less likely to succeed in affecting non-state-sponsored terrorist groups such as al Qaeda. And perhaps the most important—and challenging—task is working with imperfect allies (such as Saudi Arabia and Pakistan) that are crucial to the overall effort.

The Millennium Threat

In late 1999, after about a year on the job as ambassador for counterterrorism, I started to get frustrated with the status quo. My friend Dick Clarke was fighting a relentless bureaucratic battle in Washington to take down bin Laden through military or intelligence operations. I wasn't convinced that his efforts would bear fruit, but I shared his fear that the chances of another attack were increasing with every passing day.

With Y2K on the horizon, the cyber world was full of doomsday scenarios. The public and private sector spent literally billions of dollars preparing for an event that turned out to be a big nothing. In the counterterrorism world, though, we were concerned about al Qaeda taking advantage of the chaos associated with Y2K—or perhaps pursuing millennial terror aspirations themselves. I was very skeptical of the millennial target date for al Qaeda because the year was 1420 on the Islamic calendar, not the turn of a new century. But the intelligence community was up in arms over the amount of chatter they detected—usually a faulty indicator, as far as I was concerned. In any case, things began to happen around the end of 1999. Two events in particular sent my office into overdrive.

On the eleventh of December a naturalized American citizen named Khalil Deek was arrested in Pakistan. Deek was in possession of a computer linked to a Jordanian plot to attack Western targets. The next day, Jordanian intelligence arrested sixteen men involved with this plot. Deek's computer files revealed a plan to bomb the SAS Radisson Hotel in Amman, Jordan, along with Israeli border crossings and Christian pilgrimage sites near the river Jordan. Although not sophisticated, the plot called for an assault using AK-47s. The cost in lives could have been devastating—not unlike the 1997 Gama'at al-Islamiyya attack in Egypt in which fifty-nine foreign tourists and four Egyptians were gunned down. A tragic event for the victims and their families, the attack also had a strategic impact on the Egyptian tourist industry for years. We took the Jordanian plot seriously for those same two reasons: the potential loss of life and the economic implications for the beleaguered Jordanian economy.

Before we could exhale after the interruption of this major terrorist plot, the media frenzy surrounding another foiled plot began (Ahmed Ressam's plan to bomb the Los Angeles airport, discussed in Chapter 1). I was asked to comment on the plot on

NewsHour with Jim Lehrer with the head of the U.S. Customs Service, Ray Kelly, my future boss at NYPD. Kelly and I both spoke frankly about the dangers of this type of activity. I made reference to the Jordanian cell that had been discovered the week before and said that although two plots had been thwarted back to back, there might be others in the works, and I named Osama bin Laden as a major threat. On *NewsHour*, and later on CNN and some other shows leading up to the New Year's Eve celebration, I advised viewers to keep their plans for the holiday but report to the nearest cop if they saw anything suspicious. I repeated this over and over years later when I came to NYPD, reminding ordinary citizens that they're the eyes and ears of the police. The catchphrase "If you see something, say something" became my mantra.

The Afghan Ultimatum: Draining the Swamp

Shortly after the New Year in 2000, as the nation realized that it had indeed survived the passing of Y2K, alarm regarding al Qaeda spread beyond the CT community into the higher levels of the bureaucracy and on up to the president. Concomitantly, I began to agitate for a diplomatic move with Afghanistan—not as a substitute for military action but in conjunction with our by now endless meetings regarding bin Laden. My immediate goal was to make the sanctuary bin Laden enjoyed in Afghanistan increasingly untenable. If he was forced to move out of Afghanistan, he might make a mistake and we could grab him. At the same time, I wanted to dismantle the Afghan camps that were recruiting radical militants at an alarming rate. Trying to pick off terrorists coming out of these camps one by one was like trying to swat mosquitoes on a hot summer night in the bayou. The only way to stop mosquitoes from swarming is to drain the swamp and all other potential breeding grounds. Likewise, if we were ever going to contain al Qaeda, we had to drain the Afghan swamp. That brought my focus on their hosts: the Taliban.

I quietly embarked on a diplomatic campaign to box in the Taliban. The first step was to threaten them to get them to turn against bin Laden, and the second was to bring more sanctions against their regime, including an arms embargo. The arms embargo was really aimed at Pakistan, as its intelligence service was still supporting the Taliban in its war against the Northern Alliance. These two classic diplomatic activities were, at that point, the only weapons I had.

In the aftermath of the millennium threats, the terrorism czar at the time, Richard Clarke, held a series of meetings at the National Security Council to once again try to get bin Laden or otherwise crush al Qaeda. Ever since the United States launched the missile attacks following the embassy bombings in August 1998, bin Laden's location had been harder to pinpoint. Clarke asked CIA, FBI, DOD, and State to develop initiatives to bring bin Laden and al Qaeda down. In response to his call for action, I began to draft a demarche, or formal diplomatic statement, to the Taliban leadership. The message was simple: the Taliban would be held completely accountable for any future acts of terrorism committed against the United States by al Qaeda. In other words, if we were attacked again, we wouldn't limit our retaliation to specific al Qaeda targets as they scurried into mountain caves; we'd hit Taliban targets.

I drafted the message with Clarke and we got it approved through all the various strata of government, right to the cabinet level. I was a bit surprised that nobody seriously opposed the message—I thought I'd have a hard time getting it passed. But it sailed through. I'd hoped it would be presented to the Taliban by a higher-level official, but it fell to me to deliver my own demarche. Since we lacked an embassy in Kabul and had no official contact with the Taliban, I couldn't use the standard diplomatic means for delivering my message and had to hunt around the foreign policy community for someone who'd get me in touch with them. As it turned out, our best contact was through Voice of America (VOA), the government's overseas broadcasting service. I'm still not sure why we went through VOA—perhaps they had the best language capability—but they managed to arrange for me to speak with the

Afghan foreign minister, Wakil Ahmad Mutawakil. As foreign minister, he was the official recipient of a demarche, and it was thought that he was one of the more reasonable apparatchiks within the circle of the Taliban's leader, Mullah Omar.

I called Mutawakil in January 2000. After a few short pleasantries, I told him I had instructions from the highest level of the U.S. government. I asked him if he understood what that meant, and he said he did. I then told him that if al Qaeda, or any group associated with al Qaeda, attacked the United States again, we would hold the Taliban completely responsible for that attack. Again, I asked him if he understood what I meant.

At this point Mutawakil began to dissemble in a way I'd been quite accustomed to hearing from Taliban leaders in New York and Islamabad. He told me that the United States and the Afghan people were great friends, that they appreciated our support in ousting the Soviet Union from Afghanistan, and that they wanted friendship with the United States. But he also said bin Laden was a guest of Afghanistan and that they could not expel him. He offered again to try bin Laden under *sharia*'s law if we could provide them with evidence of his role in the East African bombings.

I explained how U.S. courts had clearly proven this point and asserted that this was no longer up for discussion. Osama bin Laden was responsible for the East African embassy bombings and many plots since then—and was very actively launching attacks from his Afghan sanctuary. Mutawakil insisted that bin Laden was no threat to the United States, that they had him under control, that bin Laden would issue no more statements and not support any operations from Afghan soil. I told him that bin Laden was in fact known to be directing his operatives in violent initiatives as we spoke.

I then told the foreign minister a story to try to drive my point home. I told him to imagine that he lived in a house in my neighborhood. "Imagine if an arsonist lived in your basement," I began, "and every night that arsonist left your house to set fire to my house and then returned to his sanctuary in your house. If you were fully knowledgeable of his activity, you'd be held accountable for the crime of arson." I then drew a direct parallel to the relationship between the Taliban and al Qaeda. "They're in your house, you are protecting them, and they're launching terrorist operations against us," I stated emphatically, "and *we hold you fully accountable* if there is another attack against the United States." I reiterated that this message came from the highest levels of our government.

We ended cordially, but he got the message. I was exhilarated. This was a serious message formally given to the Taliban by the U.S. government. I really didn't expect Mullah Omar to heed the warning, but I felt that if al Qaeda hit us again, we'd be prepared to take our response directly to Afghanistan and the Taliban regime.

Empty Words

Al Qaeda did hit us again about six months later in Yemen with the attack against the USS *Cole*. But we did nothing in response. We didn't hold the Taliban accountable, as I'd promised Mutawakil we would in that important phone call. When I left office at the end of December, CIA and FBI had still not formally attributed the attack to al Qaeda, at least within the channels I was in. Five years later, when I read the 9/11 Commission's report, I was surprised to learn that there were many good indicators of al Qaeda involvement in December 2000. However, by mid-January 2001, right around the time of the transition from Clinton to Bush, CIA and FBI finally concluded the obvious: that the USS *Cole* was an al Qaeda operation. My demarche still stood as official U.S. policy for the last few weeks of the Clinton administration and for eight months of the Bush administration, until September 11.

When the United States invaded Afghanistan after 9/11, bin Laden was forced to scurry across the Afghan border at Tora Bora. Prior to 9/11, I believe that bin Laden was prepared to evacuate Afghanistan for Pakistan, but he probably thought he'd be able to stick it out in southern Afghanistan and bog down American forces in a protracted war, eventually wearing us out, as he'd done with the Russians. However, the massive invasion forced him into the rugged tribal areas of Pakistan, where he began to reconstitute his operation in a new sanctuary, Wajiristan.

By early 2003, there were signs that al Qaeda was rebuilding some of its infrastructure in Pakistan. Most important, the training camps were back. At the camps terrorists are trained in key skills such as weapons, explosives, and tradecraft and are also able to network with like-minded operatives. In addition, they're further radicalized by ideological leaders and receive strategic direction and tactical planning support from the central network. This very dangerous situation is largely out of the reach of American power. Because of Pakistani sensitivities, the United States has had to tread very softly in those terrorist-infested areas.

State Sponsors of Terrorism: Diplomacy's Success

Diplomacy failed with regard to the Taliban and Pakistan prior to 9/11. However, diplomacy has had a very successful yet unheralded role in diminishing state-sponsored terrorism, particularly since the George H. W. Bush administration. Modern American counterterrorism policy evolved during the 1980s as the Reagan administration faced a series of crises. Iran and Syria were supporting terror in Lebanon through bombings, hijackings, and kidnappings. Meanwhile, Libya was causing trouble, bombing a discotheque in Germany frequented by American servicemen and blowing up Pan Am Flight 103 over Lockerbie, Scotland. The North Koreans also were brazen, attacking the South Korean presidential delegation as it visited Burma in October 1983 in a blast that killed twenty-one and wounded forty-six. Sudan, a haven for all sorts of terrorists, was put on the watch list in 1993. Iraq, traditionally the most inactive of the state sponsors of international terrorism, rounded out the rogues' gallery.

The 1980s and early 1990s were active years for the traditional state sponsors of terrorism—Iran, Syria, Libya, Sudan, and North Korea. But since then, with the significant exception of terrorism directed against Israel, these countries' governments have all dramatically reduced their support of terrorism. Libya, Sudan, and North Korea went from actively and shamelessly supporting terrorist events to giving up the instrument of international terrorism entirely. Each has its own reasons for eschewing terrorism, but without question, one of the primary factors in driving terrorism out of these countries' foreign policy has been the pressure of international diplomacy and the threat of sanctions.

Iran and Syria are different, of course. Both are active supporters of terrorism against Israel. But, as I discussed in Chapter 4, even these countries are restrained in their use of active terrorism. They can get away with supporting terrorist groups in their activities directed against Israel and the occupied territories because of the general support the Palestinians have in the international community. So it could be posited that the Iranians and Syrians support terror in Israel because the Europeans let them, but when they stray outside of Israel, the threat of sanctions drives them to restraint.

When I first took my post at S/CT in 1998, Libya's terrorist activity was placed squarely on my front burner by a rather unorthodox messenger—the unrelenting families of the victims of Pan Am Flight 103. Libya has been viewed as a case study in the success of diplomacy and sanctions in terrorism, but it isn't a perfect solution, as the murderous thug Muammar al-Qaddafi is still in charge there and the families of the victims of Flight 103 have not gotten full restitution. Nevertheless, Libya has not committed a large-scale terrorist attack since the 1980s and has begun to meet its obligations to the families of Pan Am 103 victims.

In the past several years since 9/11, Libya has come in from the cold with regard to terrorism. Some have suggested that the Iraq war was a defining moment for the Libyans' decision to renounce terrorism and play a very cooperative role in exposing the nuclear and missile proliferation of Pakistan and North Korea, respectively. But few in official Washington subscribe to this idea. They know that Libya's path out of terrorism has been a long and winding road that began a long time before the 2003 invasion of Iraq. It began as a result of a variety of forces, including relentless U.S.

diplomatic pressure and sanctions. The war in Iraq actually had very little to do with this long-simmering development.

During the 1980s Libya was very actively engaged in terrorist activity, along with the Palestinians, the Iranians, Hezbollah, and the remnants of left-wing European terrorist groups such as the Red Brigades and the IRA. According to Robert Oakley, a former ambassador for counterterrorism and State Department official, the U.S. government was very worried about Libyan terrorism in 1984 and 1985.

We had reports that there were Libyan hit squads loose in the United States.[1] The Libyans were using a surrogate terrorist for hire, Abu Nidal, to conduct bombing operations in the airports of Rome and Vienna in December 1985. The administration responded by putting two aircraft carriers into Libya's Gulf of Sidra, which quashed a few small attacks that were made against them by boat and plane. Qaddafi escalated and called for his intelligence operatives to respond. One of the successful operations was the bombing of a nightclub that was frequented by American soldiers in West Berlin. We responded by bombing Tripoli, and as a result, the Libyans laid low for a while. However, several years later, in December 1988, they struck again and exploded a bomb in the checked baggage of Pan Am Flight 103 en route from London to New York. More than 270 people from 21 countries (including 189 Americans) were killed.

Like the attack on the USS *Cole,* the Pan Am bombing happened during a presidential transition period, and the definitive proof of who perpetrated the act wasn't clear until after Ronald Reagan left office and President George H. W. Bush was handed the problem. Bush departed dramatically from Reagan's military response to the Berlin club bombing. Instead, he took a much more deliberate legal approach. Painstaking Justice Department officials gathered forensic evidence and over a two-year period built an ironclad case against Libya. The evidence was brought to the UN, which consequently approved economic and diplomatic sanctions against Libya in 1992. No further military action was taken against Libya.

Over the next several years, Libya slowly but deliberately got out of the terrorism business. The international sanctions, weakened by the fact that they didn't include Libyan oil, had a definitive impact. American sanctions were much stronger, including an embargo against Libyan oil and the barring of all American oil companies from working in Libya. The combination of sanctions—wide, relatively weak ones from the international community coupled with tough ones from the United States—seemed to work. Other factors played a role as well. Qaddafi seemed to mellow somewhat in his old age. Although he continues to support various dictators in Africa, he's toned down his confrontations with the West considerably. Another factor is that Qaddafi has always been a secular leader. He was one of the first to see the threat of al Qaeda not only to the West but also to his dictatorship. In fact, when I was at S/CT it surprised me that only one country had a formal warrant out for the arrest of Osama bin Laden prior to 9/11, and that was Libya.

The Libyan outreach began in 1999 and 2000 without my knowledge. In fact, had I known about it I would have fought it. But the Libyans, with the support of the United Kingdom and Egypt, were trying to mend fences with Washington. The process inched along for years, and after 9/11, when they decided to provide very important information on the A. Q. Khan nuclear network, their alliance with the West in the current war on terrorism was formalized.

Libya has not quite been fully rehabilitated, and they are still on the list of state sponsors of terrorism. But in spite of the grief the downing of Pan Am Flight 103 caused so many, Qaddafi has been ostensibly absolved of that crime. The good news is that in this case diplomatic measures proved to deter future acts of terrorism by Libya. And I suppose it is worthy of note that a terrorist can renounce his former ways. For me, notwithstanding his rehabilitation with our government, he is still responsible for the deaths on Pan Am 103, and, in my book, the statute of limitations has not run out.

The case with Iranian terrorism in the 1980s is also interesting. Imagine the reaction if a country today were accused of blowing up three of our embassies, kidnapping a CIA official, killing an American colonel on a UN peacekeeping force, and kidnapping untold numbers of other Americans. Well, that's exactly what the Iranians did in the 1980s, and they basically got away with it. In fact, by means of terrorism, and without penalty, they accomplished their rather limited objective of driving the Americans out of Lebanon.

Ironically, at one point in the hostage crisis, we were providing arms to the Iranians so they would use their influence with Hezbollah (their surrogate) to get our hostages out. Ambassador Oakley talks about that time with clear regrets for its effect on American policy. The Americans didn't attack, according to Oakley, because the Reagan administration didn't have clear proof, but just as important, we didn't have any good targets in Iran. And even if we had, we weren't sure what the attacks would achieve. Eventually an implicit deal was cut with the Iranians: we backed out of Lebanon and they stopped the terrorist activity. Eventually the approach Oakley and the administration took worked. The terrorism by Libya stopped, and Iranian and Syrian terrorism was greatly curtailed. In 2001, just after 9/11 and before the Iraq war, Oakley made a prescient analysis of the lessons of the Reagan years with respect to terrorism. He said:

> The lessons we learned are applicable now: building coalitions, picking your target carefully, being able to justify your target, making sure that you have a successful operation when you undertake it, calculating the political downside as well as the military effects . . . I think that we have to . . . understand that we're not going to stop all terrorism for all time. That's one thing that stands out.[2]

The Sudanese Proposition

The case of Sudan was another messy one I grappled with when I was at State. In 1999, the new counterterrorism guy at CIA, Cofer

Black, approached me about Sudan. The Sudanese had made overtures; like Libya, they wanted to come in from the cold and break free from the sanctions we issued after the assassination attempt on Egyptian president Hosni Mubarak in 1995. Ironically, Mubarak was far more willing to forgive Sudan for its actions than we were. Perhaps he understood Sudan better than we did; although the same government was in charge there, the influence of the radical clerics had diminished dramatically by the late nineties. Sudan was in the process of reverting back to its normal thuggish but secular state.

The administration had broader concerns with Sudan, primarily with the killing fields in the Darfur region. Sudan was important to the conservative movement in Congress because of the Christian right's concerns about the religious persecution and tremendous suffering associated with ethnic cleansing of its Christian population. I was sent to meet with Kansas senator Sam Brownback, who, as a member of the Senate Foreign Relations Committee and the African Affairs Subcommittee, had led a congressional delegation to Sudan that year. Brownback cared more about Sudan than virtually any other member of Congress and was an influential voice on the subject. In his office, I convinced him that our mission was not your typical diplomatic junket or a chance to get cozy with thugs such as Sudanese strongman Omar Hassan al-Bashir. My team would make sure the mission stayed focused entirely on counterterrorism issues.

Brownback and his conservative colleagues took us at our word and gave our mission their full support. Much to the credit of our Congress, I have found more often than not a little effort in the way of communication (even on sensitive and classified missions) goes a long way with our legislators. However, if you leave Congress out of the process, they are likely to be much more resistant when they find out about your activity.

After several trips to Sudan, the prospect of reopening the U.S. embassy in Khartoum looked promising, and we did so, on a temporary basis (but not officially). The Sudanese not only wanted to get off the terrorism watch list, they really didn't like the jihadis and genuinely wanted to be rid of them. But at the end of the day the Sudanese government was unable to dispel groups such as the EIJ and Hamas. As a result, the embassy was never reopened and the initiative ran out of steam. Nothing was achieved on the humanitarian front either; millions were to die in Darfur in the years ahead. I'm not sure an embassy would have prevented this, but I'm certain that by pulling out we diminished our influence there—and our understanding of what was going on, in terms of both terrorism and human rights.

Diplomacy's Role

Diplomacy, backed by strong sanctions, can be an effective tool in constraining state sponsors of terrorism. However, in dealing with a recalcitrant regime such as the Taliban and a fanatical and unconstrained organization like al Qaeda, diplomacy has its limits. I dealt with both of these groups through diplomatic channels, but in the end it took decisive military action to remove the Taliban and destroy al Qaeda's Afghan sanctuary. That said, military solutions are not always feasible, especially in a world where al Qaeda hides within the borders of legitimate countries without the governments' consent. Ongoing diplomatic work with every nation involved or impacted by radical Islamic terrorism has proven to be indispensable. Ultimately, the United States must forge a political environment in which local leaders will root out and disarm terrorists in every land.

Chapter 8

Foreign Intelligence Operations: Spying Abroad

YOU MAY NEVER HEAR about many of the most successful counterterrorism operations. They're conducted quietly in conjunction with foreign intelligence organizations with no Hollywood car chases, large explosions, or dramatic face-offs. When there are explosions in counterterrorism operations, they're usually rocket attacks from an armed Predator aircraft. The Predator is an unmanned aerial vehicle (UAV), essentially a small, light, robotically controlled plane that can linger around a target area for many hours waiting for the best moment to strike. Heavy reliance on the Predator is less than optimal, because mistakes that can kill or injure innocents are not uncommon, and of course intelligence exploitation isn't possible via remote control. But in many remote counterterrorism operations these weapons are the best thing we've got.

Optimally, a CT sting concludes when a known terrorist is jolted out of a sound sleep and arrested in his safe house. He's then handcuffed and taken immediately to jail, where he's interrogated within the bounds of a legal process with the hope of extracting information on other members of his terrorist organization. The arrest, trial, and incarceration of terrorist cell members is the single most important goal in global security. CIA (our principal foreign intelligence agency) and the counterpart agencies of our friends, allies, and even some of our enemies are engaged in this type of activity every day around the world. CIA has stepped up its unilateral and multilateral sting operations after coming under intense scrutiny after 9/11 for failing to do enough of this type of work, and rightly so.

Of course, CIA can't shoulder all of the blame. The U.S. intelligence community includes several other agencies, each with a distinct mission and some with much larger budgets than CIA. The National Security Agency (NSA) is responsible for signals intelligence as they listen in on phone calls, e-mails, and other overseas communications. It's also responsible for the decryption of our enemies' codes. The Defense Intelligence Agency (DIA), another huge, sprawling organization that includes its own human intelligence collection service, supports the Department of Defense with all forms of intelligence. Other intelligence agencies include the National Reconnaissance Office (NRO), which designs and launches satellites for the intelligence community, and the National Geospatial-Intelligence Agency (NGIA), which is responsible for imagery and mapping. All of these agencies play a role, but the most important for counterterrorism are CIA and NSA.

September 11 showed failures in all areas of intelligence, but the primary failure was one of focus, despite the fact that CIA's director at the time, George Tenet, genuinely "declared war" on al Qaeda in 1998. I was at CIA one afternoon in 1999 when Tenet spoke to some of his CT analysts, and that was exactly the language he used, with his famous passion. But, in fact, most of the agency was still dedicated to Cold War missions in Washington and the field. Bureaucracies change very slowly. And unfortunately, the dedicated and hardworking crew that did focus on al Qaeda was unable to neutralize the threat they posed. The collection of reliable, actionable information from inside the organization was weak, and the breakdown of information sharing between CIA and FBI concerning the travel of some of the 9/11 hijackers to the United States proved disastrous. Much of the post-9/11 discussion regarding the reform of the intelligence agencies focused on the need to improve the sharing of information. Unfortunately, the "solution" that the majority of people rallied behind was to create another massive bureaucratic layer. Soon after 9/11, the National Counterterrorism Center (NCTC) was created, and a new building was constructed a few miles down the road from CIA to house its staff. But that wasn't enough. Later, Congress created the position of Director of National Intelligence (DNI), whose staff was charged with supervising and integrating all other intelligence-gathering agencies: more bureaucracy to manage the swollen intelligence monolith. It was a classic Washington solution to a problem: create a new agency, hire more bureaucrats, and increasingly outsource the work to contractors.

The cost of these new organizations is absolutely staggering, but I've yet to see how they've appreciably helped the so-called war on terror. By the available current estimates, intelligence budgets have doubled since 9/11. There are some tremendously dedicated and talented people in these organizations, but as I've said before, I'm convinced we could have fought this war with no budget increase, just a shifting of funds to counterterrorism and a new focus on the problem. At NYPD, we built two new organizations because we hadn't been in the CT business prior to 9/11, but we did so *within the existing resources* of a shrinking police department, for which the major expenditure is its personnel budget. As I discuss in greater detail in Chapter 9, Ray Kelly had to make serious cuts in other programs to finance the new CT mission, which was focused on collecting intelligence, sharing information, and acting upon it in a timely manner.

I can't overemphasize the importance of intelligence in CT work. Allow me to take you on a tour of intelligence operations, starting at the ground level and moving up through every echelon of the intelligence business. And as you will see, relative to the billions of dollars in new money being spent, most of the effective operations are not that expensive.

Basic Intelligence Operations: El Salvador, 1985

I received my introduction to international intelligence operations while serving in the U.S. military in El Salvador. In the early

1980s, El Salvador was a Cold War battleground for the Reagan administration. Although now just a historical footnote, at the time El Salvador and Nicaragua were front-page news, representing some of the more controversial components of Reagan's foreign policy. In 1984, while stationed in Korea in the demilitarized zone (DMZ), I volunteered to return to Central America, this time to El Salvador. During my previous Special Forces tour I'd worked extensively in Central and South America and was eager to go to the primary Cold War battleground. My former Special Forces company commander in Panama, Major Cecil Bailey, was stationed at the embassy in the capital, San Salvador, and was looking for veterans of the region to help the local army get control of the countryside. So from the heavily armed demilitarized zone in Korea, where I served in a mechanized armor brigade as part of a fifty-thousand-soldier force, I volunteered for a direct transfer back to the mountain jungles of El Salvador, where I'd be operating out on my own.

At the time, the Reagan administration feared that El Salvador and all of Central America would fall to the self-avowed Marxist revolutionaries inspired and supported by Fidel Castro and his Cuban regime. The issue raised a domestic political ruckus. The Democratic leadership in Congress vigorously opposed U.S. intervention in El Salvador and succeeded in limiting the administration's involvement to the deployment of fifty-five advisors. I was one of the fifty-five.

It was sometimes a lonely job, especially in the remote area to which I was assigned. The majority of the U.S. advisors were in the capital; only two Special Forces soldiers were stationed in each of the six regions of the country, one of them being the capital region. I was one of ten advisors stationed outside San Salvador in the middle of a bitterly fought rural insurgency. My post was in the northern province of Chalatenango, where I was reunited with my good friend and former Special Forces teammate, Sergeant First Class Juan Gonzalez. Juan was stationed at a subordinate headquarters about four miles from the Fourth Brigade Headquarters, which would be my home in El Salvador. For about seven months in 1985 and 1986, Juan and I were the only Americans who stayed in our zone overnight. Others would come from the embassy, congressional delegations, and the press, but they'd fly in by helicopter for a day and fly right back out again. Few would help appreciably in their brief visits. A delegation from *Soldier of Fortune* magazine came and went, then mailed me a box with a ninja crossbow and some fighting stars in it. I guess they thought I was creeping around the jungle in black pajamas throwing ninja stars at the enemy. Instead, my local training sergeant and assistant shot the arrows and threw the stars at some birds out in the back of the M-16 range on a quiet Sunday afternoon until they lost them all (and they didn't hit a single bird).

One exception to the parade of useless visitors was adventurer and conservative lobbyist Andy Messing. After his visit, Andy brought donated, old, but completely serviceable incubators for premature babies for the local hospital. This gift was the most significant piece of foreign aid I was able to deliver to my region in the six months I had been there, and it did not cost the American taxpayer one cent.

During my second six months, I was assigned another Special Forces sergeant, Staff Sergeant Stan Brown, and a permanent CIA officer. A few military intelligence sergeants from Panama would come in for a few weeks at a time. So there I was, alone in my small dusty office, with only intermittent electrical power and well water that I disinfected with a bucket of swimming pool chlorine. There was no American air support, no artillery, nothing—just me and my Salvadoran counterparts. We were equipped in basically the same way as the guerrillas: with an assault rifle and a few magazines of ammunition. We had no real airpower, for the air was controlled by the Salvadoran air force and they couldn't be counted on. There was no artillery support to speak of; although the three 105-millimeter howitzers at my base were good for making a large bang, hitting something depended on random luck. We had no real mobility advantage, only a few trucks that were very vulnerable to ambush. So we mostly moved by foot. Our chief advantage was we'd been better trained in both weapons use and small-unit combat tactics. My Salvadoran troops could fight very well in the mountain jungles; the guerrillas were no match for them in direct combat. What worried Stan Brown and me was the surprise attack.

The military base where I was stationed was overrun by guerrillas three times during the war, once before I got there and twice after I left. The first attack, in 1983, was the worst disaster in the history of the Salvadoran military. The guerrillas stormed the base, killed more than a hundred soldiers, looted the national ammunition storage facility that was located there, and held the compound under siege for almost three days before they were repelled by air and ground power from the capital. And, as I mentioned in Chapter 1, six months after I left my replacement was killed in the March 1987 attack.

For me and my troops in Chalatenango, intelligence was not only crucial to successful long-term operations in the zone but the key to our very survival. When I arrived at the U.S. embassy in San Salvador, I received about two days of orientation from military and intelligence officials stationed in the capital. I was shown the intelligence support I would get from national assets to help me do my job. I'd be provided signals intelligence of intercepted radio communications of the insurgents in my zone. I was also given "target packages" about enemy encampments in my zone that showed detailed satellite photos of the guerrilla camps. I was impressed by this briefing, naively thinking that the huge American intelligence machine with its sophisticated technologies was going to give me a great advantage against the guerrillas.

After a brief orientation in the embassy, I was flown by helicopter to my home for the next year, an army base compound called El Paraiso—"paradise" in Spanish. El Paraiso was the headquarters for the Fourth Brigade of the Salvadoran army and was named for the small, dusty town adjacent to it that had been wrecked by several years of war. It had hardly been a paradise in its best days, which were long gone by. Although it was only about twenty miles from the capital, most of the roads were controlled by guerrilla forces, so traveling there by jeep wasn't permitted. Upon landing in "paradise," Major Ed Philips and I reviewed the intelligence support packages coming from the U.S. embassy. At first glance the packages were impressive, consisting of extensive folders with satellite images of enemy camps up in the mountains and analysis of their capability and plans. But Ed scoffed at this stuff, telling me that the intelligence always came too late to act on or gave us useless information about camp emplacements we already knew about but couldn't get to because the roads and trails leading up to the camps were heavily mined with improvised explosives. The guerrillas' antipersonnel land mines, the primary threat to our soldiers at the time, prevented our troops from moving freely through guerrilla areas even when we were confident that we possessed superior firepower. Every Salvadoran soldier had a buddy who'd lost a leg or foot from one of these improvised mines. These devices proved to be the great equalizer for the guerrillas and kept us off their backs.

Ed and I later met with Sergeant Juan Gonzalez, my old partner from my A-team in Panama who'd driven (against policy) down a dangerous road over to the brigade from his headquarters. Juan confirmed what Ed had told me about the intelligence support from the embassy, only in more colorful language. He was in the process of building his own human intelligence network in the zone from the ground up. But he had very little resources with which to do so. What Juan was doing to obtain actionable intelligence was far more productive (and considerably cheaper) than what the national programs were doing. He was establishing a network of undercover soldiers and paid civilian informants, the most prized information obviously being anything that would help prevent the insurgents from overrunning our compounds at night. The operation was on a shoestring budget at first, with most of the funding coming out of Juan's meager sergeant's salary. But the handful of soldiers didn't cost much to run, just occasional bus fare and lunch money. It was the same for the informants—a little lunch money and an extra bonus for those who provided useful information. Juan started his program by paying out of his own pocket, but over time, as the operation became more sophisticated, he was able to get some financial support from CIA.

CIA presence in my province was minimal. The head office, known as "the station," had assigned my headquarters a circuit rider, so named for the rounds of trips he made to different camps to collect information. He'd fly in by helicopter every week or two and conduct a perfunctory briefing with me, then proceed to meet with the Salvadoran brigade commander behind closed doors, leaving me outside. Unlike me, he had cash available to pay his sources as necessary. This guy was getting the latest reporting from the field and catching up on political machinations occurring in the country with my commander, who was a constant plotter of political intrigue.

I figured out two things very quickly: one, CIA was there to collect national intelligence, and two, I wasn't in the loop for the high-level political stuff going on in the capital. Quite frankly, I was more interested in locating the bad guys in my zone who were trying to kill me and my soldiers than I was in seeing the big picture. For the first six weeks, the commander and circuit rider ignored me and I ignored them, focusing on training my soldiers and pushing operations into the remote mountain areas of my zone.

Early on in my assignment, I was introduced to signals intelligence, or SIGINT. The guerrillas in El Salvador controlled the remote mountain area, keeping the Salvadoran army at bay with their land mines. To coordinate their activities and alert their comrades of approaching soldiers, the guerrillas communicated by handheld radios. U.S. Air Force planes flying out of Panama intercepted these communications and downloaded them to an operations center in San Salvador. The operations center then sent the data from these intercepts to our radio room with a very crude secure transmission device. The secure line couldn't manage voice communications, but we were sent numbers representing the time and grid coordinates of the intercepted transmissions. It was interesting but not of great use to me until a second and far more useful CIA officer showed up at the brigade. This time the new CIA guy decided to reside on the compound (at least a few overnight stays during each week), which changed his perspective immediately. He became much more interested in the local tactical situation when his life was on the line.

The new CIA officer showed up in Chalatenango with an intelligence sergeant from the U.S. Army in Panama. They had some money and a mission to establish intelligence fusion centers. What, you may ask, is an intelligence fusion center? Ours consisted of two extra rooms built in the brigade HQ space, a few big maps on the wall, and a few large file cabinets. The CIA official bought a few new air conditioners and a bucket of paint and soon the fusion center was the nicest office in the headquarters (the air conditioner in my office was broken). I had the Salvadoran colonel assign a few smart guys to the office and we got to work. Juan supplied a steady stream of human intelligence, or HUMINT, to the operations room, while the aircraft were giving us dots (communication locations) to post on the map. We were literally connecting the dots of enemy locations based on radio transmissions and informant reports.

I learned early on that the value of SIGINT wasn't only the content of a discussion but also the location of suspect conversations. Once we learned locations we could conduct surveillance operations and find the bad guys. (Twenty years later, I employed a variant of this method with NYPD searching for terrorists in New York City by accessing phone records and tracking the terrorists' calls. You don't always need to know what a person is saying, but it can be crucial to know *where* he is saying it, whether it be a mountaintop in El Salvador or an apartment in Brooklyn.) Using the data from these radio transmissions, the brigade was able to map out its military operations more effectively, allowing us to put relentless pressure on the guerrillas.

Juan's HUMINT operation foreshadowed another thing I'd do much later in my career. He started his program with a simple geographical and demographic analysis, beginning with a review of the locations where we knew or suspected guerrillas were operating. We then ascertained how we could establish coverage of that zone so we'd know when the enemy passed through and who supported them. We looked for people in our unit who knew the area and could identify possible sources of information. We recruited into our program people who could travel to those areas without raising suspicions. And we developed undercover soldiers to be our eyes and ears as necessary. In short order, Juan had established a human intelligence network in the key areas of our department.

It wasn't a very glamorous or complex network, but it was dangerous work for those reporting from the hot areas, and we did our best to train them. Starting from scratch, Juan ran a course in the basics of spying—or "tradecraft," as it's known in the business—for his small group of intelligence officers (which I later emulated for my detectives at NYPD). We had no current manuals to run the course, just some old, stained Vietnam-era stuff that Juan had scrounged up. This gave us a starting point; the rest we made up as we went along. As self-taught HUMINT collectors, we found it really wasn't that complicated. When your life is at stake, you tend to be very motivated to get things done. We needed to keep the pressure on the guerrillas or they'd be able to attack our bases. We knew we couldn't defeat them in the short or medium term, but we were determined to keep them off balance.

The primary means of information gathering involves various types of human sources, the most important of which are confidential informants and undercover agents. The difference is simple: an undercover agent is a member of an intelligence agency—FBI, CIA, police, and so on—and the confidential informer is a civilian. A true undercover agent isn't just some cop running around in civilian clothes with a fake name. He's a master of tradecraft with a false identity that can stand the test of his adversaries' investigation. In other words, he lives a full life that cannot be tracked back to his real identity as a government employee. In FBI and police operations, deep undercover officers are used to penetrate organized crime and drug organizations. The further up the chain of command they penetrate, the more sophisticated their false story needs to be.

A basic cover for an overseas agent might involve a diplomatic or foreign-service backstory, something under the aegis of the American government. This gives the agent diplomatic protection, which safeguards the agent in the event that his or her cover is blown. When the United States and the Soviet Union caught each other spying during the Cold War, it normally resulted in the mutual expulsion of intelligence operatives from both embassies. Such persons would be declared persona non grata by the host country and promptly deported. In CIA, non-official-cover operatives have a much better chance of infiltrating an intelligence target, but their disconnection from the embassy also means they lose their diplomatic protection and run the risk of long-term imprisonment or worse. An NOC has very deep cover and may operate within a country with the knowledge of only one or two officers in the entire CIA office. It isn't easy to set up an effective NOC, but once established they are extremely valuable to CT work around the world.

Levels of Intelligence Operations

The three different levels of intelligence collection and analysis used by military planners are strategic, operational, and tactical. Strategic-level intelligence helps leaders make broad national security decisions. For example, the decision to take down the Afghan sanctuary of al Qaeda was based on the strategic intelligence that identified Afghanistan as the heart of their operation. Operational-level intelligence is a step down from the strategic and looks at regional issues or broader movements in counterterrorism. For example, in NYPD counterterrorism, our operational-level intelligence defined and studied the radical movements that were influencing young recruits and inciting them to violence. Tactical intelligence involves ground-level activities directed against an individual or cell.

I was fortunate to have an opportunity to work at all of these levels during my career, and each level helped me to better understand the massive intelligence industry. After I left El Salvador, my life took a very different trajectory. I went from seven straight years of overseas tactical missions to sitting in a lecture hall in the School of Foreign Service at Georgetown University, where one of my graduate school professors, Madeleine Albright, taught me how to think through the political, economic, and social issues pertaining to national policy. After graduation, I was assigned to the Guatemala desk at the Defense Intelligence Agency. I was bored out of my mind at DIA, but managed to wrangle my way into some counternarcotics work during my spare time, which was considerable. Through this work, which my boss didn't even know I was doing, I was invited to brief a White House–sponsored panel on the Colombian cocaine industry (which was becoming a national security issue after the Cold War ended). This contact led to my next assignment, which was in the White House as an intelligence support officer for NSC staff dealing with what was then known as the "drug war." (In our national politics we Americans like to have "wars": war on poverty, war on drugs, war on terror, etc.)

In 1989 I began working for the national security advisor, Lieutenant General Brent Scowcroft, in the office that had been reconfigured after the Iran-contra scandal (in which Marine lieutenant colonel Oliver North sold antitank missiles to the Iranians in exchange for the release of our hostages being held by Hezbollah in Lebanon). My immediate boss, Randy Beers, was a holdover from the Reagan administration's cleanup of that mess. He worked in room 302 of the Old Executive Office Building, Ollie North's old office. Above Randy was David Miller, a former Westinghouse executive and two-time ambassador in Africa. My job was to provide all-source intelligence to their office in support of counternarcotics and low-intensity warfare.

It was during this assignment that I was introduced to the huge intelligence machinery in person. The White House staff had a very sophisticated computer network that enabled me to receive secret-level reports from all the national intelligence agencies, including CIA, DIA, and NSA, directly to my desktop computer. Some reports, particularly from NSA, were so sensitive that they had to be hand-carried and read in front of an NSA officer, then taken back to their storage locations in the West Wing of the White House.

Every night, a computer program would do a keyword search of the thousands of intelligence reports that would come in from the field. I would then scan about two hundred to three hundred cables when I arrived at my office, print out about twenty or thirty of the most important, and bring them to the attention of my bosses, Miller and Beers. It was a great job. I learned to appreciate the vastness of the intelligence community and was particularly impressed with the haul of information we got from NSA. I was underwhelmed by the CIA reporting, but I also understood that I wasn't getting all of the good stuff, which was restricted to people with a need to know. The intelligence community came up with these compartmentalized programs to protect their sources, but in my experience, they were far too constrictive in their sharing. This hypersecretive mentality caused a degree of blindness within the CIA that would prove devastating on 9/11.

Strategic-level intelligence helps direct national strategy, sets priorities, and helps policy makers shape effective policies and programs to support our national security goals, but the operational level is equally important. While working at NYPD, the most interesting work I did at the operational level involved the radical Islamic movements that were generating conscripts for potential terrorist cells in New York. As we studied these organizations, we found that there wasn't much on them at the federal level, but we saw them operating in New York City and traced their radicalizing and violent influences. Although they're not officially pegged as terrorist groups, organizations such as al-Mujahiroun and Hizb ut-Tahrir motivate and provide organizing platforms for terrorist activity. They teach a radical but not outwardly violent brand of Islam and point potentially violent individuals toward more militant organizations, often overseas. We tracked these organizations in the region and abroad. And in 2004, we held a joint conference with the British Metropolitan Police in New York City to review these movements on both sides of the Atlantic. In addition, R.P. Eddy and the Manhattan Institute provided a team of intelligence analysts that supported our work with timely and accurate reports on this and other fast-breaking issues.

At the tactical level, the key functions are running informants and informant networks—not unlike the work Juan Gonzalez did in El Salvador. The first step is to know your enemy at the international, regional, and local levels. Then you can begin to target your actions. Based on an understanding of the threat and your local community (whether it be in El Salvador, New York, or Pakistan), you then develop a collection plan.

At NYPD, we wanted to know our neighborhoods in different ways than they were previously known in the Department. Based on our knowledge of radical Islam, we looked for indicators of that ideology in certain neighborhoods. It wasn't enough to simply look for the most radical imams preaching hate in mosques, for much of that rhetoric had been squelched due to FBI scrutiny. Instead, we looked on college campuses, in coffeehouses, and in bookstores where radicals congregated. From there, we looked for persons plotting illegal action, such as planning to kill infidels whom they claimed were responsible for crimes against their brothers. At that point we could begin an operation. Informants and undercover agents were then used to identify others that might be involved in plotting criminal activity.

Foreign Intelligence Operations: Unsavory Alliances

CIA is responsible for making sure our foreign partners support us with useful intelligence. However, foreign intelligence agencies always look to their own national interest first. Also, at times the United States must work closely with countries that are outwardly antagonistic toward us. In these cases CIA must build common ground with a lesser enemy in order to deal with a more imposing one. For example, after we invaded Afghanistan, we worked with Iran, also an enemy of the Taliban. Although the goodwill was short-lived, this temporary cooperation demonstrates the nature of diplomacy and intelligence: our enemies are often very flexible when an alliance is necessary or convenient.

In the terrorism business, particularly with regard to al Qaeda, we're generally able to obtain solid support from foreign intelligence agencies in finding radical cells because al Qaeda has no support from any government. But the task isn't always easy. Some local intelligence officials are underpaid, underequipped, or otherwise ill-suited to the task. Some are also quite unsavory. Although we've forfeited much of our moral high ground with the scandals surrounding U.S. military torture practices and questionable detention policies, we maintain standards of human rights and legal process far higher than most of our allies do. But CIA must work with foreign agencies, good and bad. Failing to do so because we disapprove of their tactics will leave us more exposed to future terrorist attacks.

Our foreign intelligence operations function from within and outside of our embassies to accomplish these tasks. However, for CIA to operate where there is no U.S. embassy is extremely difficult. Most CIA officers operate without deep cover and need an embassy to provide them the diplomatic permission to operate. Without an embassy, our operations are sadly reduced, and we're often blind to what is happening in places we really need to watch.

The unfortunate practice of rebuking rogue regimes by pulling our embassies from their capitals can be rather self-defeating, yet this punishment is the standard diplomatic means of expressing displeasure with a country. Somehow we feel better after withdrawing our embassy because it sends a message that we're dissatisfied, but ultimately we lose our best information and diplomatic channels. This self-defeating policy is something I have never understood, even as a former diplomat. Right now, the U.S. government does not have embassies in Iran, North Korea, and Sudan. It's no wonder we're so clueless and operationally inept in these parts of the world. I argued this point often when I was at the State Department. Once I was asked if I would have kept an embassy in Nazi Germany during World War II, and I replied that if I thought it was safe for our diplomats, absolutely yes. And I would have run intelligence operations against the Nazis from our embassy in Berlin. Of course, embassies are often expelled by the host nation, but I wouldn't leave unless expelled, especially in hostile countries. That is where we *most* need embassies.

Prior to 9/11, we had no embassy in Afghanistan and none in

Sudan (where al Qaeda had been based previously), so we were blind to much of al Qaeda's activity. Also, because of human rights issues, our intelligence agencies had weak relations with Algeria, Egypt, and Yemen. Those countries hold information that can help us to better understand and potentially thwart al Qaeda. We won't know what we're dealing with if we don't interact with hotbed countries.

Central Asia, 2000

As ambassador-at-large for counterterrorism from 1998 to 2000, I was given the task of convincing our friends and allies to work together for our mutual interests—and, in doing so, to uphold the standards of behavior that we expected of a government. Easier said than done.

One of my trips took me to the strategically important area of Central Asia. These newly independent states were eager to build a relationship with the United States and put some distance between themselves and their former masters in Moscow. I remember walking into a room full of counterterrorism officials from a country I won't name, but it was in Central Asia and ended in "stan" (that leaves five possibilities). I whispered to my assistant Nicole Bibbons that there must have been a strict requirement that you had to have a size twelve head and an eighteen-inch neck to be a counterterrorism official in this country. She added in a whisper that it also helped to wear loud, off-color polyester suits. As I looked across the table at this crew, I took a deep breath. My mission, as it had been earlier on a trip through the region with the secretary of state, was to convince these guys that we should partner in the fight against terrorism. I had the unenviable job of telling them that respect for human rights was required by international law, important to the long-term success of their programs, and a sine qua non for their expanding relationship with the United States. I also knew that the security of Americans, at home and abroad, was to some degree in their hands.

One of the highlights of the trip was visiting a police unit that had been responsible for detecting the smuggling of radiological materials across an international boundary. Although there was no link to terrorism (it was just a criminal garbage-dumping process), it certainly caught the attention of the intelligence community when the story broke. The local police were very proud, since they'd detected the materials with the help of a handheld radiological detection device provided by a DOD program. The problem of loose nukes in the "stans" was still very much a big issue at the time, and this sting seemed to validate the program's effectiveness. So, even without a connection to terrorism, it is in the best interest of our CT policy to be plugged in around the world if we want to find the terror buzz.

Lacking Imagination

In 2002, I was often asked why if John Walker Lindh, the young American captured on a battlefield of Afghanistan, was able to get inside al Qaeda and meet bin Laden, why couldn't one of our CIA operatives? It's an obvious question, and a good one not asked frequently enough of our intelligence operations: why haven't they been able to penetrate these organizations?

The fact is we should have been able to do so. We should have been sending informants up the chain for years. But we're unable to do so for a number of reasons. One of them I discussed in detail with regard to domestic intelligence: our standard for deploying operatives is too risk-averse. We deploy agents against al Qaeda as if we're going up against the KGB because our outdated methodology, developed while we were operating against the Soviet Union. We had to be extremely careful because the Soviets had sophisticated programs and technology by which our agents could be detected, jeopardizing our larger operations or causing international embarrassment. So we learned to be very careful with our assets. But al Qaeda isn't even a country, and it has virtually no ability to conduct counterintelligence operations (for example, penetrating our intelligence operations). This doesn't mean we should be reckless, just significantly bolder in recruiting and deploying agents against the terrorist target.

Let's take the case of a hypothetical potential source, Mr. Ahmed Khan. The would-be Mr. Khan is a Pakistani citizen who came to the United States illegally eight years ago and was recruited by NYPD after he was arrested for credit card fraud. Khan was asked to report back to NYPD if he finds any pockets of violent activity in his neighborhood. A few weeks later, Khan bumps into a group of radicals associated with a bookstore and café in Brooklyn that has radical materials. As he gains their confidence, the leaders of the cell ask him if he is interested in going on a pilgrimage to Pakistan, where he will meet other "brothers" and perhaps receive radical ideological training with an organization that has known ties to terrorism. If he makes it through this passage, he may be asked to attend some paramilitary training to defend the brothers against the infidels. It is now in our interest to get this guy abroad, where we hope he can make his way up the chain, even gaining entry into al Qaeda. We know he's a questionable character; he is an illegal alien with a criminal past. His passport and identity are false. But he also has family in the United States and does not want them to get deported. This is the type of guy who might be recruited to do a long-term penetration of al Qaeda. He certainly couldn't have penetrated the Soviet or Chinese intelligence agencies, but perhaps he could be useful as a spy on al Qaeda.

But to employ the services of a character such as Khan, we'd have to take risks. We might have to give this criminal false papers and a cover to get him back into Pakistan. This would be dangerous work for him, but it would be voluntary on his part and he'd be paid. We wouldn't want to send an agent like this until he was fairly well tested. But we shouldn't wait too long, or opportunities to infiltrate al Qaeda will pass us by. Does this sound simple? In many ways it is, but in my experience it isn't happening with enough frequency, creativity, and prudent risk. Too often a potential case like this is shot down by fearful bureaucrats in Washington and abroad. And that's why, in part, we have consistently failed to penetrate the organizations that threaten us.

We also need to encourage foreign liaisons to recruit operatives that can travel to the United States and be used to penetrate hostile local cells—and then reverse the direction to get people back overseas. Al Qaeda is doing the same thing now, trying to recruit people to enter our country. We need to be faster and better at recruiting people who can enter into their organization at all levels and in all countries where al Qaeda operates. If we do it enough, over time we'll get people in position to provide us with information we can act on.

We need to be patient and take a long-term view if we're to penetrate these groups. We've been in Iraq now for several years, and I would hope we're seeding all of the potential terrorist organizations there with informants. Some may lie dormant for years as they work their way up the chain, but it's this type of investment in human penetration of terrorist organizations that will protect us in the future. It is probably more difficult now than it was prior to 9/11 to get someone up into the al Qaeda central organization. However, there are plenty of feeder organizations. We read of cases where Europeans are receiving training in camps in Pakistan. We need agents in those camps, and we need them now.

The most significant CIA station in the world today is in Pakistan, currently our most important yet flawed ally in counterterrorism. It's the current home of bin Laden and much of the Taliban. Some of the most important arrests against al Qaeda have been made in Pakistan, including Ramzi Yousef (the leader of the World Trade Center attack in 1993), Khalid Sheikh Mohammed (the 9/11 mastermind), and major al Qaeda inside operatives such as Abu Zubaida and Abu Faraj al-Libi, both captured in the past several years. These successful operations have been usually conducted as joint actions, involving U.S. intelligence and local intelligence and police forces. In most of these cases, a combination of human intelligence, normally provided by locals, and signals intelligence, often provided by the United States, leads to closing in on an operative. With a little luck, and perhaps a hot tip from a source or a quick hit on a telephone intercept, a person of interest can be found. Then it is normally a local operation to take down the house and affect the arrest. Rarely is there any loss of life.

Embassies Are Not Enough

Simply having embassies inside rogue regimes is not enough. Obviously, Americans associated with an embassy can't operate in deep cover. That work is left to the NOCs. The CIA station chief is normally under official cover. In other words, he's announced as an intelligence official to the host country, as is their chief of intelligence in Washington, D.C. This may seem strange, but it's normal protocol.

NOCs can operate with much greater flexibility than embassy-based personnel. Unfortunately, over the years, the use of NOCs was minimized in favor of more traditional CIA work. CIA has dramatically expanded its NOC program since 9/11, but it will take many years to build the type of intelligence infrastructure we need.

NOC operations are very sensitive and difficult for me to discuss in an unclassified forum. But to illustrate the type of capability we need, I'll go back to the Iran hostage rescue mission to describe a classic NOC operation. Although this wasn't a CIA operation, the principles are the same. It began when the U.S. Army's Delta Force was planning to rescue the American hostages in Iran and needed an inside presence. The plan was to fly from an aircraft carrier in the Indian Ocean into Iran in a remote desert location, named Desert One. From Desert One, the unit would move by helicopter to a location outside of Tehran, where they'd be moved by truck inside the city. To get the trucks to that location, the commander, Colonel Charlie Beckwith, asked Major Dick Meadows to infiltrate Tehran undercover as an Irish businessman to make the arrangements. And he did. We'll never know if the operation would have been successful if they proceeded from Desert One into Tehran; but Dick Meadows appeared ready to go with his part of the plan.

Although this wasn't a traditional NOC operation, you can imagine that if in the future a Special Operations unit needs transportation in a remote place in the world, it would be beneficial to have some capability already there to support the operation. One of the reasons Secretary of Defense Donald Rumsfeld expanded DOD's own intelligence capability after 9/11 was so they could directly support these types of operations and not depend on CIA.

The NSA Wiretap Controversy

Shortly after September 11, President Bush authorized NSA to expand its listening program. Prior to 9/11, NSA was authorized to listen to all phone calls between two callers if they were both overseas, even if they were U.S. citizens, as long as the conversation was intercepted outside of the United States. They could also listen to an international call between a foreign country and the United States, again as long as the communication was picked up overseas. They were prohibited from listening to a foreign phone call if it was tapped from U.S. soil. After 9/11, President George W. Bush authorized NSA to listen to international calls from within the United States as well. It did not change their requirement to get a warrant to tap purely domestic calls.

Although the exact nature of the program wasn't well understood by either side of the debate, this lack of knowledge did not quell the formation of very strong opinions. To President Bush's critics, it was another example of how the president had overstepped his authority since 9/11, recklessly trashing the U.S. Constitution, whereas on the other end of the political spectrum, any challenge to the president's authority to listen to our phone calls was deemed unpatriotic and considered "giving in to the terrorists." Very few seemed to understand the problem at all, nor was anybody willing to work toward a reasonable compromise; too many political points were being scored by both sides.

At New York University, where I work at the Center for Law and Security, we attempted to clarify what exactly the NSA program was and lay out its pros and cons. It wasn't easy, for the very subject was so shrouded in secrecy it was difficult to determine what the program actually did. In a report we published in early 2007, we tried to describe the program in clear language. I argued that a compromise was easily within reach if the Congress and the administration would trust each other, a tall order in today's Washington. Let me remind you that the primary addition President Bush made to the NSA's authority was to allow NSA to intercept a foreign phone call (between the United States and a foreign country) from within the United States without a warrant. The same call could be monitored from overseas without a warrant. As a CT practitioner, I strongly support this choice because it enhances our ability to prevent future attacks. Had the president asked Congress for this privilege explicitly, and implemented close congressional oversight to prevent abuses, he would have received their support and avoided much of the negative controversy that was generated.

NSA will have a huge role in the future of counterterrorism. Although many terrorists are careful not to talk about operational issues on the telephone, it's almost impossible to live in this world today without a phone or e-mail, even if you're a terrorist. Obviously, phone intercepts with real content are crucially important, but phone calls also give us lots of other information about a person, including his location and the individuals and groups with whom he associates. This data and, when available, the actual content of a phone conversation are crucial tools for counterterrorism investigators.

In addition, the Internet is increasingly important to terrorists. As their physical sanctuary comes under increasing pressure, terrorists are forced to communicate within their networks in virtual space. The Internet is used for networking terrorists around the world. It also has two other important roles for the terrorists. One is the increasing use of the Internet to spread the hateful ideology of the violent movements. Prior to 9/11, preachers such as Abu Hamza used his rights of free speech to spew hate on a soapbox in central London. Others also openly advocated hate and violence (although few as blatantly as Abu Hamza). Public displays such as this have diminished dramatically since 9/11 in the United States and since July 7, 2005, in the United Kingdom and other parts of Europe. Instead, terrorists are increasingly using the Internet to spread their ideology. Another troubling issue on the Internet is the information that can be found—including bomb-making instructions. This is particularly worrisome for the future of making improvised weapons.

The Future of Counterterrorism Intelligence

The future of our counterterrorism programs will depend heavily on our ability to monitor the information that is out there in an effective and legal manner. It doesn't take a lot of resources to run a human intelligence network, just a little creativity and a lot of motivation. In El Salvador, Special Forces sergeant Juan Gonzalez built an effective network on a shoestring budget; NYPD did the same with a shrinking overall budget. The most effective operations take advantage of locals, employing volunteers to watch and listen. In New York City we had plenty of volunteers, but we didn't wait for them to come to us. We employed some rather creative methods to find people who would cooperate with us.

Spying can be a sordid business, but it is the key to our success in defeating al Qaeda's immediate operational capability. The subject should be discussed more openly; only then can we fully understand its importance and inherent risks. Good intelligence operations must be conducted with great operational security. Leaks are unacceptable and oversight must be thorough, both from within an intelligence agency (by lawyers and internal investigative agencies) and by the legislative and judicial branches of the government. I'm convinced that executive branch leaders at the local, state, and federal levels can form bipartisan partnerships with oversight committees that will strengthen our intelligence ability while ensuring that our civil liberties are protected.

Chapter 9

Domestic Intelligence: The Spy Game at Home

AMERICANS LOVE MOVIES, TV shows, and books about spies and secret agents. They love it when their heroes take huge risks, put pistols in the faces of the bad guys, and blow up the villains' headquarters in spectacular flames. But in real life, most Americans are uncomfortable with the notion of spying, particularly at home in the United States. They cherish their personal privacy and don't want the government peeking into their private lives. The right of privacy is jealously protected by liberals, conservatives, and moderates alike. Not only do we mistrust spying, we don't even like talking about it as public policy. I found it interesting that after 9/11 most of the discussion about intelligence focused on information sharing. Although there was some discussion about expanding human intelligence, there wasn't much discussion about the details of the murky world of collection.

As I've illustrated over and over, the key to counterterrorism is intelligence. And the primary work of intelligence is the collection of information. Once data is obtained from within terrorist organizations, or at least from around the periphery of such groups, that information must be reported as soon as possible and properly documented. From there, the sharing of the information is largely taken care of by computer systems that provide access to the appropriate analysts.

So why have we not discussed publicly the details of domestic intelligence collection, aka spying? Two reasons. First, those who are personally involved in domestic intelligence don't like to talk about it. By their silence, they protect their trade secrets and diminish the notion that Big Brother is watching the American public. Second, those who do discuss counterterrorism and shape our policy—foreign policy experts, journalists, and pundits—don't really understand the business. They have a hard time penetrating the smoke and mirrors of the intelligence world, so instead they rely heavily on speculation and uninformed guesswork. I've seen enough action in intelligence work to share the concerns of operatives who'd rather keep the details of their work mum. But even though I feel reluctant to open up the box, by peering into a small window on the world of domestic intelligence I hope to illustrate its central importance to counterterrorism.

NYPD: Bold Leadership for Big Blue

NYPD's intelligence operations provide part of that window. Without getting into all of the details of these sensitive operations, I can tell you that the boldness it took to build NYPD's intelligence capacity speaks volumes in itself. I'll give you the basic story line of NYPD intelligence, but my allegiance to the organization and my concern for the continued effectiveness of their programs prevent me from sharing specifics. With a little imagination, you should be able to fill in the gaps.

Three months after 9/11, newly elected mayor Michael Bloomberg appointed Raymond W. Kelly as the police commissioner of New York. Kelly is a former Marine and Vietnam veteran who holds the distinction of having risen from police cadet to commissioner. This was Kelly's second turn at the helm of NYPD. During the intervening years he gained valuable federal, international, and private-sector experience. Immediately upon taking office, Kelly set out to transform NYPD counterterrorism and intelligence programs to meet the new post-9/11 challenges. His determination to reform the Department was driven by a firm conviction that in the wake of September 11, NYPD could no longer completely rely on the federal government in the areas of counterterrorism and intelligence as before. Several key decisions on Kelly's part made it possible to create in New York City one of the world's most effective counterterrorism forces.

First, Kelly made an enormous personnel commitment to FBI's counterterrorism program. In virtually all jurisdictions outside of New York City, FBI completely dominates the business of intelligence operations against domestic terrorism threats. In fact, the Bureau contends that they have sole jurisdiction for that mission, and any law enforcement agency that wants to join in the effort is obligated to do so as part of the web of joint terrorism task forces (JTTFs) FBI has established throughout the country.

Kelly knew that FBI, with its enormous infrastructure and huge financial and human resources, had inherent advantages that he could never duplicate at NYPD. FBI in New York is plugged into the national intelligence databases and to other JTTFs around the country. Kelly wanted to be part of that network, so he dedicated enough NYPD police officers to effectively pair up with their FBI New York–based counterparts. This gave Kelly complete access to all the federal counterterrorism programs. For their part FBI also benefited enormously. They got a large number of knowledgeable veteran cops (from narcotics, vice, homicide, organized crime, etc.) to team with the Bureau's younger and more formally educated agents. In all, Kelly assigned more than a hundred streetwise detectives to FBI, with supervisors at every level from sergeant to captain to chief, dwarfing any other commitment made to FBI nationally. Most police forces, including departments in Los Angeles and Chicago, assigned only a handful of officers.

Participation in a JTTF is a great deal for local police agencies, and most are glad to sign on. FBI provides company cars, gas, parking, and tolls for cops to get to and from work—a valuable perk for the average cop, who often commutes as long as one hour to the office, each way. The cops also get decent office space and top-secret clearances. In addition, these local cops are granted limited federal law enforcement powers as well as impressive-looking credentials they can flip open like FBI agents on TV to wow their cop buddies, friends, families, and suspected criminals.

Perks notwithstanding, Kelly was unwilling to relinquish full control of counterterrorism activity to FBI's JTTF. So, in addition to his commitment to the JTTF, Kelly re-created the Intelligence Division within NYPD, separate from FBI. This was a huge decision. The idea of a local police department running a major counterterrorism intelligence operation was unheard of in the United States. But after announcing the division's creation, Kelly took an even bolder step: he recruited and hired David Cohen to run it. Cohen, a thirty-year veteran of CIA, had been head of the Agency's clandestine service, the spymaster for the largest and most sophisticated intelligence operation in the world. Cohen is modest, even self-effacing at times, and is focused entirely on results—the exact qualities Kelly was looking for in an intelligence director. After Cohen's appointment as deputy commissioner in the Intelligence Division, the ex–CIA man and Kelly quickly established a close working relationship and personal friendship. The commissioner kept a very tight rein on operations but always gave Cohen plenty of room to improvise. Under Cohen, NYPD intelligence ranked right up there with the French, British, and Israeli operations, and in some important ways has even surpassed them. Cohen took prudent risks in coupling seasoned veteran detectives (most of Irish and Italian ethnicity) with younger talent from NYPD's fastest-growing ethnic groups: Hispanics, African Americans, and Middle Easterners (many of them Muslim). He applied years of CIA techniques to the local level and bypassed some of the more stringent bureaucratic obstacles.

Kelly's third major reform was his expansion of the Department's counterterrorism mission. As deputy commissioner for the Bureau of Counter Terrorism, I commanded its two components: the NYPD unit within FBI and the new Counterterrorism Division (which was responsible for training, critical infrastructure protection, public outreach, and a few other programs). Prior to my turn at the helm of the Counterterrorism Bureau, Kelly had hired retired Marine general Frank Libutti for the job. Libutti returned to Washington about a year after he got NYPD's counterterrorism unit up and running, and I inherited from him a great team. Of course, Cohen, Libutti, and I were all recruited to come to NYPD because of 9/11. We weren't sure what we were going to do; we just knew that it was important work, and with Kelly in charge, we wouldn't be spinning our wheels in another Washington bureaucracy. We wanted to be where the terrorists were likely to strike, making sure they couldn't follow through on their plans.

In selecting outsiders such as Cohen and me, Kelly took a chance. Most police departments would never hire a former CIA official to run a program. First, as a rule, programs are run only by cops, and neither Cohen nor I was a cop. Second, appointing a CIA man could generate suspicion and criticism from both left- and right-wing political groups. But Kelly understood the enormous benefit to bringing in Cohen and took the risk. Mayor Bloomberg also deserves great credit. Even if the police and the public had their biases, Kelly had Bloomberg's full support. I suppose it was easier to push through controversial appointments in New York City, where the smoke from the Twin Towers was still bringing tears to our eyes. But bold leadership is what the city needed, and Kelly and Bloomberg delivered.

There were other pressures on Kelly as well. The Giuliani administration had presided over a drop in crime so extraordinary that few believed it could be sustained. In a way, Bloomberg and Kelly were set up to fail. The ranks of NYPD had risen to record high numbers by the end of Mayor Giuliani's term, and in the aftermath of 9/11, the surge in cops was unsustainable. The city's economy was reeling from the effects of the attacks, and Mayor Bloomberg had to balance a budget. He and Kelly knew that the force would have to be cut back, an ominous portent given the Department's new obligation to simultaneously push crime rates down while simultaneously protecting the city from a terrorist attack. It was in the context of this intense external and internal pressure that Kelly made the difficult decision to devote existing resources to counterterrorism while his department was shrinking.

In contrast, the federal counterterrorism bureaucracy began to expand at an enormous rate, and any agency that could claim some piece of the terrorism world was running up to Capitol Hill to get new terrorism funding. Previously starved programs, including the one I ran at the State Department, were flush with staff, offices, and expanded budgets. In divying up the ballooning homeland security budget, it seemed, no preference was given to places considered at high risk for terrorism attacks; New York City was just one of many contestants waiting in line for this heavily sought-after pork. But instead of depending on the federal government to provide resources for homeland security, Kelly made an immediate and enormous commitment to counterterrorism at NYPD using the resources he had at his disposal.

Kelly knew that for Cohen and me to fulfill our distinct missions, we would need some of the Department's best personnel. All were volunteers selected from a highly competitive pool of specialists. They had put thousands of felons behind bars throughout the city and were now dedicated to the counterterrorism mission, which included helping me, a relative outsider, navigate both the city's streets and the many twisting avenues of NYPD politics. Many of the officers who came over to my Bureau were legends within the Department; when they joined the CT mission, the city's crime-fighting capacity took an enormous hit. The staffing of Cohen's team also severely depleted resources. Kelly had resolved to transform the Department quickly, and to do that he needed his very best. He was reminded of the urgency of this challenge every day as he drove past the enormous hole in the ground at the World Trade Center site, which was a short distance from his apartment.

Kelly was also careful to keep a tight rein on non-cops such as Cohen and me, who had no prior experience with the intricacies of police work or the politics of either the Department or New York City government. To keep us out of trouble, he surrounded us with some very smart police chiefs, but we were clearly in charge of our divisions. This was a refreshing change for me. In my previous job at the UN I had felt I was constantly fighting the bureaucracy, even with my own subordinates. At NYPD, Kelly empowered us to effect rapid change. It's a mandate that's easily issued but, in my experience, very rarely accomplished within most government bureaucracies, owing to the profusion of independent power sources and agendas.

It's truly a testament to Kelly and all of NYPD that despite the drain on the Department from staffing Cohen's and my programs, crime continued moving downward at record levels. In fact, in the first five years of Kelly's term overall, crime levels dropped another 17.7 percent and homicide levels reached levels as low as those of the early 1960s.

The Showdown Between NYPD and FBI

Kelly's unprecedented innovation pushed law enforcement in New York into uncharted territory, and initially, this new paradigm didn't sit well with FBI. While FBI was happy to welcome into the JTTF so many quality NYPD detectives, they were less thrilled about Cohen's unilateral mission. Other local jurisdictions that attempted to expand their counterterrorism mission outside of the JTTF were crushed (New Jersey, for one). But that wasn't going to happen at NYPD. During the first three years of the Department's counterterrorism program the tension grew, rising to a peak by the end of 2005.

Hollywood often portrays local cops and the feds as fighting over jurisdiction of crime investigations. Sometimes the moviemakers exaggerate the conflict, but make no mistake about it: the tension not only exists but is inherent in our political system. The existence of multiple organizations at the federal, state, and local levels with overlapping missions inevitably leads to tension and competition. As frustrating as this may be, in my opinion it beats the alternative of having one national police force under a central authority, as many nations do. When I came to NYPD in 2003, I gained a new appreciation for the way we do things in the United States of America. The Department considered itself quite independent of the federal government, and it had the size, talent, and capability to retain its independence. But NYPD also understood its limitations, and often reached out to the federal government for assistance from the Drug Enforcement Agency, Coast Guard, CIA, and even FBI. However, under Kelly's direction, NYPD would never completely subjugate itself to the federal government when it came to its primary mission: protecting the city of New York.

NYPD was in conflict when I arrived. Department detectives were feuding with FBI, and my NYPD detectives assigned to FBI were also doing battle with their brother detectives in NYPD intelligence. Although these tensions reached a peak during my tenure at NYPD, they eventually simmered down, and relations were markedly improved by the time I left. The seriousness of the task before these CT professionals demanded that they work out their differences, but I imagine that the relationship between FBI and NYPD will never be completely harmonious. One detective was so disgusted after working with FBI that he resigned and went back to work on an investigative squad on the mean streets of Brooklyn. This is a very rare move; the perks at FBI are just too good for most cops to resist. The Bureau's enticing power over its junior police partners at the local level adds to the animosity felt by the cops. But NYPD is a different animal. The creation of the NYPD intelligence unit, independent of the Joint Terrorism Task Force, wasn't very popular among FBI agents. It represented yet another flash point in an already strained relationship.

FBI director Robert Mueller was well aware of the rift. Kelly, Cohen, and I all had deep contacts in Washington, D.C., and we let it be known that the conflict was serious enough to affect operations, which was clearly unacceptable to both NYPD and FBI. In addition to our grievances, some agents in the Bureau's New York office were also complaining bitterly to their headquarters in Washington.

In a way, it was fortunate for NYPD that this showdown with FBI didn't happen until 2006. Three years earlier, when Cohen took over the Intelligence Division at NYPD after 9/11, his office wasn't much more than a protection service for high-level dignitaries who visited the city. It wasn't really in the counterterrorism game at all. But by the time the rift with FBI got serious enough to warrant a showdown, Cohen had already created one of the largest and most innovative counterterrorism initiatives in the United States, if not the world, with very little interference from Washington.

In early February 2006, relations between NYPD and FBI had deteriorated to such a degree that Mueller came to New York to see for himself what the issues were. When Mueller entered the NYPD conference room flanked by three of his most senior staff, Commissioner Kelly greeted him formally. Cohen and I sat by Kelly's side. The issue at hand was NYPD's independent counter-terrorism effort, and the main brief of the day would come from Cohen. Because one of my responsibilities was to integrate over one hundred NYPD detectives into FBI's JTTF, I had my share of issues with FBI as well. But that morning's focus was on Cohen's team. Cohen's independent unit was a particular irritation to some of the senior leadership of FBI, who'd been accustomed to calling all the shots concerning any counterterrorism investigation launched within the United States. But that was no longer the case in New York City, and NYPD was big enough, tough enough, and good enough to face them down.

Cohen took Mueller and his staff through a two-hour briefing on NYPD intelligence program. He laid out the details of under-cover recruitment and training, innovative informant identification and development programs, the prison program, the overseas program, and other operations of the division. It was clearly a tour de force, and Cohen didn't even get into all NYPD's ancillary programs, such as the growing cooperation we had with local police forces in New Jersey and New York. Cohen showcased a program that was massive and extremely innovative, but most important, he proved that his team was covering the city effectively. The NYPD intelligence program was created by a career intelligence professional, empowered and emboldened by Commissioner Kelly, and supported by a team of very able NYPD detectives.

Mueller was impressed. He listened to Cohen with great interest and asked some very good questions. At the end of the briefing, Mueller conceded that FBI had things to learn from NYPD. This was a remarkable statement, completely uncharacteristic of FBI, and one I give enormous credit to Mueller for making in front of his key deputies. Above all, the meeting justified the very legitimacy of NYPD's independent counterterrorism intelligence operation.

After Cohen's breathtaking overview of NYPD intelligence program, Mueller laid down the law. He congratulated Cohen on establishing a terrific organization and instructed his staff to embrace Cohen's programs, not resist them. In fact, he invited Cohen down to Washington to brief his senior leadership. I'd respected Mueller from his reputation in George H. W. Bush's administration in the 1990s, but my estimation of him grew considerably that morning. It wasn't easy for him to make these concessions. His subordinates, all career agents with about twenty-five years of service per man, didn't flinch as he spoke. In fact, they seemed to welcome Mueller's attitude, at least on the surface. Most important, though, Mueller's promise took hold and our relationship with FBI improved significantly.

However, in the days following the meeting, we picked up on some blowback from FBI headquarters. There was grumbling about Cohen's ability to accomplish things by operating "out of bounds." Some at the Bureau rationalized that certain FBI programs weren't as effective as Cohen's because the feds "played by the rules." NYPD dismissed this as sour grapes. Cohen had always operated under state and city legal guidelines for investigations that were modeled after the federal guidelines of the Patriot Act, the same guidelines FBI followed. If NYPD's programs were more innovative than FBI's, it was a direct result of Cohen's creative initiative, along with the backing and sometimes cajoling of Commissioner Kelly, who kept Cohen and me constantly moving forward with our programs. To me the difference was a product of (Kelly and Cohen's) leadership and the talent of their NYPD detectives.

NYPD Intelligence: Looking for the New York Angle

NYPD intelligence has received a lot of press attention in the past several years, much of it regarding the overseas program. As the name implies, the overseas program sends NYPD detectives to posts in nations around the world, including Israel, the United Kingdom, Canada, Spain, Jordan, France, and Singapore. This is a great program, even though it often gets NYPD in trouble with FBI and the local U.S. ambassadors. But the police forces in those countries appreciate the cop-to-cop relationship with NYPD, and the program is thriving. The overseas program was never designed to compete with CIA or FBI, as some in the press have implied; that would be absolutely counterproductive to the shared mission of these forces. As Commissioner Kelly often said in defense of the program, NYPD detectives were looking for "the NYC angle" on any given issue that might not be at the center of the radar for our federal partners.

The Madrid train attack in March 2004 is the perfect example. NYPD responded to that incident immediately because we were keenly aware that al Qaeda might be conducting a multicountry attack, as they've done before. (Recall the African embassy bombings.) We were also concerned about copycat bombers striking in New York City. Detectives from my and Cohen's offices were on the scene in Madrid within eighteen hours of the blast, looking for the New York angle. Obviously, we had a massive train system to protect in New York, so we were focused on the details of this attack, in contrast to FBI and CIA operatives, who were more interested in investigating the case with an eye toward its broader implications for U.S. interests and policies. Our issues were very specific: we sent transit cops to Madrid to review what did and didn't work in protecting those trains. Nobody in FBI or CIA has experience in protecting a train system; it's simply not their responsibility. The New York angle, in this case, pertained to subway security procedures that FBI and CIA had no interest or experience.

Within twenty-four hours, we'd made adjustments to our security procedures in New York based on what we'd learned in Madrid. Two immediate changes were made. First, based on reports that the van holding the attackers' backpack bombs was several blocks from the entrance to the train station, we pushed out our patrol perimeters a few blocks beyond the subway stations. Second, we knew that someone had seen suspicious activity that was indeed the terrorists at work, but hadn't reported it. So we ramped up our public awareness program, imploring New Yorkers to keep alert in and around the subway trains with the catchphrase "If you see something, say something." After our team returned from Madrid, we prepared an extensive analysis of the attack and its implications for our transit security programs. These studies became an integral part of our planning and were soon incorporated into our threat-based programs and strategies.

The Herald Square Plot: Jokers or Killers?

There is one NYPD case that has been well reported by the *New York Times* and gives a window on the world of NYPD intelligence: the trial of the men involved in a plot against the Herald Square subway station in the summer of 2004. *New York Times* metro reporter Willie Raushbaum, an aggressive and experienced reporter, covered the case closely. In the end, one of the defendants pled guilty and the other went to a jury trial, where he lost. The trial itself reveals much about the importance of intelligence in the fight against terrorism.

In 2004, an election year, George W. Bush strategically selected New York City and the backdrop of the 9/11 attacks for the site of the Republican National Convention that summer. NYPD and the U.S. Secret Service prepared painstakingly for over a year for this enormous undertaking. At the time, the country was at war in Afghanistan and Iraq, the al Qaeda threats were high, and throngs of protesters and anarchists were planning to descend on the city and wreak havoc on the convention. NYPD geared up for the challenge. Our planning included detailed procedures for managing delegates, their buses, tourists, and protestors.

The Herald Square case also commenced about a year before the convention, in September 2003. It started in the manner of many NYPD cases, with an individual trial, in this case, that of a twenty-two-year-old Queens man named Shahawar Matin Siraj.

Siraj initially came onto NYPD's radar when a source for the Department reported that Siraj had discussed a potential act of violence against the city. But at first the details were a bit vague. It soon became apparent that Siraj was indeed planning violence, not just spouting anti-American or anti-Bush political diatribes. At NYPD, we didn't have the legal authority, the time, or the inclination to investigate political opponents of the U.S. government. If we had traveled down that path, we'd never have gotten anywhere in protecting the city from actual terrorists. Instead, we focused solely on those people who were conspiring to support or commit acts of violence. Siraj fit this profile.

Siraj and his accomplice, nineteen-year-old James Elshafay of Staten Island, were the two defendants in the Herald Square case. Raushbaum reported on NYPD informant named Osama Eldawoody who first came across Siraj at a bookstore next to the Islamic Society of Bay Ridge, Brooklyn. According to tapes made available during the public trial, Siraj asked Eldawoody about making bombs and provided him with a CD-ROM on how to make conventional explosives. He said at one point, "I will teach those bastards a lesson."[1] The second defendant, Elshafay, was a hapless tag-along with only a ninth-grade education who'd been prescribed drugs for depression and schizophrenia. He'd made general complaints about the Iraq war, Abu Ghraib, and U.S. Middle East policy, and it was determined that he actively took part in the plot.

In later conversations, both men can be heard repeatedly discussing plans to plant bombs on the Verrazano-Narrows Bridge and at subway stations. One of the defendants had drawn a map of the bridges and police precincts on Staten Island. The other declared he "was ready for jihad."[2] Commissioner Kelly also informed the press that "backpacks were obtained with the intent of putting explosives in the backpacks."[3]

As the Herald Square plot developed, the press reported that the would-be terrorists twice conducted surveillance of the station, drawing diagrams of entrances and exits. With the aid of his NYPD handlers, our informant, Eldawoody, secretly made videotapes of the plotters in action. On the stand, Siraj admitted that the plot was his idea but said he didn't want to place the bomb on the subway, though he would accompany someone who did. The *New York Times* reported that throughout the case, "Mr. Siraj's behavior seemed to alternate between shrewd, bumbling and bizarre."[4] The defense accused the informant of manufacturing the crime, citing the fact that Eldawoody had been paid nearly $100,000 by the Department over the course of three years.[5]

A very strong case was made by the prosecutors based on the testimony of the informant. But later in the trial, the U.S. attorney's office brought to the stand an NYPD undercover detective who really bolstered the prosecution's arguments—and also opened a window into NYPD's intelligence program. The undercover cop, given the pseudonym Kamil Pasha, had filed more than a hundred reports on the case, providing great detail as to what had occurred. According to Kamil's testimony, he'd come to this job straight out of the Police Academy and within three weeks was reporting in the bookstore. (To his credit, Cohen allowed his carefully recruited detectives a degree of operating room, and they came up with results.)

After a four-week trial, Siraj was convicted by a jury and sentenced to thirty years in prison. Before the case went to trial, he and his lawyer had foolishly turned down a ten-year plea deal. I guess they thought the entrapment defense would work, but it didn't. The case has been scrutinized and criticized, as have all post-9/11 cases in the United States. And perhaps the critics were right; perhaps these guys weren't capable of pulling off a real operation. We'll never know for sure. But I would venture to say that if Mohamed Atta and a few of his cohorts had been arrested in Hamburg one year prior to the 9/11 attack, the same people who criticized the outcome of the Herald Square case would have cried entrapment for Atta and his friends as well. After all, who would believe that a band of untrained radicals armed only with box cutters could hijack commercial airplanes and fly them into the World Trade Center, the Pentagon, and the White House? "Clearly a laughable plot," these critics would have said, "cooked up by over-imaginative cops and spies." NYPD cops constantly reminded me that everyone in jail claims to be innocent—that they never knew a perp who didn't say he was entrapped.

But what can we learn from this case? First, it illustrates how NYPD intelligence covers the city's hot spots for radical activity—in this case, a bookstore in Bay Ridge, Brooklyn. Initially, NYPD had an informant in the store who discovered that Siraj was planning violence against the city. To strengthen the case, NYPD introduced an undercover cop into the cell by way of the informant. The trial showed that this was done only after it was well established that Siraj was already getting specific about his violent intentions. The undercover cop was trained to ensure that he collected evidence against the suspect in a legal and aboveboard manner. The jury concluded that there was no entrapment and that the two defendants did intend to attack the subway system.

This was a well-run police operation that included well-placed informants collecting vital information and the bold insertion of an undercover agent into the cell. And it worked. It worked also because the undercover cop was a twenty-four-year-old New Yorker of Pakistani descent, not a blond, crew-cut FBI agent from Topeka, Kansas. From the first, Cohen's aim was to tap the human talent of NYPD, with its ethnic diversity and solid training, and quickly deploy it when needed. There were risks, but they were managed. The young undercovers were very closely supervised by a veteran detective and sergeant, which minimized the risk of a mistake or the penetration of NYPD by a double agent.

The FBI Joint Terrorism Task Forces

FBI has fifty-six field offices around the United States, which are generally located in the biggest cities of each state or region. Most of these field offices have a JTTF. After 9/11, a major influx of new resources was dedicated to terrorism and the JTTFs. At FBI most of the expansion into terrorism came from a massive infusion of new funding, unlike NYPD, which relied on redistributed funds and personnel to grow its CT programs.

The New York office of FBI is the largest by far and was the first to establish a JTTF. The New York JTTF grew out of the 1970s-era Arson Task Force, organized by FBI with NYPD and other agencies to investigate arsons and terrorist bombings in New York (recall the attacks conducted by Puerto Rican nationalists in 1975). After the first attack on the World Trade Center, the New York office became FBI's lead for al Qaeda investigations. This was not only in recognition of New York's direct involvement in the attack but also another indicator that FBI didn't regard the threat as a national one. After 9/11 the Washington office of the Bureau took on al Qaeda and made it a national priority, but the New York office remains a major player.

My introduction to the New York office began in 1998, shortly after I began the counterterrorism job at the State Department. Richard Clarke, the White House counterterrorism czar at the time, recommended I go up to New York and meet with John O'Neill, the legendary FBI agent and al Qaeda specialist, and his number two guy, Pat D'Amuro. The prosecutors in the New York office, headed by Mary Jo White and Patrick Fitzgerald, were also known for their expertise and dedication to the al Qaeda mission.

Clarke was right in his assessment; there was nobody in Washington with more expertise and dedication to countering al Qaeda than those in the New York office. During my 1998 visit, O'Neill took me to see the defendants in the East African bombing case who were locked up in a cell in New York City awaiting trial. These were the killers of our State Department personnel, and I was personally interested in their convictions. So were O'Neill and D'Amuro. I also got a taste of O'Neill's legendary rite of drinking and carousing at all of the New York hot spots. I returned quickly to Washington, but it took me about three days to fully recover from that hangover. O'Neill was unfazed. O'Neill later died at the hands of the enemy he knew so well while working as head of security at the World Trade Center on 9/11.

When I took the job with NYPD, I was given command of NYPD's Counter Terrorism Bureau and NYPD's contingent within

FBI's New York office. My first priority was to work with FBI. I had more than 120 detectives assigned to me who were working in FBI's headquarters across the street from NYPD's headquarters. Some of the cops were very aggressive, take-no-prisoners types who were already beginning to wear out NYPD's welcome with FBI when I arrived. I quickly ascertained that though my detectives could be a bit abrasive with the Bureau, there was merit in their criticisms of FBI. First, FBI was still not sharing information, not with NYPD detectives assigned to my counterterrorism unit and not even with FBI offices in other cities. FBI retained a law enforcement culture in which each agent was fairly autonomous. Their purpose was primarily racking up convictions of various low-level nobodies rather than gaining insight on the bigger picture so as to connect the dots of a larger plot. This resulted in poor coordination of efforts and sharing of information—major shortcomings for a counterterrorism intelligence program.

A blatant example quickly hit my desk. In July 2003, my first summer in NYPD, the JTTF was involved in a major investigation that reached from the streets of Asia back to the streets of Manhattan. Security reasons prevent me from revealing all of the details of the case, but I'll try to summarize the pertinent points. The JTTF in New York, following up on leads from international intelligence sources, arrested a suspect as he was working late one night in his office. Based on this arrest and some initial statements the defendant made to NYPD detectives, another man was arrested in Asia.

As it turned out, the suspect's computers contained a wealth of useful information about his other connections to al Qaeda operatives. But it wasn't until late August, over six weeks later, that we were made privy to the data collected from his computer. The device contained addresses, names, and phone numbers associated with New York, including New York City area codes and partial addresses that only a New York City cop could identify as New York City addresses. And it took six weeks to get the data to my office! This was completely unacceptable. This guy had been arrested and investigated in an emergency situation based in New York, but relevant information wasn't coming back to the city's law enforcement in a timely manner.

Instead of working together, agencies battled one another over who could interview the suspect. Emotions were running high particularly between FBI and CIA. I was told at that time that the FBI al Qaeda team still had no direct access to Khalid Sheikh Mohammed (the principal architect of 9/11), almost a year after he'd been arrested. I found this to be outrageous. Equally outrageous was the fact that NYPD, with its tremendous interrogation skills, hadn't been able to take a run at the man arrested in Asia, particularly since his compatriot in New York City was simultaneously being questioned by NYPD cops to great effect.

These wasted opportunities put me and my NYPD chiefs at direct odds with our FBI partners across the street. In some ways I commiserated with them, in that CIA was treating them shabbily by denying their agents access to key persons of interest, but they were playing the same game with us. We wanted to know the New York angle immediately. This example, and others like it, confirmed a suspicion I'd had in my many years dealing with intelligence: that the problem of information sharing is a problem of reporting. Investigators, whether with CIA or FBI or NYPD, must be required to report what they know quickly, and to provide raw data (such as the dump of phone numbers from someone's BlackBerry) in a timely manner. Proper classifications must be made on the document, and then the material must be put into the electronic files for review by analysts with the appropriate security clearances.

Notwithstanding this glaring problem of information sharing, my real concern was always with collection. The Washington community was obsessed with information sharing in their efforts to fix the intelligence apparatus after 9/11. This important issue falls within the comfort zone of Washington policy types who specialize in the rearranging of bureaucratic fiefdoms, the drawing of wiring diagrams, and the flow of paper. But unfortunately, the more important issue, collection of intelligence, didn't get enough discussion. Even if the sharing mechanisms are perfect, without a good collection you've got nothing.

As I approached this challenge at NYPD, I addressed problems in information sharing, but not in the usual sense of breaking down walls of secrecy and compartmentalization of information. The problem was largely a lack of good reporting. FBI agents and NYPD detectives, like their colleagues in police forces elsewhere, generally don't like to write, and so, specific data was not being recorded, much less shared, throughout the system. This problem has been largely solved by bringing hundreds of civilian analysts to FBI to turn this information into usable documents.

One area where I made headway was in urging my detectives not to rely on the same old informants, some of whom made a nice living spinning yarns. I encouraged them to find our blind spots in the city instead. Once a source was tapped, we had to report what we found. Did I mention that cops don't like to write? (Indeed, that's why they became cops and not newspaper reporters.) However, a good intelligence officer must write up everything religiously and get it into the proper database as soon as possible. At NYPD this was something that was always lacking, and the result was that, as an organization, we often didn't even know what we knew. Finally, I pushed for face-to-face coordination between NYPD intelligence and FBI, including the NYPD detectives assigned to the JTTF. These goals seem easy enough to attain, but each change was difficult to implement because it ran directly into the cultural conflict between intelligence and law enforcement.

Tradecraft Training: Intelligence Operations 101

As part of our effort to create revolutionary and sustained change at NYPD, Cohen and I embarked on a joint training program between his intelligence unit and my CT unit. Our goal was to capture this program in a syllabus so that we could more quickly and effectively train new personnel for our respective units. I'd noticed that many of my best detectives were retiring in 2004 and 2005, and I didn't feel that we were institutionalizing our knowledge. I also knew from my time in the military and as an adjunct professor at

Georgetown University that teaching is a great way to truly master a subject; getting up on a platform and talking to thirty people for a few hours requires real preparation. So we created a formal teaching program in which our seasoned detectives taught new officers assigned to the JTTF. The preparation in itself was a useful exercise for even our most experienced investigators, and their insights were invaluable to the next wave of NYPD.

These courses offer a great perspective on the work that we did at NYPD, since they spell out what we did without being specific about sensitive cases or areas of investigation. One course we established was called "Tradecraft for Asset Handlers." It covered basic intelligence operational skills for detectives managing informants or undercover cops investigating terrorism cases.

The course began with a fundamental grounding in the basics of Islamic culture, taught by Daniel Rudder, the Columbia University–trained expert I introduced in Chapter 3. The course was designed for and limited to those detectives who were actively engaged in managing informants or undercover operatives. We focused primarily on the Sunni extremism of al Qaeda and associated groups, and we compared it to the Shia extremism of the Iranian fundamentalists and Hezbollah. We analyzed variations in extremist thought to show regional differences driving terrorist movements. Another class included Islamic and Arab cultural awareness training designed to sensitize investigators who might be dealing with informants and other sources. The courses were taught by experts from the federal government, contractors, and cops who spoke the native languages of the various regions of interest.

Once a solid background in the relevant ideology and culture was achieved, the training shifted to the skills that many of our experienced detectives had developed in other disciplines such as undercover narcotics, organized crime, and vice. A great deal of time was focused on techniques of elicitation, debriefing, and interviewing. Unlike military or CIA briefing procedures described in press accounts after 9/11, NYPD's specialty was coaxing information out of people. An NYPD detective approaches a perp with two assumptions: first, that he'll start out lying, and second, that he really wants to tell his story. One challenge unique to counterterrorism work is that we're often investigating people before they commit a crime. Fortunately, this problem is usually overcome because the people who are subject to our counterterrorism investigations are almost invariably breaking the law in some form or fashion. The most gifted closers at NYPD could extract information from a suspect with a mix of threats (of maximum prosecution), flattery, and just plain persistence.

Some of our training came from State, DOD, and CIA personnel. One course on interviewing techniques was taught by a retired CIA employee who'd been one of the Agency's most experienced polygraph administers. In all of our training, we provided the legal guidelines in accordance with NYPD and New York state law. For instance, one block of instruction was on the guidelines for recruiting confidential informants, or CIs—the bread and butter of investigative work. CIs are law enforcement's window onto the worlds of narcotics, organized crime, and in our case terrorism.

The tradecraft training then moved into more advanced levels as the instructor provided insights into how to communicate with assets. Obviously, in communicating with an asset, you don't want to drive up to the front of his house in an unmarked police car with a big radio antenna. Nor do you want to employ "secret squirrel" techniques that just draw more suspicions. Sensible places to meet and exchange information are recommended, with specific suggestions offered.

Developing asset networks is yet another more advanced stage of training. Once again, the same basics that I learned in the Special Forces—and that my detectives knew from their experiences with organized crime—came to bear, but were rejiggered slightly to fit a different environment. Investigators are trained to always verify a CI's reliability by testing or cross-checking his information with known data. The very best confirmations come when an undercover agent is able to be at the same location without the knowledge of the CI. Liars, exaggerators, and ineffectual CIs are easily identified in this manner.

A separate skill set is used for those managing undercovers. Undercovers are different from CIs, of course, because they're members of the police department, and they give case managers great confidence in a given set of information. But obviously there are limits to the number that can be deployed. Another limiting factor is the time it takes to fully infiltrate a cell. CIs get into the proper areas faster, but you never have as much confidence with them. Managing undercover cops requires a different set of rules, guidelines, and skills. It's a very specialized area, one reserved for only the most experienced and trustworthy officers. Obviously, the very life of an undercover is in the hands of his handler.

Case studies and practical experience are, of course, hallmarks of the training. Detectives, sergeants, and lieutenants give real-life examples of tradecraft and review how to establish cover stories so that our informants will be skilled in staying undetected as they move up the chain of command within the organization they're infiltrating. FBI, to their credit, participated in the training as students and lecturers.

The Vanity Fair *Fiasco: FBI and the State Department*

Although I arrived at NYPD having had a generally good relationship with FBI, several incidents were always present in the back of my mind and colored my impression of the Bureau. During my first days on the job as the Coordinator for Counterterrorism at the State Department, I'd been confronted, for example, with a troubling press piece that provoked strong traction in FBI and CIA. A dubious *Vanity Fair* article authored by David Rose, which many within FBI and CIA believed accurately reflected the facts, suggested that the State Department had blocked a Sudanese offer made through FBI to arrest two individuals associated with the East African embassy attacks. Rose claimed that the offer had been blocked in the week following the attacks, thereby preventing us from gaining access to a host of information on al Qaeda and its leadership.

Initially, I believed the story and set out to find out how this had happened. According to the article, the Sudanese had approached the State Department two days before President Clinton was planning to bomb Afghan camps and a Sudanese pharmaceutical plant both in retaliation for the embassy attacks and in an attempt to kill Osama bin Laden. At the time, the president was caught up in the Monica Lewinsky scandal, and the bombing was believed by some to be a convenient diversion from that mess. So the logic was that some "weenies" in the State Department were in collusion with the White House to keep the case active so that the bombing could go forward and divert press attention from Monica and her soiled dress. The stink from the *Vanity Fair* story continued to linger, even though nobody could find the unnamed officer who'd turned down the Sudanese offer, and over time a rumor circulated that the culprit was a low-level official in the Africa Bureau.

I was a bit suspicious, but since the story kept lingering and perpetuated an image of the State Department as an entity blocking the real CT guys from doing their job, I was determined to find out who had squandered this intelligence opportunity and make sure it never happened again on my watch. I began rumbling around the Africa Bureau like a bull in a china shop trying to find answers. How could anyone at State have turned down this offer at the same time the secretary of state, Madeleine Albright, was burying members of her staff who'd been killed in the assault? With the full support of the secretary, I relentlessly patrolled the corridors of the State Department hoping to find the guilty party. I was ready to start chopping off heads all the way up, even if it included that of my good friend Susan Rice, the assistant secretary of state for Africa. I'd known Susan for five years, and although there was always controversy around this sharp-elbowed young upstart, she never shied away from a tough issue. I couldn't imagine, therefore, her passing up an opportunity to gain such valuable information from the Sudanese. After all, it was *her* people in the Africa Bureau who'd been killed in the attack, not FBI's or CIA's or DOD's.

After a few days of ranting around the State Department, I began to question the veracity of the story. I went back to my colleagues at FBI and asked them if they could tell me who had blocked this action. Had a cable or a memo been written? This was big stuff, and most bureaucrats would want credit for the action. Who'd made this contact? Was there any paper trail? Had the director called the secretary of state on such a hot subject? Who was the weasel in the Africa Bureau who'd blocked the initiative? All of these questions came up empty.

To this day, I'm not sure exactly what happened, but as a result of this fiasco, I sent a clear message to the FBI and my other partners in counterterrorism (at the White House, DOD, CIA, and so on) about how they should proceed if they wanted the State Department's support for CT action. My main message was clear: "If you have a counterterrorism issue with the State Department, it must go through *me* first, the ambassador for CT. I will get a quick and almost always, supportive response from my boss, Madeleine Albright. Any phantom request turned down by some other official (high- or low-ranking) on CT does not constitute an answer from the State Department. And if you appeal to another section of State, I'll suspect you're shopping around for a no answer because you didn't really want to execute the mission at hand—and shame on you." This isn't to say that the State Department was always the tough guy, for I'd have my own issues *within* the Department over the next several years. But when it came to direct-action missions during my watch, State would always support them.

This incident was part of a pattern I'd seen develop in how bureaucracies deal with very difficult issues. Normally what they do is look for another agency to do the dirty work—or block their action—to get off the hook. This is the exact opposite of what I'd learned while I was a cadet at West Point. A popular textbook at the Academy, *The Essence of Decision* by Harvard professor Graham Allison, showed that during the Cuban missile crisis, different agencies looked to solve the problem of Cuban missiles with their own assets. They viewed the problem through their own particular lens. The Army wanted a land invasion, the Air Force an aerial bombardment, and the Navy a sea blockade. CIA wanted a covert action, and the State Department wanted more diplomacy. That "let's use *my* tools" philosophy may have been true then, but my experience with government agencies taught me that when it comes to today's tough issues, the exact inverse is true. Typically, State wants to use military assets to solve humanitarian issues and other problems. The military normally is wary of anyone advocating the use of their assets (with reason), and if they're forced to act, they'll insist on an option with such overwhelming force that it becomes impractical. Covert action, either by CIA or FBI, is normally very difficult to conduct and is often fiercely resisted by these agencies. Sanctions, which involve economic pressure, are usually resisted by the Treasury Department. My task would be to prod other agencies to act with their levers even as I prodded my own agency to act with its levers.

Comparing NYPD and FBI

By now my prejudices are surely obvious to you: I have tremendous respect and admiration for the people I worked with at NYPD, but my experiences with FBI have left me with mixed emotions. Both organizations have strengths and weaknesses, but these differences underscore the value of NYPD to the overall New York City intelligence collection. With regard to organization, structure, and mission, NYPD and FBI attack the problem differently, and ideally, they should function in complementary roles.

For example, the JTTF gets leads from the federal government through agencies such as CIA. If an al Qaeda operative is captured in Pakistan and gives up a name of an accomplice in New York City, FBI gets the case handed to them on a platter by CIA. It's a tremendous advantage for them. But it also makes them a bit reactive and focused on individual cases. In contrast, NYPD intelligence must be more proactive. It doesn't get gifts over the transom from CIA, so it digs around the city's hot spots. NYPD takes a grassroots approach to finding sources and winds up covering areas FBI ignores.

FBI agents are plugged into the national databases and have access to vast resources. They're college-educated and trained to get as many convictions as they can, and they work closely with U.S. attorneys to build airtight cases. NYPD detectives are less formally educated but tend to be older and more streetwise. They usually come from NYPD crime units and possess great knowledge of the communities within the city. There is simply no better experience for an investigator of any law enforcement agency that can be gained than in the streets and detective squads of NYPD. One of my most important contributions at NYPD was bringing these two groups of CT warriors together. And tension was not necessarily a bad thing; it meant that two agencies with inherently overlapping jurisdictions were aggressively pursuing their job. When I hear that another city's police department gets along perfectly fine with FBI, I am a bit suspicious.

We made a real effort to ease the conflicts, primarily through working groups of detectives and agents where NYPD and FBI actions overlapped. Coordination between NYPD and FBI was never easy. In fact, it was almost always a struggle. In the past two years, coordination has improved dramatically due to the leadership of Joe Demerest, FBI's current head of JTTF. He is widely admired by cops and FBI agents alike—a rare feat.

Chapter 10

CBRN: Real Danger or Overhyped Threat?

CHEMICAL, BIOLOGICAL, RADIOLOGICAL, AND nuclear weapons can enable a terrorist organization to achieve a strategic impact on our nation in a single attack. These weapons, known by the acronym CBRN, have been sought by terrorists for a long time. But fortunately, until now, their efforts to attain even one such weapon have been largely ineffective. Even the most successful CBRN attacks have been less lethal than a single handgun can be against the same target. However, the potential lethality of these substances and their ability to seriously disrupt our lifestyle demand that we retain a high level of focus on the CBRN threat, even if the likelihood of its manifesting itself is currently low.

Nuclear weapons represent the most serious threat, but because they remain for now solely in the hands of nations, their containment is primarily a nonproliferation issue, with a different set of experts weighing in. As a CT practitioner, I believe that crushing terrorist cells and organizations helps prevent nuclear proliferation, but, in general, I tend to focus on the less devastating but more likely terrorism scenarios. This entails preventing and responding to a terrorist operation that employs a weapon of mass *disruption* as opposed to a weapon of mass *destruction*—that is, a radiological or "dirty" bomb rather than a nuclear explosion.

While at NYPD, I was acutely aware that the radical cells I was tracking in New York City, or others that I was aware of across the United States and in Western Europe, had people within their ranks with the education and professional experience needed to acquire very dangerous materials and transform them into terrorist weapons. I worried every day that a cell might be formed with the motivation to conduct such an operation and that it might link up with a person of that caliber. For example, a medical technician or radiologist would know about the large quantities of cesium-137 in a cancer treatment machine. A maintenance manager in a large research hospital would know the location of and security procedures for handling deadly strains of bacteria, such as anthrax or smallpox. A construction engineer would be aware that some of the devices used to measure the depth and density of the bedrock of a major construction site emit powerful X-rays with significant quantities of radioactive isotopes such as cobalt-60. Are there radicals out there with this type of specialized background? The answer is an emphatic yes. Are they involved in a plot to use these materials? That I haven't seen, but I worried about this for three years at NYPD, and I still do.

At NYPD, we created a small but very skilled group of people dedicated to dealing with the issue of CBRN weapons. As always, we founded our priorities on a realistic assessment of the threat based on case studies and a careful review of the national intelligence about terrorist capabilities and intentions in this area. The good news is that the record of terrorists using these weapons is one of futility.

An example worth reviewing is that of Abu Issa al-Hindi. Hindi was the guy who conducted the reconnaissance of Wall Street, the Citigroup Center in midtown Manhattan, and other targets in Newark, New Jersey, and Washington, D.C. His capture briefing set off the orange alert craze of the summer of 2004. Hindi, an Indian national and Islamic convert, had strong jihadi credentials. He fought in Kashmir against India and wrote a book about his exploits during that conflict. But Hindi, like many other potential terrorists, was either unable or unwilling to take the next step of assembling a conventional or other type of bomb. He spoke of improvised explosives and even had fanciful ideas about a radiological weapon. But between the spring of 2000 and the summer of 2004 when he was apprehended, Hindi had not moved beyond the talking phase of the operation. He never returned to the United States to follow up on his reconnaissance, never really assembled anything resembling a hit team, and was content to brief leaders about possible scenarios. Though his concept of extracting radioactive materials from thousands of smoke detectors was flawed and even comical, he was supposed to be one of the "stars" of al Qaeda.

Even so, we had to deal with a whole range of other scenarios sent to us by the Department of Homeland Security, which must have had too many underworked staffers or overpaid consultants. At NYPD we had to set priorities. We needed to make grounded judgments on the types of weapons most likely to be used by a terrorist cell. As part of the process we tried to push our imaginations a bit (as al Qaeda did in their 9/11 plot) and anticipate other weapons al Qaeda might deploy in the city. In fact, we created a massive and intense CBRN program to try to prevent a CBRN attack or mitigate one if it happened.

When I arrived at NYPD, one of the first things Commissioner Kelly asked me to do was organize some tabletop exercises relating to terrorist scenarios. He was unhappy with a previous tabletop exercise that was run by an expensive contractor but didn't accomplish much. So I went back to my office to collaborate with my team. We decided to do a series of in-house tabletop exercises starting with the most realistic of the CBRN threats. We conducted a series of exercises over a one-year period involving multiple scenarios, including the plague (stolen from a lab), a radiological bomb (made from medical materials), and a chemical attack (from chemicals common in the tri-state area). Each scenario assumed a homegrown cell with a weapon that was acquired and manufactured in our region and transported into the most densely populated areas of the city. It was a sobering process, but one that gave us an appreciation of the threat and provided some direction, something we weren't getting from Washington.

The Radiological Threat: The Dirty Bomb

Though the threat of a nuclear weapon being deployed against the city was my worst nightmare scenario, I was much more concerned about a less devastating but far more likely scenario: the use of an improvised radiological device, or "dirty bomb." For this reason, Commissioner Kelly expended a great deal of time, energy, and resources evaluating the radiological threat and carefully considering how to respond to it.

In 2004, I learned that HBO and PBS had teamed to produce a movie called *Dirty War,* a docudrama about a dirty bomb explosion in downtown London. HBO generously provided NYPD with a copy, and Commissioner Kelly agreed to show it to the executive staff on a Friday afternoon. The movie, an outstanding and realistic production, definitely commanded our attention. In the film, a truck bomb laced with highly radioactive cesium chloride and some other materials (perhaps the highly radioactive americium) is detonated in central London. A cloud of fallout from the blast drifts across several city blocks, contaminating hundreds of people within them. The crowd begins to panic and flee, especially as it's determined that there's radiological contamination in the device. The British police are unable to contain and properly decontaminate the large number of affected citizens. Authorities are quickly overwhelmed. By the film's conclusion, scores of Londoners have been killed or injured in the attack, and a whole section of the British capital has been rendered uninhabitable, probably for many years. The British authorities, largely inattentive to the threat before this fictitious incident, were obviously totally unprepared.

Based on the movie, we conducted several tabletop exercises and engaged in intensive training and preparation for this type of attack. The filmed scenario was portrayed in as realistic a manner as possible through the use of both British and American consultants whose understanding of the issue was similar to ours. Within the next year, my team of experts at NYPD continued to reach out to the nation's experts, particularly at the national laboratories, on how we should respond to such an event. Washington officials were of little use. Several different agencies were very interested, but they bickered over who was in charge of the nuclear program, and we could find no one to help us with the most realistic problem: how to respond to an incident in New York City.

We met with some of the nation's top scientists, including those who were actually conducting tests of radiological weapons. At that point we discovered that all of our planning assumptions were wrong. What we learned was somewhat heartening. When a dirty bomb goes off, two kinds of radiation are released. First, large chunks of radioactive material scatter in the square block or so around the bomb. These chunks contain gamma radiation—referred to as "shine" by our scientist friends—that is dangerous to anyone in its immediate proximity. The second type of radiation, sometimes known as "fallout," spreads over a wider area and consists of radioactive particles attached to pieces of dust or other airborne debris. These particles are dangerous only when ingested into the body either by inhaling the contaminated dust, by eating contaminated food, or through contact with a cut or lesion in the skin. The alpha and beta particles of fallout can't penetrate the skin, but once inside the body they can be very problematic or even deadly.

What we learned from these scientists was that the alpha and beta particles actually fall to the ground much more quickly because of their heavy molecular weight compared to air. The danger from fallout, or floating particles of contaminated dust, wasn't nearly as severe as I'd previously assumed. The real problem came from the heavier, more radioactive gamma particles. But these particles were less likely to become airborne and would probably be thrown by the blast no farther than a block or two from the crater. This bit of scientific information, not known to anyone in Washington, dramatically changed all of our planning assumptions. Although made in good faith, the movie dramatically overhyped the threat of a dirty bomb in London and gave a false impression about how a city should respond. The blast radius would be much smaller and the fallout less harmful. As a result of what we learned—and because we never got any clarifying guidance from the Department of Homeland

Security (DHS)—we developed our own protocols. Instead of trying to decontaminate thousands of panicking city residents, authorities should guide people away from the blast area and direct them to go home and do a self-decontamination: take off their clothes and put them in a plastic bag, take a shower (without allowing any of the water to enter the mouth), and await further instructions. I'm still not sure this protocol is completely correct, but it was the best we could do with the information we had, and we had to have a plan. My first priority, of course, was to prevent a dirty bomb from being built. But we also needed to be prepared to react quickly and professionally if one was employed against us. Lives would be at stake, as would the future ability of the city to bounce back, both physically and psychologically.

The one area in which DHS had a robust program was in the area of response. NYPD took full advantage of the program, as did many other municipalities around the country. Every cop was outfitted with a basic protective mask, and we trained another ten thousand cops to operate around a contaminated area in full protective suits. This was an enormous undertaking, but we got it done. If there's an incident in New York City tomorrow, there will doubtless be some confusion, as there is during any major crisis. But I'm sure that the Department will have the capability to handle the situation. Federal funding for training and equipment certainly helped—but it was the relentless pushing of chiefs Phil Pulaski and John Colgan that was primarily responsible for building this very credible program.

Chemical Weapons

Chemicals weapons, if properly deployed, can be lethal, and their effects are normally immediate. Unlike biological or radiological poisoning, an individual will know immediately if he or she is attacked by chemical weapons. Chemical weapons, although deadly, are easier to contain than radiological weapons and usually can be cleaned up with relative speed. Another fortunate characteristic of chemical arms (or, for that matter weapons-grade biologicals) is that they're difficult to manufacture without the support of a sophisticated state-run program.

The most important terrorist chemical attack in recent years was perpetrated in the Tokyo subway system by the radical cult Aum Shinrikyo. On March 20, 1995, the group sent five of its members into the subway system in Tokyo during the morning rush hour. They carried small plastic bags of fluids that when mixed would release sarin gas on five crowded trains. The attackers used sharpened umbrella tips to puncture the bags and release the fumes, which killed 12 people, seriously harmed another 54, and adversely affected at least another 980.[1]

Aum Shinrikyo is a cult, primarily based in Japan, that at its peak had tentacles throughout the world. As a so-called religious organization, the cult had protection under Japanese law and was involved in massive undetected illegal activity prior to the subway attack. The group's fanatical leaders hoped to ignite armageddon with their attacks.

The initial band of Aum Shinrikyo members first assembled in a yoga class that blind acupuncturist and New Age guru Shoko Asahara and his wife taught in Tokyo during the mid-1980s. They followed no single religion, drawing instead on various teachings of Buddhism, Hinduism, Taoism, and Christianity. The group gained official recognition as a religious corporation under Japanese law in 1989, despite an initial denial from the government and a series of complaints from the families of several Aum Shinrikyo devotees.

The group was involved in several incidents of violence before the subway attacks, including assassinations and kidnappings. They began experimenting with chemical agents in 1993. A year later, the group released sarin gas in the Japanese city of Matsumoto, killing seven people (the authorities investigating the incident initially declared it an accident and failed to implicate the group).[2] Estimates of the group's size at the time of the 1995 subway attacks vary, but most place the number of members in the tens of thousands, although only a few were terrorists. Many of these devotees were highly educated scientists and engineers. Reflecting the makeup of its vast membership, Aum Shinrikyo's financial resources were enormous. Reportedly their assets totaled roughly $1 billion worldwide.[3]

The good news is that even though Aum Shinrikyo possessed enormous financial and scientific resources and operated with virtual impunity under Japanese religious freedom laws, their chemical attack wasn't catastrophic. Yes, twelve people died, but more could have been killed had the terrorists opted to use automatic rifles or even a couple of handguns. The chemical nature of the attack did cause panic and forced the shutdown of the subway system for a time, but the public recovered fairly quickly. Clearly, Aum Shinrikyo's objective of causing mass panic and some sort of apocryphal response was a failure.

Biological Weapons

The threat of biological weapons was brought home to the United States in the immediate aftermath of September 11. Ground zero was still smoldering when the rest of the nation was hit by another terrorist attack. A week after 9/11, letters containing spores of *Bacillus anthracis,* which causes the disease anthrax, were sent through the mail to media targets in Florida and New York. Two of the letters arrived at the New York offices of NBC News and the *New York Post* with notes that read:

```
09/11-01
THIS IS NEXT
TAKE PENACILIN NOW
DEATH TO AMERICA
DEATH TO ISRAEL
ALLAH IS GREAT
```

A month later, two more anthrax-laced letters were sent to the Washington offices of senators Tom Daschle and Patrick Leahy. They contained identical notes:

```
YOU CAN'T STOP US.
WE HAVE THIS ANTHRAX.
YOU DIE NOW.
ARE YOU AFRAID?
DEATH TO AMERICA.
DEATH TO ISRAEL.
ALLAH IS GREAT.
```

Seven letters are believed to have been mailed, but only four were ultimately found. Two different kinds of anthrax were used in the attacks. The letters to NBC and the *Post* used a coarse, less-threatening grade, while the letters sent to Washington had contained deadlier anthrax powder. Five people were killed in all: an editor at the *National Enquirer,* two employees in a mail facility in Washington that handled the Daschle and Leahy letters, and two more whose contact with the letters has never been determined.

In my opinion, this attack was conducted by someone with experience in biological weapons programs and access to military-grade anthrax spores. It wasn't al Qaeda, because bin Laden's MO is to kill without warning. This theory is shared by most analysts in NYPD (and we had our own hunches about who was involved). The terrorist sent a letter with the spores to warn the recipients, knowing that if caught early, anthrax is often treatable with antibiotics. However, the attacker didn't anticipate all of the consequences of his treacherous warning, and innocent people died. The attack was probably staged as a post-9/11 warning that the country was vulnerable to biological attack.

The weapons-grade anthrax powder was sent by normal mail. Our modern and very efficient mail system has letter sorters that speed letters along a track, assisted by puffs of air. It was during this sorting, with its short blast of air, that some of the anthrax spores (which were very fine particles) escaped the envelopes and landed on letters that didn't include warnings. It appears that the first letters were sent out in late September 2001, just weeks after the 9/11 attacks, though the spores in those were of a slightly lower grade. Incredibly, law enforcement and public health officials were very slow in recognizing that in fact the country was under biological attack.

So the mad scientist upped the ante by improving the quality of the finely powdered spores and sending it to the U.S. Congress. This finally got people's attention. For years FBI thought that the quality of the anthrax, particularly in the later attacks, pointed to a link with government biological programs and that the perpetrator was probably embedded in one as a scientist or technician. To my great surprise, in late 2006, five years into the investigation, FBI reversed this assumption and has since broadened the search beyond the biological weapons community. No explanation has been given as to why the Bureau's thinking changed.

The chief lesson of the anthrax case is that it's possible—but difficult—to conduct a biological attack on a mass scale. Anthrax's main advantages lie in the ease with which it can be made and stored. While people who are infected are not contagious, the spores are capable of contaminating a building or other enclosed place. This can take months to clean up, as was the case with the Hart Senate Office Building. But to have a catastrophic effect on the United States, however, a huge quantity of anthrax would be required.

Improvised Explosives: Still the Weapon of Choice

Improvised explosives are still the weapon of choice for terrorists. And although they may not have the stigma of a chemical, biological, or radiological event, they still can be enormously damaging physically and psychologically, especially if a series of attacks can be sustained over time. At NYPD we tried to counter the threat of improvised explosives by going after the materials, ammonium nitrate for truck bombs and hydrogen peroxide concentrate for backpack bombs. For these reasons I include my discussion of explosives with CBRN.

Terrorists generally use two types of bombs: big truck bombs against buildings and multiple smaller backpack bombs against enclosed targets such as trains or airplanes. NYPD analysts studied hundreds of terrorist incidents to get a clear-eyed assessment of what types of attacks we might anticipate. After mastering the terrorist modus operandi, we then focused our study on explosives science and the mitigation of blast effect to help us develop reasonable, informed policy judgments.

Improvised explosives aren't complicated, and that's why they're so popular with terrorists. The Defense Department refers to a truck bomb as a VBIED, or vehicle-borne improvised explosive device. I'll use a simpler nomenclature for three main bomb types: truck bombs, backpack bombs, and suicide belts. Of course, a car, boat, or airplane is a variant of the truck bomb—just another way to carry a large explosive load. Most terrorists prefer electronic detonation, especially suicide bombers, but Ramzi Yousef and Timothy McVeigh both used a time fuse (similar to a firecracker fuse) in order to get away from their truck bombs before they exploded.

Each bomb type has its strengths and limitations. Truck bombs are the most problematic because they can be built in a remote location and then transported to a target with relative ease. Backpack bombs, although less lethal, can be smuggled onto a train or into any crowded, enclosed place. And belt bombs were designed by Palestinian terrorists in response to improved security measures implemented by the Israelis. Belt bombs pack an even smaller charge, normally less than ten pounds (as compared to a backpack bomb, which can carry up to twenty-five pounds of explosives), so they can be more effectively smuggled to a target.

Big truck bombs are usually made with nitrate-based fertilizers, which are relatively stable and can be purchased in large quantities at farm supply stores. Smaller backpack bombs are normally made of peroxide-based improvised explosives. They too can be made of readily available household and industrial chemicals. However, they're much less stable than ammonium-based explosives and normally must be "cooked" in a lab. Belt bombs, such as those used by Hamas, are ideally made with commercial or military-grade explosives, but they can be used with improvised ingredients by experienced bomb makers such as those employed by Palestinian terrorist groups.

More complex bombs require more sophisticated infrastructure to produce them. For this reason, such bombs are more often found in war zones such as Iraq, Afghanistan, or the occupied Palestinian territories where terrorists hide and function amidst chaos. War zones also provide easier recruitment for suicide bombers. Peacetime environments in the West are more difficult operating areas for gathering materials, establishing sophisticated labs, and recruiting suicide operatives, although it has been done and will be done again in the years ahead.

Timothy McVeigh was operating in an area where there was no vigilance against this type of activity. He was able to build a massive truck bomb and deliver it to the target with relative ease since there was no security in place. Conversely, Hamas must use small bombs because it's difficult for them to hide a large bomb factory with its major signature. They must use small bombs hidden on a terrorist's person to deliver the bomb to the target in a tight security environment. In Madrid and London there was moderate but not very tight security. Backpack bombs could be manufactured locally (such as in the Leeds safe house for the London bombers) and carried into an enclosed public place that was easily accessible. The terrorists selected mass transit to maximize the psychological effect on large numbers of people and to increase the attack's economic impact.

Operation Kaboom, Winter 2005

My first experience with improvised explosives came while I was in training for the U.S. Army Special Forces in Fort Bragg, North Carolina. During the last phase of my training, my team was tasked with building an improvised bomb and blowing a crater in an "enemy runway," which was really a dirt road in the woods of North Carolina. It was a cold and rainy night; there was no moon or stars. The rain was falling hard and anyone in their right mind was covered up, including most of our opposition "troops"—a group of regulars from Fort Bragg's Eighteenth Airborne Corps.

I recall combining the ammonium nitrate fertilizer we had bought at a local farm supply store with a few quarts of motor oil to make a volatile mix. (Fertilizer-based explosives were also used by Timothy McVeigh at Oklahoma City and Ramzi Yousef in the first World Trade Center attack.) We had the help of military grade C-4 to boost the bomb and it generally worked, although a good bit of the slurry didn't detonate and was scattered around the farmer's open field.

The second time I worked with improvised explosives was in El Salvador. We were just finishing a double-barrier fence around the compound where I was stationed in the mountain outpost of Chalatenango. I had a team of about six soldiers that had been well trained in explosives by my predecessor, and they wanted to increase the security of the fence by planting mines around it. However, Claymore mines (the U.S. Army version of a portable land mine) were expensive and in short supply and saved for carrying on patrols. To mine the double fence, we'd have to resort to improvised explosives.

None of the techniques we used was very difficult. We employed extra C-4, commercial dynamite, and a series of trip wires and triggers through the zone. Many of the techniques we copied from the guerrillas, who were world-class experts in making improvised land mines. Ours would only be put in the area between the two fences, never outside of that zone. Of course, mines and fences are only part of a defensive strategy, and when the human element is asleep the technical one is easily penetrated. This double fence was penetrated six months after I left, resulting in the death of my successor.

Nearly two decades later, in my NYPD office, Chief John Colgan, Inspector Mike O'Neil, and I came up with an idea to test how hard it would be to put together a truck bomb in New York similar to the one that was used in the first World Trade Center bombing or the one constructed by Timothy McVeigh. I wanted to know if it was any more difficult in a post-9/11 environment. I explained to O'Neil that I wanted him to put together a small team of "terrorists," and that they could not cheat. I told him I wanted the team to use knowledge acquired from open sources (usually the Internet). The purchases of material were to be made by ethnic cops, not burly white guys (although a terrorist can certainly fit any physical profile). In fact, I wanted one of our Pakistani detectives to purchase the explosive materials, rent vehicles, and secure storage facilities.

I took the idea to Commissioner Kelly, knowing he might reject it; it would eventually get out that we constructed the bomb, and this might cause embarrassment. But Kelly immediately understood the value of the exercise and approved the operation. O'Neil and one of his captains, Joe Cordes, supervised the mission (which was dubbed "Operation Kaboom") methodically. The results were frightening: in ten weeks, ten guys with about $10,000 were able to construct a ten-thousand-pound bomb in New York City. To complete our experiment, we decided to put the bomb to the test.

It was a cold winter afternoon on the NYPD firing range at Rodman's Neck, a day reminiscent of that frigid night at Fort Bragg where I'd had my first experience with IEDs (though this time I had the comfort of a heated car waiting for me at the end of the exercise). The small range overlooked a section of New York's inner harbor off a small isolated peninsula on the far edge of the Bronx. For the third time in my life, I was testing improvised explosives, this time with materials assembled near the city of New York. When the explosives ignited, I had proof that if a New York terrorist cell wanted to do the same thing, they'd find it all too easy.

After the July 2005 attacks in London, we decided to test how difficult it would be to obtain large quantities of high-percentage hydrogen peroxide, an ingredient used in those bombs. Hydrogen peroxide–based explosives are inventions of necessity. They're harder to assemble, require a basic laboratory, and aren't very reliable (as was demonstrated in the second London bombing). But they can be built in relatively small spaces. So we again put together an undercover team of cops, this time including an Egyptian female cop who worked in my front office and also an officer of Pakistani origin. We were able to order large quantities of the peroxide over the phone with the flimsiest of covers. We didn't even bother to get a safe house. Instead, we asked that the barrels of the materials be delivered to a street corner in Brooklyn. Again, we were successful. The truck delivered the bomb-making materials to our

Egyptian detective, who, in a long white raincoat and sunglasses, looked like she'd been cast in a B-grade terrorist movie. Not a single question was asked! Like the truck bomb exercise, this exercise was both sobering and more than a little frightening.

Sustained over a period of time, attacks using conventional explosives such as these (as well as commercial- and military-grade explosives) can have a strategic effect. So there are some important steps that need to be taken to protect the nation from bombs. First, it should be much more difficult for would-be terrorists to get bomb-making materials; as our exercises show, this is far too easy. In addition, certain key targets in our urban settings should be protected with integrated security structures (to avoid creating the sense of an armed camp).

A Comprehensive and Realistic CBRN Strategy

The specter of terrorists using weapons of mass destruction continues to haunt the counterterrorism community. The bad news is that al Qaeda and its associated groups have clearly shown their intent to use such weapons. They've plotted the use of anthrax, chemical devices, and improvised radiological bombs. They've also deployed some chemical weapons in attacks in Iraq, though with minor effect. However, there's good news also. Although al Qaeda was trying to develop a rudimentary anthrax program prior to 9/11, there is no evidence today that they have a viable program. High explosives, although often not included in this grouping of materials, remain the weapon of choice for terrorists, and similar strategies for preventing CBRN programs (denying materials) can be applied to high-explosive weapons as well.

What, then, should be our strategy for confronting this threat? First, the federal government must remain focused on preventing the proliferation of nuclear weapons. This is a separate discipline led by a different team. CT officials contribute indirectly to a nonproliferation strategy by preventing any one terrorist organization from developing, acquiring, storing, or making military-grade weapons. In my view, the only way to prevent al Qaeda from establishing weapon-making capability is to crush their cells.

While those of us at NYPD worried about our ability to respond to a CBRN attack, we were much more occupied with preventing one. That led us into the business of local nonproliferation of dangerous materials, an unprecedented move for a local police force. Nobody in the federal government was taking local nonproliferation seriously in the three years after 9/11 (they were focused almost exclusively on nukes). To their credit, the Department of Homeland Security slowly started to get with the program. Assistant Secretary Vayl Oxford worked hard with NYPD to provide a comprehensive ring of radiological detection devices around the city and other initiatives. They should be credited for their initiative and practical approach.

But the overall progress on the broader issue has been painfully slow and marked by bureaucratic infighting between the agencies involved with nuclear materials and the Nuclear Regulatory Commission (NRC). The NRC, which is responsible for managing nuclear materials nationwide, has put forth a weak effort to regulate the nation's radiological materials related to the medical and engineering fields. This unfortunate reality is due to the fact that the NRC is dominated by nuclear industry people who are reluctant to mandate the type of security and regulatory measures necessary to safeguard our radiological materials. The regulation of these sensitive materials must be taken out of the control of the industries that manufacture them. DHS, as weak as it is, is probably the best place for this mission.

The CBRN threat is very real in New York for at least two reasons. First, we've already experienced a biological attack—the still-unresolved 2001 anthrax attack in which five New Yorkers were hurt and one was killed. Second, as one of the most densely populated cities in the United States, New York, and Manhattan in particular, provides an ideal target for this type of weapon. At NYPD, we built a massive and comprehensive CBRN program based on five pillars: (1) a realistic threat assessment, (2) use of the most advanced (experimental) environmental detection devices, (3) a local nonproliferation strategy that makes dangerous materials more difficult to acquire and turn into a weapon, (4) a massive response and mitigation strategy in the event we're attacked, and (5) a management process for the training, logistics, and general readiness required to keep the whole program moving.

Prior to 9/11, NYPD possessed a remarkably sophisticated capability to respond to CBRN incidents, the foundation of which was its Special Operations Division and Emergency Service Unit. This group of highly trained and experienced cops could operate in contaminated and very dangerous sites. They'd been given sophisticated equipment to protect them in the event of a CBRN attack, and they were trained regularly in its operation.

Of course, detection depends on the ability to narrow down where a weapon may be hidden. This can be difficult, because once a terrorist has a weapon there are nearly unlimited places to store it and just as many targets. So in addition to conducting normal intelligence operations to find terrorist cells with CBRN capability and intent, we worked hard to safeguard our materials. For bioweapons, that was not easy. Our first attempt to find dangerous biological pathogens stored in the city was rebuffed by the Centers for Disease Control in Atlanta. However, through persistence, we learned where the most dangerous pathogens were stored and worked with the Department of Health and these storage facilities to, at a minimum, increase awareness. We also made some progress in getting them to ramp up their security procedures. However, mandating protocols for the securing of hazardous biological substances wasn't really NYPD's job, so our meddling was continually met with resistance. But we kept on pushing; it was too important to let go.

Chapter 11

The Department of Homeland Security: Searching for a Mission

SHORTLY AFTER 9/11, TERRORISM became the dominant political and partisan issue in America. Both of the major political parties, the pundits, the press, and Congress (all of which had largely ignored the threat of terrorism prior to 9/11) were suddenly eager to take ownership of the issue. Although a brief period of political unity ensued as the nation pulled together in the weeks and months after 9/11, by the summer of 2002 the partisan rhetoric of terrorism had begun to heat up. Two years later, in the summer of a presidential campaign, the political rancor surrounding the politics of terrorism reached a fever pitch.

The front-loaded primary schedule of that election year narrowed the race early on, and by summertime the nominating process had been reduced to a mere formality. Senator John Kerry accepted his party's nod in Boston at the Democratic Convention on July 29, 2004. A month later, President Bush would take his turn at the Republican National Convention (RNC), scheduled to take place from August 30 to September 2 in New York City. This was unusually late in the summer for a convention, and the timing and location were no accident. President Bush would make his case to the American people with terrorism front and center on his agenda. The gaping hole at ground zero would serve as a stark reminder of the damage terrorists are capable of doing and of

Bush's commitment to preventing another attack in the United States. It was a massive event, fraught with security challenges from terrorists and anarchists blending in with crowds of delegates and legitimate political protestors. The RNC had been designated a national security special event, which meant that the Secret Service was the lead federal agency to partner with NYPD.

Other than the big job of securing the RNC, it was a typical summer for the counterterrorism community. Washington analysts were reporting all sorts of terrorism chatter, as they always seem to do during summertime. For lack of a better definition, "chatter" refers to a nebulous measuring by analysts of an increase in phone calls, e-mail conversations, and ramblings within suspected terrorist cells—indicating that something might be afoot. In all my years in counterterrorism, I've never put a whole lot of credence in chatter or other speculative reporting. I'm interested in specific information that I can act on, not rumors. Sweeping statements and broad generalizations simply don't help us defend against real threats. In the summer of 2004, various offices in the Department of Homeland Security (DHS) were providing warnings for every conceivable type of attack and target, from subways to ports to shopping malls to iconic buildings. Attacks, they announced, could come from cars, trucks, airplanes, or even bicycles. This didn't help us at all in New York. We were accustomed to working with specifics, and our cynicism regarding DHS grew with every vague warning they produced. We were doing all we could in New York, but absent something specific, there wasn't much more we could do. We began to view DHS's blanket warnings as "CYA"—"cover your ass"—statements in case any one of a million threat scenarios they hypothesized actually materialized.

The Wake-up Call, August 2004

In the politically charged summer of 2004, we got something specific. On August 1 we learned from our sources at FBI that CIA had recently been informed of a major Pakistani intelligence operation that had uncovered an important al Qaeda cell. Interestingly, the Pakistanis had conducted the raid weeks before, but they withheld the information for a time because they were concerned about the all-too-common American tendency to leak intelligence information to the press too quickly. We were glad to get the information when we did, because in this case, the suspicion that it had been leaked would prove to be prescient.

Earlier in the summer, Pakistani intelligence had raided an al Qaeda safe house in a remote mountain area of western Pakistan, capturing several suspects and discovering a computer holding thousands of pages of encrypted documents. In one of the files, they found details of a disturbing plot to attack several buildings in New York City as well as in Newark, New Jersey, and Washington, D.C. At the time I was in East Hampton, Long Island, enjoying a few coveted days of vacation with my wife and kids. I was oblivious to this new intelligence report until David Cohen called me one evening around dinnertime and alerted me to it. At NYPD, we were used to these types of threats coming and going all the time, so he recommended that I stay in touch, but he didn't think it was necessary for me to return to the city. But the telephone kept ringing through the evening, and I sensed from my conversations with Cohen and members of my staff that Washington was becoming very agitated.

At about 1:00 A.M., I told my wife that I needed to cut short my vacation. I drove back into Manhattan at 90 miles per hour and arrived at my apartment around 3:00 A.M. After two hours of sleep, I was awakened by a call from Chief Jimmy Waters, the police chief assigned to FBI's JTTF who reported directly to me. Jimmy confirmed what Cohen had told me the night before and told me that a report was expected to come in soon over the JTTF's top secret computer terminals. Waters had said that documents had been recovered in Pakistan, and they appeared to contain a detailed attack plan on the New York Stock Exchange and some other targets.

That morning, FBI was convening a meeting at its headquarters downtown to review the documents. The head of the New York office of FBI, Pat D'Amuro, invited Ray Kelly, Dave Cohen, and me to a meeting to review the documents together—a generous move on his part that was greatly appreciated by NYPD. When we arrived, we were informed that a cabinet-level meeting was to take place that morning in the White House situation room and that the New York office of FBI was to sit in by secure phone. D'Amuro had arranged with FBI director Mueller for us to be present during the call, another generous act by the Bureau. I was sure glad I'd driven back to the city the night before; I wouldn't have wanted to miss this.

When I arrived downtown at FBI headquarters, I bumped into Cohen getting a cup of coffee on the street corner and we went up to the secure facility, known as "the SCIF"—secret compartmented intelligence facility. We entered a room filled with NYPD and FBI bosses, quickly got a copy of the relevant cables, split them up, and began reading them as we sipped our "street" coffee (neither of us drinks Starbucks). As I read the first one, the hair on the back of my neck began to rise. The cables appeared to be "target folders" for prominent buildings in New York and Washington, including a detailed reconnaissance of the New York Stock Exchange, in lower Manhattan, and the Citigroup Center, in midtown Manhattan. I noted that the person who'd written this report was very literate, seemingly a native English speaker of British or Australian heritage. The manner in which the report was structured suggested that it might have been part of a PowerPoint presentation. I thought it could have been written by someone with a military background. If we were dealing with someone in al Qaeda with British or Australian military experience, I thought, this could be a nightmare scenario.

The person had a detailed attack plan. He'd researched the leadership of each firm being targeted, and at first it appeared he'd actually penetrated the Citigroup Center. We didn't know the date of the report, but we knew it had been briefed to al Qaeda leadership somewhere in Pakistan in early 2004. We assumed (incorrectly) that the reconnaissance had been conducted recently. In the briefing, the operative appeared to have a photo of a conference room in one of the buildings and perhaps had even conducted reconnaissance on a specific room.

After this initial scan, Cohen and I were very concerned and could see why Washington was spun up. The conference call to discuss the threat would begin in two hours, so we began to pass the cables back and forth between ourselves, quickly digesting the scope of this plot against some of the most critical targets in New York City. But as we pored over the details laid out before us for the next hour or so, something began to seem not quite right. By the time the conference call began, we'd begun to have doubts about the seriousness of this plot.

Cohen had been working with this type of intelligence report for over thirty years, and although I didn't have that depth of experience, I viewed him as a Special Forces soldier trained in sabotage operations. While the guy who'd conducted the surveillance was very literate and glib, he'd created little more than a graduate school report on some famous buildings. Most of what he had reported could have been gleaned while sitting in the Starbucks across the street from the Citigroup Center (perhaps our would-be terrorist sipped the expensive stuff).

The report began to take on a much less ominous tone. The more I read it, the more I knew we weren't faced with an imminent threat. At that time, we couldn't pinpoint the exact time of the reconnaissance, but a few days later we got pictures from the brief and we were quickly able to confirm that the recon had taken place well before 9/11. A few NYPD detectives and FBI agents were able to determine the exact date the photo was taken by identifying a flag that was being flown outside the New York Stock Exchange in honor of a foreign visitor. As a result, we concluded that this reconnaissance was at least three years old, conducted before 9/11, when New York City was a very different operating environment for terrorists.

DHS Goes Public

The Washington–New York conference call began at about ten o'clock that morning. In attendance were national security advisor Condoleezza Rice, deputy secretary of state Richard Armitage, defense secretary Donald Rumsfeld, CIA deputy director John McLaughlin, Homeland Security secretary Tom Ridge, and FBI director Mueller. They told us that a suspect had been identified and that he was somewhere in the United Kingdom, but not under active surveillance.

This was very good news, but before I could exhale, to my astonishment Secretary Ridge said he was going to go public with specific warnings concerning the four buildings, which included the New York Stock Exchange, the Citigroup Center, the Prudential building in Newark, New Jersey, and the International Monetary Fund headquarters in Washington, D.C. We in New York were flabbergasted.

First, this was a British and Pakistani investigation, and if specifics of the plot were released, it should be done by them. The individual responsible might recognize that his plot was compromised and "go to ground," meaning he'd try to escape and evade capture. We risked blowing the British case before they were even able to put hands on the subject. There was some discussion of this in the conference call, and Ridge responded by saying that the details were already in the *New York Times.* I scrambled to find and reread the morning's article and found no such details in print. I wondered how the Brits and Pakistanis would react to our announcing information regarding ongoing investigations. Commissioner Kelly interjected this very point on behalf of NYPD, but his plea fell on deaf ears. Ridge was going public, and he did so at two o'clock that Sunday afternoon. The FBI raced to inform the security directors of the various companies involved, and NYPD followed behind them to discuss what security measures would be provided (FBI couldn't help them with that). Most important, the British scrambled to find Abu Issa al-Hindi, the suspected plotter. The Brits knew his general whereabouts, but he wasn't under active surveillance when Ridge went public with the plot details.

Fortunately, Hindi was no James Bond. He was a serious Kashmiri veteran for sure, but not a real terrorist operative. British authorities picked him up the next Tuesday following his regular visit to his mother in London. If the public release of the plot had allowed Hindi to escape, it would have been a major embarrassment for Ridge and the entire U.S. government. The Brits and Pakistanis were furious but kept mum. So what explains the actions of that day? There were several factors at play, and all shed light on the bureaucratic politics of homeland security.

Since its inception, DHS has had an identity crisis. They thought they were to be in charge of homeland security, but they never really were. In the case of Hindi, Ridge probably thought he needed to show leadership by sharing the threat information publicly. And, of course, moving first put him in the headlines. Some suggested that Ridge decided to go public for political purposes, but I don't agree with that; I think he sincerely believed there was a threat. But he also enjoyed the spotlight as he stood before the national press, and he had to be aware that as security threats went up, so did the president's approval ratings. People in the Kerry campaign called me specifically and asked if I thought Ridge was hyping the Hindi threat for political purposes. I said no, for at the time I thought he'd just made an honest and understandable mistake, and in fact, I was still a bit nervous about the plot myself. But the hyped-up characterization of this plot certainly helped the Bush campaign. Everyone was aware of the direct correlation between Americans' fear of terrorism and their inclination to support the president. In retrospect, it is easy to see now that the Hindi threat was indeed overblown. Cohen and I recognized this within hours of the intelligence release. But it took many months for DHS to lower the orange alert—the most important months of the presidential campaign. Was it deliberate? At the time, I did not speak up, because it was not clear to me that it was. It still isn't.

NYPD Battles DHS

A year later, New York City experienced its own conflict with DHS over threat scenarios. In this case, NYPD was accused of hyping a threat by DHS officials. I'll let you decide if the criticism was warranted. It was the summer of 2005, and Mayor Bloomberg (our boss) was running for reelection that fall. Bloomberg was ahead by about thirty points when FBI and NYPD were informed by an Iraqi source about a plot to attack the NYC subway system. Such an attack against the subway was without question my biggest worry. The report told of several people in Baghdad who were planning to come to New York and meet with others who might already be in the city. Cohen and I sat down together and assessed the threat. We learned that the Department of Defense was quite serious about the report, which had been derived from one of their trusted sources. Through our connections in Washington, D.C., we got copies of polygraph reports that indicated that the informant wasn't lying. In addition, we were told that although the source didn't have an extensive track record in reporting international threats such as this, his previous reporting had been reliable about 50 percent of the time. As a result, we became much more interested and began to review possible strategies to counter the threat, though we remained very skeptical.

Meanwhile, two things happened that prompted NYPD to take action. The FBI informed us that a local NBC news reporter had gained access to the entire story (as you'll recall, Ridge was also prompted by the possibility of the media breaking the story). It appeared as if someone from within the government had read the entire report to the journalist. I was irritated but not surprised. The new FBI boss in NYC, Mark Mershon, was busy trying to keep NBC from running the story—and he was successful, at least for the time being. We were then informed that an e-mail had circulated from somewhere within DHS (the Coast Guard, it turned out) that was warning some people in New York City to tell their friends and relatives not to go into the subway system in the days ahead.

Now we had an even more serious problem. It appeared that certain people, those who were more informed or "plugged in," were privy to inside knowledge of government intelligence while it was still in the process of being evaluated. We also learned that the Defense Intelligence Agency was responding aggressively to the reports and was conducting nighttime air mobile insertions in a dangerous neighborhood in Iraq in an attempt to take down some suspects associated with the threat. As we faced this confluence of information, NBC News was getting ready to break the story—and we weren't sure what angle they'd take.

Kelly, Cohen, and I reviewed the situation, especially DIA's risky nighttime insertion in response to the information. DIA was certainly taking it seriously. Kelly was preparing to brief the mayor, so we had some tough decisions to make. Should we quietly increase subway security, or should we go public with the threat? The mayor was looking to do the right thing. Comfortably ahead in the polls, he wasn't looking for a "security bounce"—nor did he want to be accused of manipulating threat data to gain political advantage.

After his briefing with Kelly, the mayor reflected on the fact that an e-mail was already circulating regarding a subway threat and that somebody in DHS had obviously leaked secret information. Pressured by the fact that NBC was going to run with the story, Bloomberg decided to get out in front and hold a very calm and sober press conference regarding the potential threat. We all supported the mayor's decision. Kelly asked me if we should invite FBI to the press conference. I was initially hesitant, thinking selfishly that we should do it ourselves. But Kelly's instincts were usually right, so I agreed that Kelly should call Mershon. Kelly did, and FBI joined us on the podium, where we discussed the threat to the city. At the end of the conference, the mayor expressed his confidence in our security and told the public that he'd be riding the subway again in the morning. Our purpose was to get out in front of the story with FBI and keep the city calm, not hype a threat. We thought the whole event was well orchestrated. But there were others in Washington who disagreed.

DHS immediately began to snipe at our alert. Shortly after our press conference, unknown sources in DHS were being quoted as questioning the plot and the action by NYC to inform its public. We were furious. NYPD and Mayor Bloomberg had been very careful in our communications with the public on terrorism issues. It was further irritating to us that one of the key factors that pushed us to go public was the e-mail from a DHS source that was circulating in the city. We thought we had a responsibility to go public.

So when DHS questioned our actions we struck back hard. Eventually, Cohen and I were brought down to testify in a closed hearing with members of the House Homeland Security Committee, chaired by Congressman Peter King of New York, a very serious and independent thinker on homeland security issues. We were relieved to find we had King's support. Although he was a Republican, he lined up squarely against the administration in this case, and as the session went on, so did virtually every other member of his committee from both sides of the aisle. DHS was hammered by both Republicans and Democrats, and we felt a great sense of justification.

Did we jump out in the press too early? Perhaps, but I knew that the mayor was uncomfortable with the entire equation and was trying to do the best thing for the city. I did not sense for a minute that he sought political advantage, not when he was so comfortably ahead in the polls. Yes, we did like to manage our messages to the city, and that may have pushed us forward, but I have no apologies for that rationale. We attempted to open a low-key dialogue with the city on terrorism issues, keeping people alert but not scaring residents, investors, or tourists out of the city.

DHS: Identity Crisis or Inferiority Complex?

The main problem with the Department of Homeland Security is evident in its name. Securing the entire nation is simply too ambitious a task for one organization to claim. From its inception, DHS has had major overlap with FBI, and FBI isn't about to cede any of its authority to an upstart organization. For many years FBI was the lead agency in conducting terrorism investigations—the heart of the domestic counterterrorism business. FBI has an enormous infrastructure to accomplish that mission with its nationwide network of JTTFs. They have secure facilities and a broad partnership with state and local police forces. When intelligence leads come from overseas, such as a phone intercept from NSA or a lead on a stateside suspect from CIA, FBI gets the information and undertakes the mission. This puts them in the lead position on almost all serious domestic cases.

The Department of Homeland Security was conceived by a mandate from Congress that was pushed through as a result of 9/11. They were given a very expansive mission on paper and, under their aegis, a hodgepodge of new organizations was born. The DHS mission statement says that the primary mission of the Department is to prevent terrorist attacks within the United States.[1] The same document gives the Department the responsibility to distribute "warnings and information to state and local government personnel, agencies, and authorities and to the public."[2] This typical Washington document is five hundred pages of malarkey that does nothing but further confuse the situation. Nobody but a Washington lawyer can even begin to read it. However, nothing in that mandate trumps the authority of FBI. FBI is still the lead agency for terrorism investigations; they're the ones with the classified information and the mechanism for sharing that information. Ironically, DHS is still routinely criticized for not fulfilling its mandate regarding information sharing. But they lack the ability to do so. That's the job of FBI and JTTFs, which have the information, the infrastructure to handle classified information, and the means to share it with state and local governments. DHS is left on the sidelines pouting. This inherent conflict between DHS and FBI was present from day one, and DHS hasn't gotten over it yet.

The Homeland Security Act of 2002 further complicated matters by stating that "responsibility for investigating and prosecuting acts of terrorism shall be vested not in the Department, but rather in the federal, state, and local law enforcement agencies with jurisdiction over the acts in question."[3] This statement shows an incredible ignorance of the counterterrorism business. After giving DHS the mission to prevent terrorist attacks in the United States, Congress kept the real action within FBI, which reports to the Justice Department, not DHS. FBI has further powers vested in them through the federal government in that the Justice Department reserves the right to take all terrorism investigations and criminal proceedings into the federal judicial system. Again, DHS is left standing on the sidelines. According to my Washington sources, Secretary Ridge made a strong bid with President Bush to supersede FBI's authority, but lost. At NYPD, we considered the entire DHS mess, and Commissioner Kelly decided to support JTTFs while we ran our own investigations. Although terrorism is a federal crime, the plotting, building, and detonating of a bomb in New York City breaks state and local laws, giving us the full right and responsibility to protect ourselves from those attacks. And that's exactly what we did.

Problems with the distribution of information ensue because often the information comes from another agency, such as CIA, leading to an inherent conflict regarding who should be in charge of sharing that information with the public. In other words, who would be the face of counterterrorism in America? This was a big issue in the years immediately following 9/11. In more recent years, current DHS secretary Michael Chertoff and former attorney general Alberto Gonzales showed less desire than their two predecessors to be the first to get on TV, so the issue has subsided a bit. But the conflict between FBI and DHS continues at the operational level.

In my estimation, the Washington office of DHS hasn't yet proven its worth. During the first years under Tom Ridge, the Department tried to define itself as the public face of homeland security, with its color code of warnings and frequent press conferences. They immediately set up the Transportation Security Administration (TSA), a brand-new entity, and instituted more rigorous inspections at our airports—an obvious response to 9/11. The Department has also doled out millions of dollars in homeland security pork to state and local authorities around the country—unfortunately, with very little effect on our overall security. Many fire departments around the country got shiny new trucks and information centers were set up to share low-order information with local police departments, but these funds did little to support the real CT business of running informants and investigations. In DHS's second administration, Michael Chertoff has taken a much lower profile on threat announcements and has begun to redefine the Department within the Washington bureaucracy. But from my perspective in New York (which is admittedly limited) DHS still hasn't made an impact on our homeland security that is commensurate with the time, money, and energy expended.

DHS overextended itself and failed in a huge bureaucratic mission grab. They hoped that their legislation would trump the Justice Department authority and overtake the massive FBI infrastructure. That was not to be. At the same time they failed to appreciate that within the massive agencies they inherited, there *was* one important mission where they did have the lead jurisdiction and infrastructure to do something meaningful: border security. These agencies include the old Customs Service, the old Immigration and Naturalization Service, the U.S. Coast Guard, and TSA. Had its name reflected its primary mission, DHS might have been called the "Department of Border and Transportation Security." That mission would have been plenty for one organization to handle, and carrying it out would have been a much more realistic goal than the broad and nebulous aim of maintaining "homeland security." Unfortunately, DHS was given jurisdiction over other missions when it was created, so it has under its aegis the Federal Emergency Management Agency (FEMA) and the Secret Service. DHS is also responsible for supporting state and local government with funding. These separate missions overwhelm DHS's staff, resulting in poorly executed missions (as was evident in New Orleans during Hurricane Katrina).

DHS and Domestic Intelligence: More Dysfunction

The Department of Homeland Security is an awkward mix of various state and local functions and several fiercely independent federal agencies. I see the Department as two general groups. The first is "DHS Central," which are those offices located at Washington, D.C., headquarters. Their primary function, it appears to me, is to engage in Washington bureaucratic battles, as opposed to actually chasing terrorists. I refer to the second group in DHS as "the separate agencies" and include in this batch the Coast Guard, Secret Service, TSA, and the newly organized Customs and Border Protection (CBP), and Immigration and Customs Enforcement (ICE). At DHS, these organizations are often referred to as the "legacy agencies" because some of them predate the Department. They do more to engage in the CT game than does DHS Central, even if they're not the varsity players.

At NYPD, we wanted only one thing from DHS Central: money. We didn't want advice, for what they offered wasn't very useful, and we didn't want intelligence, because we already got that directly from FBI, CIA, DIA, and NSA at the FBI's JTTF. We didn't want to be bothered by DHS Central's bogus interpretations of "chatter" or other inane warnings. However, we *were* interested in the separate agencies; they had a real mission and real people in the game.

DHS agencies based in New York, such as CBP and the Secret Service, pretty much worked within their own box. You really couldn't tell they were part of DHS except for the new signs on their buildings. These organizations had a significant presence at the points of entry into New York, a narrow but very important point of counterterrorism operations for the country and for the city. TSA worked alongside them, screening passengers and luggage at our airports. And, of course, the Coast Guard was positioned in our ports. NYPD had very good relations with the Secret Service, as seen during the management of the Republican National Convention and the sixtieth meeting of the UN General Assembly. These were people we could work with.

The grandest irony of these agencies is that although they were brought together and expanded dramatically after 9/11 because of the terrorist threat, the fact remains that they don't really "do" counterterrorism. This didn't become fully apparent to me until after the Dubai port debacle. In February 2006, when investors from Dubai attempted to take ownership of some port terminal operations in the United States, it set off a hysterical and completely uninformed rage in Washington. But during this debate, which ultimately sank the investment proposal, NYPD began to turn its considerable resources and talents to the issue of ports. What we found there was a huge gap in DHS's human intelligence program. What the ports really needed was a fully integrated CIA, FBI, ICE, CBP, NYPD, and Coast Guard operation, with each organization running lines to informant networks with a particular interest in identifying a terrorist nexus. We found intelligence operations sorely lacking in the ports.

This goes back to the issue of FBI taking the lead in counterterrorism investigations. As I previously mentioned, President Bush at one point reaffirmed that FBI would continue as the lead agency in counterterrorism investigations when DHS was formed. The new DHS agencies, including ICE, CBP, and the Coast Guard, would support FBI efforts through the Bureau's JTTFs. It seemed like a reasonable decision. However, it ignored certain bureaucratic realities, effectively crippling counterterrorism investigative work in and around our sea- and airports. Why? If these agencies open up a terrorism investigation or run a terrorism informant at the port, FBI would claim authority over their case and shift the management responsibility over to JTTF, where DHS agency would be welcome to participate, but as a junior partner. The predictable bureaucratic response was for supervisors to retain control of their people and continue with their traditional pre-9/11 duties, only nominally supporting JTTFs. This was a shocking revelation, even for me, and I'm someone who regards all Washington institutions with a healthy dose of cynicism. The result was very predictable. DHS agencies provided token representation to JTTFs (a few liaison people per office) and stayed within the boundaries of their traditional business. In other words, they didn't conduct terrorism operations outside of their paltry commitment to FBI. Customs officials continued to deal with smuggling of drugs and other contraband and ICE officials with illegal immigration. They stayed clear of terrorism investigations. Fortunately, their increased size and operational activity probably helped clamp down on terrorism activity as well, but it wasn't by design.

As much as I liked the staff of the separate DHS agencies in the field, I became more troubled as I got to know how these agencies were run. The new challenge for post-9/11 law enforcement agencies is to make the transition from being purely a law enforcement agency to being an agency that makes CT intelligence operations a fundamental mission. What is not fully appreciated is that law enforcement and investigative work are related but entirely different functions. Law enforcement involves finding someone after a crime has been committed; intelligence involves finding someone before they act. Intelligence necessitates spying on suspects who may not have been involved in a crime, except perhaps conspiracy to commit a crime. The FBI had balked at this patently un-American practice, especially since the scandals of the 1960s when they were accused of improperly spying on student anti-war protesters and civil rights leaders such as Martin Luther King Jr. Over the years, they'd become very wary of domestic intelligence operations. But in the case of terrorists—especially the suicide terrorists—there is often only one shot to get them, and this requires aggressive intelligence operations before the attack.

DHS agencies, such as ICE, the Coast Guard, and CBP, should dedicate much more time and resources to running sophisticated HUMINT operations with the goal of protecting their areas of responsibility: the borders, airports, and seaports. These intelligence operations should be run both independently, as they were at NYPD, *and* in conjunction with FBI. For example, ICE and the Coast Guard should be coordinating with CIA to establish human intelligence networks along the supply chain. From a factory in China through a port in Dubai or Amsterdam and into the terminals in New Jersey, HUMINT networks should be looking for illicit activity, including the movement of terrorist personnel or materials through logistics systems. While at NYPD, I was astonished to see how little of that was being done, and how business around our ports on the intelligence side hadn't significantly changed since 9/11. Any change, if it was occurring, related to the infusion of technology, such as installing radiological screening systems for containerized materials passing through the port.

I support these initiatives but am deeply troubled that counterterrorism officials and politicians put too much confidence in these technological solutions without the grunt work of HUMINT collection. Another of the most immediate problems with the emphasis on containerized shipping is that thousands of completely unregulated noncontainer ships come into New York Harbor every month. On my first Fourth of July at NYPD I recall going out on a NYPD harbor launch to get a sense of our maritime defenses and to enjoy the view of the fireworks. I noted all of the container ships waiting in line in the harbor, their entrance carefully managed by the Coast Guard, Customs, Immigration, and the terminal operators. But the smaller watercraft, which on the Fourth of July may number in the many thousands, were completely unregulated. Even today they come in and out of the harbor with no controls, and some are as long as a hundred feet and as heavy as a hundred tons.

In a sense, what's going on in our seaports echoes the well-known problem in our airports. Just as commercial aviation is tightly managed while commercial contract air is full of holes, so too are our ports, containerized shipping carefully scrutinized (most of the time) while the rest of our maritime traffic is given an all-access pass. Simply requiring every small craft to send out a beacon that can be monitored by the Coast Guard would help enormously. Not only would it address safety issues (a beacon would help the Coast Guard rescue a ship in distress) but it would give us some sense of who's out there in our waterways. Right now we have no clue.

Redefining DHS

DHS is still searching for a mission, still floundering. The core function of DHS is defined by the separate agencies: Customs, Immigration, the Coast Guard, and airport security. They all work to protect our borders, and that's exactly what DHS should be focused on and held accountable for. As I indicated earlier in this chapter, the Department should be streamlined and renamed the Department of Border and Transportation Security. They should jettison secondary missions, including FEMA, and the role of providing support (which is mostly pork) to state and local governments should be spun off. Support to states and locals should go back to the White House Office of Homeland Security, where it resided prior to the creation of DHS. FEMA should be a separate agency with a mission to clean up all messes, from natural disasters to massive terrorism events. This important work certainly warrants greater attention than it receives under DHS umbrella.

DHS should stop trying to compete with FBI, which is responsible for domestic terrorism threats and investigations. At the same time, FBI must allow other agencies, especially DHS agencies, to conduct CT investigations within our seaports, airports, and borders without the stultifying management and oversight of JTTFs. DHS should accelerate its intelligence activities dramatically and coordinate these programs with FBI, CIA, and local authorities.

Thankfully, DHS has moved beyond its kindergarten-style color-coded warnings, but the agency continues to struggle to define itself. It should start with a laser focus on our borders, and not just with physical inspection and technologies but with investigations based on human and signals intelligence that cover our points of entry by air, land, and sea. This is a major task that isn't being effectively done today and must be jump-started immediately.

Chapter 12

Defending the Big Apple

TO SAY THAT THE September 11 attacks on the World Trade Center had a profound effect on New Yorkers is a gross understatement. For better or for worse, a few New Yorkers fled the city in the wake of 9/11 while others deepened their commitment to helping the Big Apple recover from its worst tragedy and do whatever possible to ensure that nothing like that happens again. I was definitely a member of the latter camp, but not just because I'm a New Yorker. Having spent the first twenty years of my career as a soldier, the need to be on the front lines was firmly imbedded in my psyche. Indeed, my military experience prepared me well for my work with one of the finest law enforcement outfits in the world—NYPD. In fact, working with cops to defend a city from a global threat holds many parallels to military duty. For example, while fighting a fierce insurgency in El Salvador, I was convinced that an offensive strategy was essential to keep the guerrillas off balance and keep my soldiers and me alive. Nevertheless, I never stopped working on upgrading our defensive perimeter. The same held true when I was working with NYPD.

Defenses are important to a comprehensive strategy. Although the main work of counterterrorism at NYPD was the offensive work conducted by plainclothes detectives and undercover agents, we also deployed a lot of uniformed cops in our defense. Commissioner

Kelly was innovative in developing a range of initiatives designed to keep terrorists off balance and to project an image of preparedness in the city. We focused our energy on a few key targets such as the New York Stock Exchange, the new Freedom Tower at ground zero, and the key transportation hubs: Grand Central Station, Penn Station, the Port Authority Bus Terminal, and the Staten Island Ferry Terminal.

Just as the commitment to JTTFs and the Intelligence Division diverted valuable police resources from crime fighting, so too did the defensive deployments of NYPD. But Kelly and Mayor Bloomberg remained committed in spite of the sacrifice. Although some federal funding helped offset these deployments, they cost the city millions of dollars—money that was never recovered. NYPD's overt, uniformed programs to protect the city are a case study in using whatever resources you have to do the best job possible.

"Flash-to-Bang" at NYPD

The greatest satisfaction I had in working with NYPD and for Ray Kelly was being part of an organization that gets things done. After spending much of my career in the federal government, followed by a stint inside the stultifying bureaucracy of the United Nations, NYPD was a breath of fresh air. The experience reminded me of being on a Special Forces A-team. It was a professional organization that was in the fight and getting things done.

One of Dave Cohen's favorite stories about Ray Kelly recalls an ordinary day at NYPD and is a great illustration of the commissioner at work. One morning in the daily intelligence briefing, Cohen mentioned to Kelly that it might be a good idea to post a few NYPD detectives overseas—in the United Kingdom and perhaps Israel to start (the countries with the most relevant CT experience). Cohen wanted to establish a direct liaison with our police counterparts in those key countries with an eye toward getting information on issues related directly to New York City without the filters of FBI or CIA. This was an extraordinary recommendation by Cohen, who was, after all, a veteran of the federal government. He knew his plan was certain to irritate CIA, FBI, and the State Department all in one fell swoop, yet without their approval it would be difficult if not impossible to achieve. Kelly listened, understood the potential firestorm, and told Cohen he thought it was a good idea. Cohen moved on in his briefing and let the idea marinate awhile with the commissioner. For such a bold and controversial initiative to take shape in Washington, it would require months of internal discussion within a given agency, then several more months of bureaucratic haggling, then even more months of discussion, budgeting, and personnel machinations. About two weeks later, Cohen returned to Kelly to further discuss the issue. Kelly's response was classic: "I thought we discussed this already. When will your detective be in London?" Three days later, an NYPD detective on a tourist visa was knocking on the door of New Scotland Yard in London. Within that week, NYPD had established its first international liaison office. It was new; it was raw; it was controversial. It was a brilliant idea, and the fact that it was implemented almost immediately was vintage Ray Kelly.

The time it took to move from the creation of an idea to beginning its implementation at NYPD—the "flash-to-bang" time—was lightning speed compared to what we were accustomed to in Washington. Cohen and I always had plenty of new ideas; some were good, others perhaps a bit half-baked. We'd air them with Kelly and each other in our daily morning briefing. If Kelly liked an idea, we executed the decision as soon as we left the room. If he didn't, we let it go and moved on to other issues. This was a great work environment for people who wanted to get things done, but it wasn't a place for the sick, lame, or lazy. It was also somewhat hazardous for Cohen and me, for although we enjoyed the freedom to constantly try new things, we tended to swamp ourselves in new self-initiated programs that Kelly would always ask for updates on. We were extremely busy, but it was exhilarating. Although we didn't have a big influx of post-9/11 cash from the federal government, we did have a lot of talented NYPD cops who were willing to join in this important work.

Kelly never forgot anything Cohen or I told him (and we forgot a whole lot of stuff). He was always taking concise notes in a small agenda notebook he carried with him to all meetings. Those yearly agendas hold the history of Kelly at NYPD, and what a fascinating story they must tell.

NYPD Shield

At one of our morning meetings, I told Kelly about an FBI program called INFRAGUARD, a national effort designed to reach out to the private sector. We were very skeptical of it, for its main event seemed to be a golf outing that appeared to be little more than a networking opportunity for FBI agents to make contacts with private-sector employers for whom they'd work when they retired. For private security officials, it was an opportunity to get out of their offices, meet with their old buddies, and tell their bosses they were plugged into FBI inner sanctum. We hadn't been notified of the initiative. I found out about it from Inspector Mike O'Neil, who'd learned about it from one of the ex-NYPD security officials who'd been invited to join.

A bit irritated, I told Kelly FBI would talk to their security officials about a lot of nothing while we were the ones who'd have to actually provide private-sector companies with support. We also had several programs of outreach to the private sector, but they were somewhat disparate. In truth, I was frustrated that I hadn't thought of the idea before FBI. Their INFRAGUARD program actually had some merit, I begrudgingly admitted.

It was June 2005, and FBI event was scheduled to take place in Washington at the end of August. We decided that morning to beat them to the punch. I met with my staff, primarily Chief John Colgan and Inspector Mike O'Neil, and by the end of the day we'd outlined an overarching program that pulled together a few of our current programs and added a few more. I was very fortunate to have John Colgan on my staff. Many of the bureaucrats in the Department took issue with his brusque style, but he got things done.

Colgan, who came out of retirement after 9/11, often reminded me that he hadn't come back to NYPD to win any popularity contests. He was back because of 9/11, because he loved "the job," and because he wanted to get things done. O'Neil, who commanded the Counterterrorism Division, would be the guy we called on to execute the programs.

Lieutenant Dave Kelly (no relation to the commissioner) in the front office came up with the name "NYPD Shield," and we created a brochure within two days and a Web site before the week was out. We formed an NYPD Shield staff, headed by Captain Joe Cordes, and assigned a handful of sharp lieutenants and detectives to get it going. Ray Kelly again bit the bullet and reassigned some talent from the Department to support the new initiative.

Forty-five days after that morning meeting with the commissioner, we had a new organization, a new Web site, a mailing sent out to hundreds of security managers, and a briefing in the auditorium to kick off the program. A similar effort in Washington would have taken at least a year. Within a few months, NYPD Shield was a mature, growing, and fully functional outreach program that included periodic briefings, training, security assessments, sharing of best practices, and the distribution of information via the Internet to private-sector companies. Although the idea began as an impetuous response to FBI's INFRAGUARD, our effort took a much different shape and became an active and vital program. Since that rushed beginning, NYPD Shield has developed and has become a cornerstone of the Department's relationship with the private sector.

The critical infrastructure in New York City is owned by the private sector, and it's their security personnel who are often the real first responders in an incident and thus the first line of defense in the event of a terrorist attack. We at NYPD understood that our defensive strategy was only as good as what we were able to achieve in partnership with the city's private-sector security people. When the safety of over eight million people is at stake, you may be surprised by how fast you can get something done.

Raymond W. Kelly took charge of NYPD when the piles of rubble at ground zero were still smoldering within a few blocks from his home. He transformed the police department, and not only in its traditional missions of fighting crime. Perhaps even more significantly, he created a self-driven force that would take the lead in protecting the city from future attacks.

One of his many innovations was the aggressive use of his primary asset: uniformed cops. In the city, heavily armed units with automatic rifles show up at key locations unexpectedly, units of transit police sweep through the subways eyeing suspicious packages or other terrorist indicators, and bags are inspected at random subway entrances. Some of the bags are subjected to chemical trace detection technologies similar to those performed at airport checkpoints.

Deploying NYPD: Counterterrorism and Dunkin' Donuts

Kelly is certainly an innovator, but he also adroitly kept Cohen's and my enthusiasm in check when warranted. He'd seen it all in his tenure at NYPD, from daring acts of bravery and service to the worst elements of a municipal union. We had our share of both, but fortunately, the good cops outweighed the "slugs," or at least were strong enough to carry them along.

In my first week at NYPD, I traveled up to Times Square to inspect a turnout formation for a counterterrorism deployment of cops at critical sites around the city. The deployments were meant to be a show of force and thus a deterrent to terrorists who might be plotting something. Before cops go on daily duty, they're subjected to a turnout briefing. As shown on television, this is normally done in the station house by a crusty old sergeant. But because these counterterrorism deployments involve a surge of cars, the turnout is usually done on the sidewalk right out in front of the cars. As a former military officer, I was accustomed to addressing a formation of troops in the open air, so I was right at home as

I briefed this group of about forty cops prior to their deployment. I told them to be alert for possible terrorist reconnaissance activity and to speak with the merchants on the street. (The coffee and newspaper vendors are usually the first to know if something isn't right in their neighborhood.) I urged them to talk to the private security personnel and enlist their support in being alert for suspicious activity. I reminded them that it was average cops who'd captured Timothy McVeigh and Eric Rudolph, two of America's most-wanted terrorists.

After finishing my brief I walked over and joined the cops, satisfied that I'd really pumped them up. Each cop had a sheet of paper in his hand, provided by the sergeant prior to my arrival. I asked one cop who'd seemed completely bored with my presentation what was on the paper he had. "These are our deployment locations," he said as he handed me the sheet.

I looked down the list of addresses they'd been given, and just about blew a head gasket. About half were Dunkin' Donuts locations and the other half were Blimpie sandwich shops! I turned to the captain and shouted, "You have to deploy cops to Dunkin' Donuts? Don't we have enough there already? Is that where bin Laden is hanging out?" I didn't know whether to laugh or cry.

Of course, there was a logical explanation. A sergeant pulled me aside and told me that there'd been a string of armed robberies at local Blimpie and Dunkin' Donuts stores in midtown Manhattan, and the cops were trying to strangle this mini crime wave. Although the robberies were fairly small, the precinct commander was getting hammered for the rising robbery statistics, and his priority was always to reduce crime. These criminal activities could bring down the city's economy just as much as another terrorist attack, so the counterterrorism deployment had been diverted to crime reduction that day.

When I related my story to Kelly the next day, he looked at me with a half smile. He wasn't surprised, knowing the pressure the precinct commander felt to stop the Dunkin' Donuts crime wave. After forty years with NYPD, Kelly was unflappable; it was impossible to surprise him with anything, even the most bizarre tales. Like when one of my cops almost killed himself downing a bottle of hot sauce on a five-dollar bet. (He should have known better—the hot sauce was named "Ass Reaper.") Kelly, a veteran cop himself, again just shook his head. He'd seen worse in his days in the precinct houses.

But Kelly was also concerned about the Dunkin' Donuts deployment because he knew that even cops who were committed to CT work would always drift back to crime fighting on the street. Notwithstanding the enormous political pressure he was under to reduce crime, he wanted the counterterrorism mission conducted with equal focus. He charged Cohen and me to keep our cops focused on their dual mission of fighting crime and preventing terrorism.

The deployment of NYPD officers around the city was received positively by the vast majority of New Yorkers and tourists who flock there, but there was controversy. Some complaints came from the segment of the population that will always be suspicious of police, and some came from those who simply thought it was a big waste of time. In defense of the program, I always described four purposes of the deployments, each equally important:

1. *To deter terrorist reconnaissance activity.* We knew from our analysis of previous terrorist operations that reconnaissance was often conducted prior to an attack. We also knew that heavy police presence was a concern for terrorists, who want to remain entirely undetected as they plan an operation.

2. *To keep the cops alert to the terrorism mission by periodically briefing and deploying them on CT missions.* We prepared briefing materials for the cops on a range of subjects, from general guidance on what types of suspicious activity to look for to summaries of recent attacks (such as those in Madrid and London) and lessons learned from those incidents. We understood that the terrorism awareness aspect of the deployment would carry over into the days and weeks ahead, when each cop undertook his normal crime fighting missions.

3. *To keep the public alert to the terrorist threat.* We instructed our officers to talk to private security personnel and vendors on the street and employ them as extra eyes and ears. The deployments were a reminder to the public that the threat is still out there and that they should remain vigilant. Our mantra to the people was that we were on the job but needed their help. We encouraged them to be alert and report anything unusual to law enforcement with the aforementioned slogan: "If you see something, say something."

4. *To promote the public affairs effort.* We wanted to spread the message that if a terrorist planned to operate in New York City, he'd have to deal with NYPD and an alert public. Our hope was that the deployments, as part of our overall strategy, would act as a deterrent for terrorists who were considering NYC for their next target.

Planes, Trains, and Automobiles

The most common target for terrorist operatives over the years has been transportation systems. Planes have an obvious appeal to terrorist groups, especially al Qaeda. For that reason I'm very supportive of most of the efforts made at our airports to protect commercial aviation. There's still need, however, for improvement of these screening systems, since we can focus our energies if we become better at profiling people and behavior that indicate a potential threat.

NYPD for a long time conducted CT patrols in our train stations. These patrols are called train order maintenance sweeps (TOMS), another of NYPD's countless acronyms that I had to learn when I began my job there. These sweeps are a deployment of about six to eight cops per station, the idea being to walk through the trains when they are stopped at the station. It's meant to send a signal—to both a potential pickpocket and a terrorist operative. The New York public, especially after 9/11, heartily welcomed the police presence. The Transit Bureau, under the assistance of CT Inspector Vinnie DeMarino, was also aggressive in many other ways in patrolling the country's largest subway system for terrorism threats.

The New York City subway system is massive. According to the Mineta Transportation Institute in San Jose, California, the United States has about 10 million rail rides per day, and 6.5 million of those occur in the New York metropolitan area. In other words, over 60 percent of all the daily train traffic in the United States is in the New York metropolitan area. And our trains had been targeted by violent Islamic radicals before, as recently as 1997.

In 1997, a couple of radicalized Palestinian young men decided they'd construct a pipe bomb and take it into the subway trains. Fortunately, one of their roommates wasn't part of the plot and, becoming aware of their scheme, went into the street looking for a cop to inform. In his very poor English, he told a cop that there was a "bomba" in his apartment. NYPD quickly swung into action and an assault was made on the house. Chief Charlie Kamerdener, current head of NYPD Special Operations Division (which has NYPD SWAT units assigned to it), was the duty officer. He reacted to the situation quickly. He sent in an NYPD team, one of the terrorists reached for a gun and was shot, and the threat was over. However, the threat to our subway system is really never over. And I constantly worried about it, even as I rode it every day. NYPD was already doing a lot in the subway system, but I was concerned we needed to do more. I seized the opportunity to push that sentiment in July 2005.

Increasing Subway Safety

On July 7, 2005, the day of the London subway attacks, NYPD reacted very quickly. In fact, one of Dave Cohen's detectives was riding in the London system the morning it was hit. He provided firsthand reports to us within an hour of the attack. Kelly immediately enhanced the security of our own system, in case this was a multinational conspiracy, as well as to protect against potential copycat attacks in New York. The commissioner deployed a large uniformed and plainclothes force into and around the NYC subway system and other key transportation nodes, such as bridges, tunnels, and bus and ferry terminals.

Whenever we had a large deployment like this, we were questioned by some. Exactly fourteen days later, Kelly's preventive actions were justified when a copycat cell did strike in London with a very similar attack—four backpack bombs carried by four suicide bombers. Thankfully, the bombs didn't go off. Although the July 21 cell was probably contemplating action prior to July 7, the first attack inspired them to take action. Only through the Brits' great fortune did the bombs not explode, sparing the UK another national disaster that July.

Later that same afternoon, Kelly held a meeting with his senior staff. About halfway into the meeting I suggested that we conduct bag checks at the train stations—*all* of the train stations. I could see some of the old chiefs rolling their eyes as I did the math in my head: six hundred stations, thirty-five hundred cops. We could do it, but it would be a drain on the Department and potentially clog up the subway system.

This idea of inspecting bags at train stations was something I'd been thinking about for a long time. I had begun to formulate the concept for the subways when I was visiting the U.S. Open tennis championships at Arthur Ashe Stadium in Flushing in September 2003. While working with the security teams at the U.S. Open, I was very impressed with how quickly and efficiently the private security personnel did their bag checks at each entrance. They were alert, courteous, and competent. They didn't waste time poking around an old lady's handbag to check her lipstick container, but they were effectively ensuring that a terrorist wasn't bringing a big bomb into the stadium. At the same time, I'm sure they were keeping an eye out for potential drunks and troublemakers who might try to bring in alcoholic beverages. It wasn't a perfect system, but in my view, it was an excellent and appropriate deterrent to any terrorist or potential troublemaker.

That was my goal at NYPD. It would be impossible to stop a perfectly disciplined terrorist. But I knew from our studies of terrorists that they weren't usually James Bond–caliber professionals; they were in fact amateurs. I was convinced that a strong showing of alert and professional cops would ward off most al Qaeda cells. It wasn't my intention to deflect them to Boston or Philadelphia, but I certainly wanted to keep them out of New York City. I knew it would be hard to implement such a program in the subway system, but I was hopeful that at least we could inspect some of the more problematic bags in the system and thereby create a meaningful deterrent. The July 7 attack in London gave me the opportunity to push the concept.

In Kelly's staff meeting, I continued to make my proposal. I could sense some support from a few others in the room. They knew the subway was vulnerable and something needed to be done. But others could only see the amount of work and commitment this proposal represented. Kelly allowed the debate to continue, and my frustration level climbed as I continued to beat back opposition and excuses. Finally, he intervened and turned to Transit Bureau chief Mike Scagnelli and told him to execute the plan to randomly check bags in the subway. He also instructed the lawyers to make sure that our instructions were consistent with Department and city guidelines and to work with Scagnelli and his team of transit cops to build the details of the program. Kelly anticipated something I didn't: the American Civil Liberties Union (ACLU) would challenge our policy. We'd deal with that later.

In typical NYPD style, the appropriate people got together immediately after the meeting and hashed out a process. I thought it was a bit cumbersome, but Cohen advised me to shut up and take my substantial victory to get bag checks into the subway system. As usual, I took his advice and the next morning, at about sixty stations around the city, NYPD was conducting random bag checks. We were careful to select one out of every five passengers. My staff included Inspector Vinnie DeMarino, who was also responsible for counterterrorism initiatives in the subway system. I told Vinnie to make sure he had alert counters at each station—and to see to it that if some young male with an overflowing, smoldering backpack rushed his way through the system, the count of five would fall on his head and not on Grandma Moses scuffling along behind him. In other words, count like this: "One, two, three . . . five. You! Yeah, you. Please let me see what's in the bag."

DeMarino assured me that his cops knew the deal and we wouldn't have to fudge the random count in any case. If a cop saw someone acting suspiciously he had every right, indeed a responsibility, to approach that person. And that was exactly what I was looking for: a physical approach to suspicious people. By putting some hands on suspicious people, we would let the potential terrorist know that we were looking for him in New York City. We also wanted the cops to *think* out there; asking to look at bags that might be suspicious was their duty.

Later we were in fact challenged by the ACLU in court. Cohen and I survived a grilling by an ACLU lawyer, but the judge wasn't persuaded by his arguments. "Yes, I know the bag checks are not foolproof," I told the judge. "They're part of a layered defense of the subway, from plainclothes detectives to uniformed sweeps to messages to the public. All together they're designed to send a message to the terrorists: 'Don't attack here because we're looking for you.' There are no guarantees, but to do less in the largest subway system in the country in the city that has been attacked twice before would be an abrogation of our duties." We won the case, and the random bag checks are still in place today.

Playing Smart Defense

If a terrorist cell is allowed to develop hidden from the eyes of the law, it will find a way to kill—especially in an open, democratic society. Defensive strategies will never be enough. Huge spending programs on protecting ports, chemical facilities, or our nation's shopping malls will have only a marginal impact on our security. We shouldn't equate strong counterterrorism policy (or toughness) with support for big-budget items. These gigantic projects will enrich a handful of defense contractors and "Beltway bandits" in Washington and only protect us marginally. However, key targets must be defended to diminish terrorists' ability to achieve strategic impact with a bomb attack.

With regard to the safety of New York City, I spent most of my time telling people to relax. One day Kelly directed me to talk to Japanese businesses in the city at the request of the consul general of Japan. I gave them both the good news and the bad news. The bad news was that NYC was a prime target for al Qaeda. The good news, for them, was that a terrorist would have plenty of very American targets to hit before they'd waste a bomb on Sony or Toyota. Al Qaeda wanted an American government building or American companies, or because of their intense anti-Semitism they might target Jewish institutions. The Japanese and other international businesses needed to be prudent but not panic—and certainly not move their offices away from New York City. They seemed relieved by my frank assessment.

I also spent a lot of time telling people to remove Jersey barriers. After 9/11, these ugly white concrete structures began to spring up like daisies all over New York City, and they were even more ubiquitous in Washington. We've spent years trying to get them removed, for not only are they ugly, they actually do very little to really protect a site from a truck bomb. A well-trained driver can plow them right out of the way if they're not pinned down in a very serious manner. And even a small explosive can blow right through a Jersey barrier, while a big bomb will turn the concrete barrier into a projectile if it didn't completely disintegrate in the blast. They provided only a minimal level of security, were an eyesore, and contributed to traffic congestion.

But there was one building I was really concerned about. It haunted me. I knew I had to do the right thing, and I wouldn't allow myself to be steamrolled. It was the Freedom Tower, the successor to the World Trade Center's twin towers. NYPD forced its redesign to prevent the construction of a terrorist magnet in lower Manhattan.

The Freedom Tower Design

The struggle over the Freedom Tower's initial design was one of the more difficult bureaucratic battles I endured while at NYPD. The entire rebuilding plan for the sixteen-acre site at ground zero was full of controversy from the beginning. It pitted against one another a variety of powerful interests with competing design agendas, including but not limited to the following: (1) some politicians, who wanted a statement of national resolve against terrorism (and a political legacy of their own); (2) families of the victims of 9/11, who wanted an appropriate memorial to their sacrifice; (3) city planners, who wanted to rectify the problems associated with the massive neighborhood disruption caused by the original towers; and (4) the owners of the real estate, who wanted viable commercial space in a very competitive real estate market. NYPD, which wasn't involved in the initial planning of the site, entered the fray late into the design stage of the Freedom Tower. We added an additional dimension to the battle: the unique security requirements of an iconic site that had been attacked twice before by terrorists.

Effective counterterrorism policy balances security measures with good city planning. If NYPD encouraged or allowed New York City to become an armed camp of barriers, walls, and closed streets, it could undermine people's confidence about living, working, and investing in this great city—and still there'd be no guarantee that security had improved. During my tenure at NYPD, I spent considerable time denying requests for Jersey barriers, ugly concrete planters, and bollards proposed by managers and security directors of Manhattan properties. As the head of counterterrorism for NYPD, I would have found it easy to encourage this bunker mentality to cover my rear in the case of a future attack. But as a citizen of the city, I was determined not to allow this to unfold.

But when I learned about the design of the Freedom Tower, I became very concerned not only for the safety of its inhabitants but of *all* of lower Manhattan, which would be economically devastated by a third attack against the World Trade Center. The initial design created not only a signature target for al Qaeda but one that was extraordinarily vulnerable to a truck bomb attack.

Meeting Mr. Silverstein

On June 29, 2004, Commissioner Kelly sent me to a meeting with one of New York City's megadevelopers, Larry Silverstein. As we pulled up to his plush midtown offices, my assistant, Detective Jimmy Fogarty, and I noted the obvious contrast with One Police Plaza, NYPD's drab, grungy headquarters. Pretty girls in short skirts greeted Fogarty and me and ushered us down plush carpeted hallways into a well-appointed conference room. The office was adorned with three-dimensional models and photo depictions of the new Freedom Tower as conceived by the master architect for the Freedom Tower site, Daniel Libeskind.

Mr. Silverstein met me with a warm smile and the friendly, confident handshake of a rich and powerful man. Silverstein was a successful New York real estate developer whose crowning achievement was the signing of a one-hundred-year lease on the World Trade Center buildings just six weeks before the Twin Towers were destroyed. Although clearly affected by the human tragedy of 9/11, Silverstein was also intent on getting back in business downtown. He had the unenviable task of rebuilding a commercially viable office building while meeting the demands of so many others—most notably New York governor George Pataki. Pataki insisted the building was going to be an "iconic structure"—in effect, a political statement about American resolve in the "war against terrorism." Silverstein was more interested in building a commercially feasible building, something I respected about him.

The Freedom Tower was part of a massive master plan for the redevelopment of the hole in lower Manhattan at ground zero. When the two towers came down, they took out the entire sixteen-acre "superblock" (which consisted of four other buildings), destroyed the adjacent 7 World Trade Center building, and severely damaged several surrounding structures, some beyond repair.

Most of the property, which I will refer to as the "old World

Trade Center site" or the "sixteen acres," is owned and controlled by a bi-state entity, the Port Authority of New York and New Jersey. It has been managed in effect by the governor of New York since the early 1970s. At that time, Governor Nelson Rockefeller championed the very controversial project, which many considered an aesthetic disaster for lower Manhattan and a needless expansion of commercial office space that would flood an already stagnant market.

In 2004, when I became involved with this project, the decision making was dominated by Governor Pataki. With his presidential aspirations alive and well, Pataki was determined to make the Freedom Tower a major part of his gubernatorial legacy, with plenty of photo ops and references to 9/11, without former mayor Rudy Giuliani hogging the spotlight. His nominal partner in the Port Authority was the governor of New Jersey, James McGreevey, who'd just resigned in disgrace over a homosexual affair with one of his staffers (McGreevey's purported lover was his first homeland security advisor, and some said his chief qualification for the job—other than his extracurricular relationship with Governor McGreevey—was that he'd grown up in Israel). The Port Authority was run by a group of people who were personally selected by both governors, and the institution was not known for great managerial effectiveness, to say the least.

The replacement building for the Twin Towers was designed by a committee of public, private, and personal interests—a formula for disaster. The master architect, Daniel Libeskind, designed the glass structure with a bent spire and wind turbines on top rising to 1,776 feet. The shape and angle of the spire was supposed to evoke the Statue of Liberty, and thus it was named the "Freedom Tower." Silverstein clearly hated the design and didn't trust Libeskind, who was handpicked by Pataki in a controversial design competition. So Silverstein hired his own architect, David Childs, who had far more experience in building tall commercial buildings than Libeskind. At the end of all the political posturing and architectural statements, Silverstein was a practical guy and knew the building had to appeal to potential tenants if he was to make a profit on his investment.

But there were many other demands to juggle as well. The families of the victims insisted on retaining the sacred ground of the footprints of the Twin Towers, and the city planners wanted closed streets to be reopened through the old sixteen-acre World Trade Center superblock. The Port Authority wanted to build a new subway terminal for its PATH trains. They envisioned a soaring edifice of glass designed by the famed Spanish architect Santiago Calatrava. Like Childs, Calatrava would have to satisfy the master planner Libeskind while designing the details of the massive subway terminal. All of these competing factors—the reopened streets, the large subway terminal, the sacred ground of the original tower footprints, and the space needed for a planned performing arts center and Freedom Center—pushed the Freedom Tower into the far northeast corner of the site.

These considerations, along with my own understanding of the prospective building's vulnerabilities, were layered in my mind as I settled into a chair in Silverstein's conference room. He offered me coffee and warm freshly baked cookies from a private kitchen high above the din of midtown traffic. I gladly accepted (more from curiosity than hunger) and again compared this delicious snack to the jumbo-sized box of stale animal crackers that was available to guests at my office back at One Police Plaza. I was thinking to myself that in five days, on July 4, Silverstein, Governor Pataki, and the mayor were scheduled to lay the cornerstone of this $1.5 billion building with great public fanfare. Only a few weeks before, when I'd been briefed on the design for the first time, I was immediately horrified by its implications for the building itself, not to mention the rest of lower Manhattan. As I finished my cookie, I thought once again, *Do I really need to go down this road?* But I knew what I had to do.

After a few pleasantries, I took a deep breath and opened the substantive part of the meeting. "Mr. Silverstein," I began, "when the Freedom Tower is completed it will be the number one terrorist target in the world, bar none." Silverstein didn't flinch. I paused and continued with my basic concerns. "The White House, Pentagon, and Congress are also top-tier targets of al Qaeda and associated groups, but they've got the advantage of enormous standoff from their adjacent streets and massive security perimeters." (In fact, the section of Pennsylvania Avenue in front of the White House, which was a major D.C. thoroughfare, was closed in 1999, two years prior to 9/11.) I added a few more warnings about the terrorist threat in an attempt to establish my credentials as someone who'd studied and analyzed this threat for the better part of his career.

I concluded with the position I'd hold for the ensuing ten months: the design of the building was extremely problematic. The Freedom Tower was projected to be a glass structure that stood only twenty-five feet from West Street, a major six-lane highway that connects Brooklyn to lower Manhattan via the Brooklyn-Battery Tunnel. Hundreds of massive trucks would rumble by the building daily, and it would be impossible to inspect them for improvised bombs. I recognized that the architects had designed a very strong core that would resist catastrophic collapse ("pancaking") of the floors of the buildings, but even a moderate-sized truck bomb would be devastating to the building's inhabitants. In addition, the building would probably need to be demolished after an attack, thereby achieving a terrorist's objectives to not only take lives but destroy the building and paralyze the financial center of the Western world. I was also concerned that lower Manhattan and perhaps all of New York City couldn't stand another blow to its financial heart. People and businesses would simply move elsewhere. Suffice to say, the security of this building had implications that extended far beyond its own foundation.

The Battle over the Freedom Tower

After rolling this bureaucratic grenade into Mr. Silverstein's conference room, I knew I was in for trouble. But Silverstein, to my surprise, was calm and polite; he understood the problem immediately. Governor Pataki was expecting to see an iron superstructure reaching up into the skies of lower Manhattan by the end of the year. As I got back in the car with Detective Jimmy Fogarty and headed back downtown, I was determined to get my arguments well in line, for although I was confident the Freedom Tower's design was critically flawed, I would have a lot of people challenging my judgment. My arguments would have to be airtight if they were to stand up against some of the most highly paid consultants and powerful people in the city.

Over the next several months, I met with many people regarding the Freedom Tower design, including clueless bureaucrats from the Port Authority, brilliant but constrained design consultants, and city and state officials, including Mayor Bloomberg. Although the mayor was trotted out for some joint appearances, the state of New York, the Port Authority, and the Lower Manhattan Development Corporation were the main overseers of the overall plan at the WTC site. Silverstein had the power of ownership, but even he had limited ability to make decisions.

During the summer of 2004, I attended several meetings chaired by midlevel Port Authority officials who presented briefs, created by high-powered, well-paid consultants, defending the design plan. After about three meetings in which these officials kept repeating the same challenges to my concerns, I realized that they'd come to one of the following conclusions about me: (1) I was wrong about my assessment of the Freedom Tower, (2) I would fold under pressure, or (3) I would just fade away over time, as most bureaucrats do.

At one point in the process, I knew it was time to play hardball. One of the Port Authority's senior executives, a seemingly nice guy and point man for the Authority in dealing with NYPD's nagging issues, indicated that the Authority was beginning to understand the problem of erecting a building that would be exposed to the street. Even so, he implied that it was too late to move the building, hence it would be NYPD's job to protect it. That's when my fuse began to burn. After all of my pesky questions, they generally acknowledged that there was a problem and then tried to deflect onto NYPD the security challenge of what I knew was a bomb magnet. That's when I almost exploded, but instead I gathered my composure and headed back to One Police Plaza to regroup. How was I to tell Kelly that not only was the building going to be a disaster waiting to happen but that NYPD was going to have to protect it?

When I arrived the next morning for my ritual meeting with Kelly and Cohen, they were completely supportive of my position. Kelly understood the basics immediately: the Freedom Tower was an irresistible target for al Qaeda, and so we'd have to stand our ground in blocking its current design plan. With my boss and partner in my camp, I retreated to my office and prepared the most effective bureaucratic weapon at my disposal: the formal letter. I drafted it, Kelly approved it, and I sent it to the Port Authority on August 31, 2004. I waited but got no reply, and was later told by their offices that they never received the letter. So I sent another letter, this time via registered mail with courtesy copies to several other key players. Although still a private letter, some of it was released to the press.

The letter expressed my dismay that the Port Authority had postponed a meeting to assess the potential risk and vulnerabilities of the site, and recommended "we expedite our discussions of these security and design issues before construction proceeds any further." I also noted that the building's vulnerabilities must be addressed in "the design and construction phases, rather than making modifications after the fact."

The issue was now in writing and all involved finally understood that our concerns could no longer be ignored. The next several months were painful, and we seemed to be making no progress. By the end of 2004, the governor's people had very artfully pulled a bureaucratic jujitsu maneuver and basically laid the responsibility for redesigning the Tower on us (otherwise presumably it would go forward as planned). Mayor Bloomberg got into the process by coming up with some ideas of his own that were actually quite creative but were ultimately rejected by the Port Authority as too expensive or otherwise unworkable.

At the end of the year, Mayor Bloomberg asked us to come up with some solutions to the dilemma. I responded with a two-page memo that included Bloomberg's option to build an aboveground tunnel around the Freedom Tower as well as two other options that involved moving the tower back from the street and building the street belowground or building a tunnel in front of West

Street, the major highway that passed by the Tower. None of these ideas went anywhere, and we were drifting into deadlock.

Meanwhile, Silverstein's people were getting desperate. To his credit, Silverstein asked for a meeting with Kelly to make one final pitch for his current plan, with his team of consultants leading the way. Kelly accepted his request for a meeting, but as always, he had a plan. He asked me to round up a group of our own outside experts to weigh in on the matter (and, we hoped, agree with our position). I quickly assembled a group with impeccable credentials. The group was led by Brian Jenkins of the RAND Corporation, perhaps the world's foremost terrorism expert. Cofer Black, a former CIA officer who'd just retired from my old job as ambassador for counterterrorism at the State Department, also kindly agreed to join. He gave our group tremendous insight on the immediate threat. We also got Jameel Ahmad, the chair of the Department of Civil Engineering at Cooper Union, who happened to be the former professor of one of Silverstein's key consultants. John Weathersby, a Ph.D. from the Idaho National Laboratory and an expert on bombs and bomb blast mitigation, gave us the scientific depth to handle any counterattack from Silverstein's consultants. Finally, we capped off our lineup with an active-duty CIA official who was an expert in current al Qaeda bomb-making capability. It was a formidable team.

The next meeting with Silverstein was held in the Federal Reserve building, another posh New York office building. Silverstein's team briefed our team on their plan as it had been laid out to me six months before. Nothing had changed. To my great relief, the team of experts we'd assembled not only seconded my analysis but upped the ante with an even more blistering critique of the building plan. Jenkins decimated the concept in his erudite, smooth baritone, and Cofer Black, in his inimitable blunt style, made my assessments of al Qaeda's intentions for the Tower seem tame in comparison. Although it wasn't apparent at the time, it later became obvious that Silverstein knew right then that he had a problem, and immediately set out to solve it without whining to us.

The Turning Point: This Isn't Your Average Building

But my problem wasn't over. The pressure was still on me to come up with a solution to a building I was beginning to feel should not be built at all. We were again tasked with finding a solution to the problem. I huddled with my two principal confidants on this project, John Colgan and Mike O'Neil. We collectively came up with the idea to give a presentation on the threat and some standards that should be applied to such a special project. I began to personally draft the body of the report, and Chief Colgan, Mike O'Neil, and the team out in Brooklyn began to flesh out the numbers. The report had two parts: a narrative that was a summary of the basic argument I'd been making for over six months, and a description of federal standards for designing special buildings.

The initial draft that I took to Commissioner Kelly was prepared as a PowerPoint presentation. Meanwhile, the investment banking firm Goldman Sachs caught wind of the controversy and decided to back out of a major development project across the street from the Freedom Tower. I was devastated. This was what I was trying to prevent in blocking the Freedom Tower plan: the loss of investor confidence in rebuilding in lower Manhattan that would result if a third attack was sustained. Now it appeared that a huge investor was backing out because of the potential for another attack. Kelly was calmer than I. He sensed that Goldman Sachs would stay, no matter how sincerely they insisted that they wouldn't. I wasn't sure that they would.

End of Story

On May 4, 2005, Governor Pataki, who was getting roasted in the press over the entire downtown project, convened a meeting with Silverstein, Port Authority officials, Mayor Bloomberg, and Commissioner Kelly in the governor's New York City office. Silverstein and his team were a bit late arriving and while the rest of us hung out in the conference room waiting for him, the tension in the air was palpable. The conference room was filled with Pataki memorabilia—man-of-the-year plaques and other "grip-and-grin" photo ops with local politicians—in an arrangement that we in the Special Forces referred to as an "I-love-me wall." Bloomberg and Pataki chatted it up while Kelly and I stood stone-faced. Silverstein finally arrived and we all took our places around the conference table. Silverstein opened the meeting with a showstopper: "We have read the recommendations of the police department and accept them in full. The Freedom Tower, as we formerly knew it, no longer exists. It will be completely redesigned." In retrospect, I could see Silverstein was a bit relieved by the outcome. He'd never really liked the original design, and although this one would cost him more money to build, he would get to design it with his new team of architects. And it's going to be magnificent.

Epilogue: Beauty and the Beast

In the end, David Childs and his very able team at Skidmore, Owings & Merrill designed a building that would withstand an enormous blast from a truck bomb. They also incorporated hugely expensive design features to ensure the safety of the building's inhabitants in a way that no other building in the world did. We'd won the battle, but it wasn't anything to celebrate. I didn't like the fortress-like design of the lower floors, and I was still concerned about the tower's height—would it beckon another aviation attack?

Our victory with the Freedom Tower was followed by some acrimony. In a press conference following the decision, Governor Pataki said New York would never "run from terrorists," insinuating that perhaps Kelly and I were cowards. Both of us are combat veterans, and as you can imagine, we didn't appreciate the comment from the governor, but we just turned the other cheek.

Although I'll probably always be unsettled by the security challenge's it poses for NYPD, the new ground zero plan is nothing short of spectacular, and Pataki and his team can be proud of the Freedom Tower when it's finally completed. The job of protecting it, however, will fall to NYPD's future leadership. I hope I made it a little easier for them—and perhaps decreased the chances that another terrorist cell will stage attack number three at that hallowed site.

Prudent Defense and Deterrence

While at NYPD I spent a lot of time talking to corporate leaders and their security personnel about the terrorist threat. Most I told not to worry; although New York City was still a main terrorist target, their particular property was probably not high on the list. There were many individuals, however, to whom I recommended precautionary measures. These big banks, other financial institutions, landmark buildings, and other classic al Qaeda targets were advised to put in place some basic security procedures. This included the screening of underground parking or the screening of vehicles entering the parking areas. Some buildings were advised to install bollards, those heavy posts that prevent a truck from penetrating a building and magnifying the blast effect of a truck bomb. We often recommended that high-profile buildings employ a front-door security package to manage the access of personnel and packages into the building.

I reminded some of the bigger targets that terrorists will evaluate their security, and if it was obviously strong, they'll pick an easier target. For example, as I mentioned in Chapter 2, in 2002 an al Qaeda cell in Turkey was tasked by bin Laden to hit American targets in Turkey, preferably the American air base at Incirlik, or Israeli ships docked in Mediterranean ports. Due to security concerns, these targets were deemed too difficult and the terrorists instead picked softer targets.[1]

Partly as a result of the Freedom Tower battle, NYPD developed a fairly impressive level of expertise in protecting vulnerable sites. Again, it was a tribute to Kelly's vision, the talent within NYPD, and the "get it done" mentality of Colgan and O'Neil. As part of this process, the Bureau of Counter Terrorism created a blast mitigation and bomb analysis unit. Commanded by NYPD Sergeant Art

Mogil—who has a U.S. Army Special Forces background—the unit has received training from some of the best sources in the world and includes a specially tailored course in bomb blast mitigation by the head of Cooper Union's Department of Civil Engineering, Jameel Ahmad—who, by the way, was born in Pakistan and received his Ph.D. from the University of Pennsylvania. Is it unusual for a Pakistani Muslim to work with a police force in this new era of counterterrorism? Not at NYPD. We embraced Ahmad, and he embraced the Department. This unit's mission was to track terrorist bomb capability and advise NYPD and the private sector on how to prudently protect the city's key assets.

Defense is an important part of a CT strategy, especially for special critical infrastructure, but I'd never expect other buildings to be built to the specifications of the Freedom Tower. All the other buildings in New York City require a much lower degree of protection, commensurate with the threat level for each building. The vast majority of buildings need only be designed to safety codes for normal construction. But for those targets that beckon al Qaeda—such as the Freedom Tower, the White House, the Pentagon, and major centers of economic activity—the appropriate investment must be made to deter an attack.

Chapter 13

Crush the Cell

Tidbits and Outrages

My friend Marianne Chambers, who worked for the U.S. Congress back in the 1980s and 1990s, would periodically produce and circulate an informal document called "Tidbits and Outrages." I always looked forward to reading this collection of humorous and at times biting vignettes about the silliness and wastefulness that goes on in Washington. It was a great little rant. This chapter contains my own version of "Tidbits and Outrages" pertaining to the most ineffectual and wasteful counterterrorism programs that have been initiated since 9/11. I've got plenty of material to work with, but I'll keep it to just a few of my pet peeves—just enough for you to get a sense of the foolishness that characterizes much of our national budget, followed by my suggestions regarding what we should really be focusing on to counter the current threat of terrorism.

I'll start with the U.S. military because that's closest to home for me. Prior to 9/11, as a retired career military officer, I was able to enter all military bases by showing my ID card at the gate. Some bases were even open to the general public back then. Sadly, those days are over. Last summer, when I approached the Marine Annex near the Pentagon in a rental car, I was first stopped by a Marine in uniform who checked my military ID card and directed me to another line because the rental car had no Department of Defense decal. In the other line, my car was inspected by contract guards who ordered me to get out of the car, open up all four doors, the engine hood, the trunk, the glove box, and my suitcase. They inspected my car and rifled through my dirty laundry before they allowed me to pass. Across the street stands a high-rise Sheraton Hotel. It has no protection, only a doorman in a red jacket who is usually busy chasing down taxis. Here's the logic: since 9/11, the military has had an almost unlimited budget, including an enormous security budget earmarked for protecting the force in its bases, so why not batten down the hatches at every base? The Pentagon cites the targeting of U.S. military facilities as the reason for tight security. But hotels have been attacked by terrorists around the world as well, and at least as often as U.S. military bases. But because the hotel has to pay for its own protection, security there is almost nil. In this case, the multistory Sheraton Hotel is actually a much better terrorist target than a rather nondescript military base near the Pentagon.

Another infamous security program is that at the Statue of Liberty. The Statue of Liberty is on a small island off the tip of Manhattan, accessible only by boat. There are no vehicles on the island except those belonging to park police. The statue is a massive metallic structure sitting atop a multistory concrete structure the size of a city block. A truck bomb would have a hard time damaging the statue, even if you could get a truck on the island. The tourists are spread out around the island and do not present a very good target for a would-be terrorist. Ironically, by far the most attractive terrorist target associated with the Statue of Liberty is the security line at the Battery Park ferry terminal. Here hundreds of tourists waiting to board ferries to Liberty Island are packed together in a queue that doubles back on itself, not unlike the security line at an airport. But the statue is iconic, you may say. Yes, but the city is filled with attractive targets that are much more accessible for a terrorist and would have far greater impact on the city. But again, the extra security is paid for by federal taxpayers (in this case the National Park Service), so the security is not surprising as compared to that at private-sector targets that must pay their own way. The security line at the ferry terminal represents a classic over-the-top procedure that is designed to look good but which actually creates another more vulnerable target.

Perhaps even worse than this is the increasing number of Washington officials rushing around the capital city (mostly to and from work and nighttime social events) in black SUVs and with a half-dozen highly trained and well-paid armed guards wearing radios in their ears. These officials have an overblown sense of importance, as only a handful of them are even remote targets for terrorists. Even if they were targets, these details would provide only minimal protection. But it has become a major perk of office, and they have become increasingly accustomed to being zipped through traffic and having doors opened and crowds parted as they go about their important and busy days of Washington meetings, photo ops, and fancy dinners. I believe this contributes to the arrogance that begins to seep into the souls of public officials who isolate themselves in the rarefied air of official Washington for too long.

These examples are small in terms of our national budget but are emblematic of the waste, abuse, hubris, and isolation that affect the government I have so long served. It's important to periodically review the initiatives we've taken since 9/11 and weed out any that haven't significantly contributed to our security. In doing so, I don't mean to disparage those who work on these efforts. In fact, I've been a part of a few less than stellar programs in my career, and if I return to government work someday, I could find myself engaging in some of my own follies. I've certainly made my share of mistakes on programs that bore little or no fruit. But that makes me all the more eager to root out the dead weight in our national counterterrorism apparatus.

I'll just cut to the chase with regard to the top three most wasteful features of the CT agenda. The following programs each involve a huge expense of time and money but haven't contributed in any measurable way to our national security: (1) the creation of the Department of Homeland Security, (2) the creation of the Director of National Intelligence, and (3) the enormous expansion of FBI and CIA budgets.

The Department of Homeland Security (Not Really)

The Department of Homeland Security was a bad idea. I have some very good friends and former colleagues working hard in that ill-conceived agency and I don't mean to belittle their service, for they're every bit as committed to the security of this country as I am. The problem with DHS isn't the people, it's the Department itself. DHS is a hodgepodge of many different agencies, some old and some new. Its primary focus, counterterrorism, places it in perpetual conflict with FBI and dilutes the strength, focus, and independence of the Federal Emergency Management Agency (FEMA). Folding FEMA into DHS and burying it in the Washington bureaucracy damaged an important agency and contributed significantly to the fiasco in New Orleans after Hurricane Katrina. My first recommendation regarding DHS is to make FEMA independent again and accountable directly to the president for major disaster management, whether such events are created by terrorists or by nature. The DHS secretary must remain focused on protecting our borders, a full-time job, and not be chasing the latest flood, hurricane, or wildfire, which is also a full-time job.

Second, as I suggested previously, I would focus DHS's mission on their core competency of border protection, including immigration, customs, transportation security, and guarding our coastline and call it the Department of Border and Transportation Security. I'd move all of the extraneous and largely ineffectual projects that DHS handles, such as support to state and local offices and critical infrastructure protection, back to the White House Office of Homeland Security. DHS needs a clearly defined mission to protect our air, land, and sea borders from terrorism, drugs, disease, illegal commerce, and any other threat to our physical and economic well-being. Domestic counterterrorism remains FBI's job, and they should be held accountable for that function. DHS should stop pretending it has the lead role in domestic counterterrorism and focus its CT efforts at our border, where it has assets and a clear mandate resides. I would then unify this new agency in much the way DOD was unified in 1986 by the Goldwater-Nichols Act. This legislation truly unified the Pentagon (the Joint Staff) and the services in the field; prior to this historic act, the Army, Navy, and Air Force ran fairly independent operations. As with the military services, the Coast Guard could keep its uniform and distinct identity and history, but its budget and operational control would be pulled into a new and truly integrated agency alongside its partners at customs and immigration. A newly organized and focused DHS (or "DBTS") could be a vital and important organization protecting our national borders, not the fragmented, bloated mess it currently is.

The Director of National Intelligence (Not Really)

The Director of National Intelligence (DNI) isn't really that; instead his title should be "the coordinator of information sharing and the chief cajoler of those agencies that actually collect intelligence and run real intelligence operations." DNI does not really run intelligence operations; those are run by FBI domestically and CIA on the international front. FBI, which reports to the attorney general, functions completely independent of DNI, and while CIA is nominally under DNI, on a day-to-day basis the director of CIA still manages the clandestine service, which is the heart of our international counterterrorism effort. CIA runs its own operations out of its headquarters in Langley, Virginia, far away from DNI's headquarters at the other end of Washington, on Bolling Air Force Base. Think of putting the secretary of defense in suburban Maryland, miles outside of the Pentagon, and try to convince him that he still runs our military services. This would never happen, but supposedly DNI can manage our intelligence and counterterrorism operations from a remote facility far away from the real operators. Even in the world of e-mail and video conferencing this does not work.

The intent in creating a Director of National Intelligence was to unify the intelligence community. The current DNI, Admiral Mike McConnell, is a smart, thoughtful, and professional career intelligence officer with tremendous integrity. But he's trying to do a big job with very limited authority. If a terrorist hit the United States tomorrow, would it be clear which government agency is in charge? Is it CIA, FBI, DHS, or DNI? This is precisely the problem: everybody and nobody is in charge. The president should be able to point to one person in his cabinet and say, "You're running intelligence operations; go find terrorists and crush their cells, both at home and abroad."

If the intent of our government is to unify intelligence authority and responsibility in the office of DNI, then he should be given full authority over CIA and especially the clandestine service, thereby eliminating the post of director of CIA (the jobs would be combined into one, as originally intended in the 1947 National Security Act that created CIA). New DNI would also have direct line authority (with the power to hire and fire) over the counterterrorism and counterintelligence functions in FBI, dramatically reducing the power of FBI director in domestic counterterrorism operations. Admiral McConnell currently does not have this type of authority over FBI or CIA, the two key counterterrorism operational units.

But I'm not against FBI; in fact, I'm for them. Their task of domestic counterterrorism must be clarified as DHS refocuses on the border. Ideally, the Bureau would report to a new and empowered DNI and would finally be unified with international counterterrorism operations within CIA, for both operations and information sharing. This would be a dramatic and meaningful step, but as much as I hate to say it, it's unlikely to happen. The bureaucratic entrenchment in Washington is just too deep. Nevertheless, another major, catastrophic failure of intelligence on the part of FBI might provide the impetus to effect this type of serious change, or to create a new organization for domestic intelligence similar to what the British have with MI-5.

In addition to this refocusing of FBI's responsibility, I'd recommend that DHS fusion centers, which are a poor duplicate of what FBI JTTFs are already doing, be shut down or merged into the much more serious JTTFs. FBI would be charged to share counterterrorism information with the state and local offices (as they already do in New York City and most of the country now). Right now, those fusion centers in the states are a hopeless distraction from real counterterrorism work and are often the focus of emergency preparedness, a FEMA function. They pride themselves on being inclusive and transparent and then complain when the "real" intelligence from CIA and FBI isn't shared with them. In fact, the real intelligence will never be shared with these centers until they match the security measures of JTTFs (and that would be a complete duplication of effort).

Bigger Budgets Mean Better Protection (Not Really)

Washington logic would have us believe that we solve problems by creating new agencies and spending tons of taxpayers' money. I disagree. As proven by the good work done under tight budgets at NYPD, leadership, focus, creativity, and prudent risk taking are more effective tools in the fight against terrorism than a steady flow of federal taxpayer dollars into already massive bureaucracies. FBI's budget for the 2001 fiscal year was $3.3 billion; by 2006 FBI director Mueller was requesting a budget of $6.04 billion for the 2007 fiscal year.[1] This included a request for $8.8 million toward the construction of a new FBI headquarters annex in Washington, D.C., to accommodate the tremendous personnel growth FBI has experienced since 9/11.

CIA's spending habits are a little more difficult to analyze because they've refused to divulge their budget since 1997. Even in 2007 when President Bush approved a law requiring public disclosure of the national intelligence budget, the House of Representatives promoted an amendment challenging it, citing national security interests as the reason for keeping the budget a secret. According to recent reports, the spending for all national intelligence operations has doubled in recent years, to a grand total of about $44 billion a year. This is a staggering sum, dwarfing what we spent to counter the Soviet empire with its massive Red Army and nuclear arsenal during the Cold War and fighting a war in Vietnam with over half a million troops deployed.

Notwithstanding these tremendous budget increases, the most important work in protecting our country since 9/11 has been accomplished with the capacity that was in place when the event happened, not with any of the new capability bought since 9/11. I firmly believe that those huge budget increases have not significantly contributed to our post-9/11 security. Of course, over time, these gargantuan budgets *will* enhance our capability, but the cost-benefit ratio does not compute favorably. The big wins had little to do with new programs. CIA's crowning achievement was the takedown of Afghanistan, conducted only months after 9/11 with the same people and organization that existed before. What made the difference was that CIA was finally unleashed in Afghanistan and around the world. The same holds true for FBI: most of the productive work after 9/11 was done within the existing infrastructure, but newly focused on al Qaeda and guided by the Patriot Act. Based on my experience in New York City, I'd say that all of the post-9/11 increases in FBI's counterterrorism business could have been supplied from existing resources within the New York office. Only about one-quarter of the agents in New York were assigned to counterterrorism, and quite frankly, nobody in NYPD could figure out what the rest were doing to stay busy, aside from periodically arresting a geriatric Mafia kingpin. New missions could easily have been taken from current units by shifting priorities rather than spending more money.

The next president should start off his or her counterterrorism effort by asking each agency (primarily CIA and FBI) to delineate its top layer of activity, representing at least 10 percent of the budget, that contributes to defending our nation from terrorist threats. Then, like most businesses that have to balance a budget, these agencies should put more resources into the high-value, high-payoff activity, eliminating the low-value, low-payoff activity. Of course, each agency will scream that everything they do is critical and to cut anything would seriously jeopardize our national security, thereby placing the blame for future failure on anyone who dares to challenge a budget increase. That kind of nonsense shouldn't be tolerated.

More isn't necessarily better. I remember what Mike O'Neil, who runs the counterterrorism unit at NYPD, told me: "Commissioner, I'd rather have a handful of quality people and get rid of the deadwood," he said. "The deadwood just distracts me and the people trying to get the job done." During our time together we worked hard to build the right-sized unit, not the biggest unit. Dave Cohen also shrank the Intelligence Division at NYPD in total numbers while creating a new and more creative organization. He did it by eliminating low-value work and focusing the good people he had on the task at hand. Meanwhile, even as NYPD got smaller overall and new counterterrorism functions were added, crime rates continued to drop. It bears repeating: more isn't always better.

What Is Working and What Is Needed?

As we assess the future of CT policy and programs, it is important to ask ourselves what has worked thus far. Beyond the obvious and important impact of the Afghan takedown, the basic intelligence work by law enforcement and intelligence operatives has made the biggest difference. American police and intelligence agents have been alert to the threat since 9/11, and it's they who've crushed the cells attempting to strike us again. U.S. intelligence has been very successful in identifying potential attackers before they can mount an attack in the West, and U.S. military forces have neutralized their capabilities around the globe. Significantly, I'm not aware of any attacks that were intercepted by defensive measures such as detectors, screenings, or patrols. Defeating terrorism has been all about finding and crushing the cells—at home and abroad. Truly, when it comes to al Qaeda, our best defense is a good offense.

Intelligence and law enforcement operations have not completely eliminated the threat, that's for sure. The bad news is that al Qaeda and other terrorist groups are clearly in ascendancy in Iraq, Afghanistan, and eastern Pakistan, and their hateful ideology is establishing deep roots in the West and around the world. It remains to be seen how much of this activity will morph into operational capability in the United States or against our vital interests overseas. Our challenge is to understand that threat and crush it before it can rise to the occasion.

Are We Ready for the Next Attack?

Unless there is another major terrorist attack, I don't anticipate that the election of a new American president of whatever party in 2008 will significantly change the way we conduct our counterterrorism business. New people will enter and there will be some tinkering around the edges, but our national structures and budgets will probably remain in place. The congressional and executive momentum is hard to shift in the short term.

So my recommendations for improving our counterterrorism efforts are offered with the full recognition that they'll have little chance of being implemented unless there's another terrorist attack and a major shake-up is mandated by the government, Congress, and the American people. Again, my primary proposals focus on two areas: revamping our intelligence collection operations and assigning clear responsibility and accountability within our national agencies.

I always try to cut through the political rhetoric surrounding the terrorism issue. Even so, I realize that I'll probably be criticized by terrorism pundits on both ends of the political spectrum. As I stated at this book's beginning, the "terrorism hype" crowd will claim that I minimize and dangerously underestimate the threat. Others will claim that my recommendations are naive because terrorism will never abate if we don't address the root causes that generate frustration, humiliation, and resentment toward America. Others who are vested in multibillion-dollar programs will argue that my approach leaves valuable infrastructure unprotected. And some will worry that my recommendations would encourage CIA, FBI, and local law enforcement to trample on our civil liberties.

To all of my critics, let me state in unambiguous terms: I *do* expect terrorists to attack us again, and I expect that al Qaeda will be actively seeking the destruction of the United States for another generation, perhaps two, before it fizzles out. However, I also believe that if we stay focused and relentless in our determination to find and crush their cells, we can limit their threat to the occasional tragic but strategically insignificant attack, and accelerate their inevitable decline into a marginalized menace. But if we reduce the pressure being applied to these cells and their organizations, they'll eventually acquire dangerous materials for even more devastating attacks, or establish an infrastructure that can sustain long-term attacks against our nation. My recommendations are firmly rooted in and shaped by this reality, and I welcome a healthy debate of these ideas, for I certainly don't think I have all the right answers. All I ask is that my critics stand on this same ground as they take potshots at my CT strategy.

The costs of an ideal offensive strategy are relatively small in terms of budgetary allocations. The real issue lies in aversion to the idea of spying at home and in dealing with unsavory intelligence organizations abroad. The challenge is to create innovative and risk-taking programs that operate within the law, have strong oversight, and allow for an occasional failure of execution. If we overly constrain CIA, FBI, NSA, and other players such as NYPD, we will find ourselves conducting another 9/11 Commission in a few years, wondering how another catastrophe could have occurred on our shores.

The effectiveness of defensive strategies such as opening up all of our containerized shipping, strangling our petrochemical industries with regulatory requirements, and barricading ourselves and our government institutions behind barriers must be carefully scrutinized. These defenses are often modern versions of the Maginot Line built by the French after World War I, which was so easily bypassed by the Nazi military machine. Walls around our critical infrastructure will also be easily bypassed if terrorist cells are able to organize a plot and construct a weapon. Getting to a good target is relatively easy; we must stop the terrorists *before* they get to that point. Some targets need to be protected, but we must recognize that not everything can or should be protected; the cost is too prohibitive.

I'll say it again: politicians should not be allowed to "be tough on terrorism" by advocating large capital expenditures (much of which tends to be pork) while ignoring the hard decisions relative to finding cells with domestic and international intelligence and crushing them with lethal force. And the intelligence discussion must focus primarily on the key activity of collecting information, not just the less controversial aspects of sharing that information between agencies. That said, Secretary Chertoff is correct in continuing his defensive focus on commercial aviation. Our airplanes must continue to be protected with tight screening of baggage and travelers, even as people complain about delays at airports. These are necessary measures, considering the continuing interest terrorists show in commercial aviation (and, quite frankly, the delays at most airports have much more to do with overcrowded runways and antiquated air traffic control systems than with security lines).

Key buildings and transportation hubs must be safeguarded from attacks with a variety of measures, but most other infrastructure only needs modest and sensible investments in security programs and technologies. The private sector will continue to find ways to do this in a prudent and cost-effective manner. We shouldn't create an armed-camp feel around our critical infrastructure—a situation that now prevails in Washington, D.C. The U.S. government should provide standards, best practices, and other assistance as necessary, but it should also be cautious not to overreact and spend billions on highly visible but minimally effective measures.

Offensive Strategies

Know the Enemy

Knowing the enemy is a fundamental principle that dates back to ancient war theorists including Sun Tsu in the East and Clausewitz in the West. A deep and thorough understanding of the adversary is critical for victory in all forms of warfare. Unfortunately, since 9/11, a plethora of "terrorism experts" have founded their analysis on guesswork rather than a true study of the enemy. The most common trap is to think, "If I were a terrorist, I would do this." We must base our analysis of the enemy on a careful study of how *they* operate and what *they* say, not on idle speculation.

One of the most common notions that arises during these speculations is the concept of multiple attacks on shopping malls during a busy shopping season, such as Christmas. Such a widespread assault would paralyze our economy since people would stay home from the malls during this critical period for our nation's retailers. Most "experts" predicted that this type of attack was inevitable. However, there are several problems with their analysis. First, it's not easy to conduct simultaneous attacks across the country. A cell large and complex enough to execute such an attack would be very vulnerable to penetration in the post-9/11 American environment. If it were easy, the terrorists would have done it already. Second, and more important, this type of speculation encourages the self-paralysis that the terrorists hope to achieve with relatively modest attacks. By whipping ourselves into a frenzy before and after an attack, we amplify the attack's impact. I always find it ironic that in continuing to hype the threat, the so-called tough guys of counterterrorism are unwittingly contributing to their own self-fulfilling prophecies of doom.

I don't think we should stand down after the next terrorist attack, even if the enemy strikes four or five malls across the country—and with the proper leadership, I don't think the country *would.* In estimating the strength of terrorists, we should never underestimate the courage and resiliency of the American people. Ultimately, I don't believe we'll cower to terrorists who are able to occasionally take advantage of our open society and kill our citizens. I hope that by understanding the real threats and the hype, Americans will be better able to distinguish between an existential threat to our well-being and a problem that can be managed.

To know the terrorist requires the study of his history and the analysis of his true modus operandi. "Experts" who don't know the history, the ideology, or even the current capabilities of radical militant Islam should be stifled. Only when one knows *exactly* who the terrorists are can one begin to project how they may operate. We must know the individuals: leaders, foot soldiers, and supporting cast. They all play an important role. Further, we must know about developments around the world and anticipate how they may manifest themselves from New York to Los Angeles and in between.

Find the Enemy

Intelligence operations are the key to counterterrorism, and human informant networks and communications intercepts are the key to counterterrorism intelligence operations. HUMINT and SIGINT programs are designed to identify the organizations and find the cells and individuals who can conduct terrorist operations. This is the only way to catch the bad guys in the planning stages and thwart their attacks before they can launch them. The use of informants and undercover agents is guided by specific laws as to when and how investigations can be conducted against citizens or residents of the United States. The penetration and collection of information from phones and computers also is legally bound. As I've said, the collection of data in the United States requires a warrant; the collection of data overseas does not. While maintaining sensitivity to our civil liberties, these vital counterterrorism programs must be kept alive and vibrant.

Another crucial point: we must not allow the Internet to become the new Afghanistan, a sanctuary where terrorists are indoctrinated, network with one another, and learn the skills of their deadly trade. We must be very aggressive in monitoring extremist Web sites and chat rooms, and we must shut down Web sites (no matter who runs them) that make available information on bomb making and other forms of violence.

When mistakes are made, it's critical to evaluate the intent of the agents involved. When FBI inspector general finds abuses of the national security letter program to get authority to investigate phone records and financial data, we mustn't jump to unfounded conclusions about abuses against Americans' civil liberties. Yes, these programs are sensitive and press against some of our most cherished rights of privacy. But from my experience with FBI, the results of public overreaction are predictable: under negative scrutiny, agents will go into a shell and do nothing. Left to their own devices, lawyers and overly cautious bureaucrats will dominate the decision-making processes of our intelligence agencies. Those who are most cautious will be rewarded and the leadership of these organizations will be filled with hidebound bureaucrats. Years from now, after an attack, we'll wonder how our intelligence agencies became so hollow.

Unleash and Then Monitor Our Intelligence Agencies

We must assign clear responsibility for intelligence operations abroad. Then we can ensure that CIA coordinates all foreign intelligence and FBI coordinates all domestic intelligence—and that the two coordinate their information, both via DNI and within their own offices. As I've said repeatedly in this book, DHS should focus its intelligence collection at the border, which requires a much more targeted approach.

CIA runs the clandestine service of our international spy activities, conducting spy operations against our enemies and coordinating the spy activities of our friends. CIA must become more flexible in recruiting and managing informants to penetrate terrorist organizations. We should be running informants up the terrorist organizations from every corner of the world, both with our own operatives and in cooperation with local intelligence operations. This isn't nearly as complex a task as penetrating the Soviet spy service (KGB) was during the Cold War. Al Qaeda has very limited, if any, counterspy activity against the United States at this time and is in many ways very vulnerable to penetration. But it takes initiative, a bit of boldness, and the willingness to make some honest mistakes. This type of culture needs to be instilled in CIA if we expect the Agency to find our enemies before they attack us.

NSA plays a critical role in finding terrorists. They shouldn't be strangled by pinheaded bureaucrats, overly cautious lawyers, and a lack of initiative from the ranks of the organization. Yes, we need safeguards to ensure NSA doesn't abuse its power, but there is no indication that they're intentionally aiming to do anything other than find terrorists. That's important, for if they were to be found abusing their powers, they'd deserve all the criticism they've been getting. What we need is an aggressive system of congressional oversight so that NSA can do their job.

The Department of Homeland Security also needs to further develop its HUMINT programs so that it can run counterterrorism investigations at our seaports, airports, and borders. Currently, if a counterterrorism investigation is run by DHS in the field, DHS staff are obligated to roll their operation into FBI activities. This must be changed. DHS agencies, especially Immigration and Customs Investigations Enforcement, must be able to run their own independent counterterrorism operations. ICE should penetrate human smuggling operations to find possible links to terrorist organizations. Smugglers should be aware that there'll be severe consequences for smuggling individuals associated with terrorist activity. Reward programs should be established for individuals who report suspected terrorists. The primary effort: crush any cell that helps terrorists slip across our borders. These operations should be coordinated with and not stifled by FBI.

The most important elements of the Patriot Act enable FBI and other agencies (such as NYPD) to open up investigations against suspected terrorist cells. If there are concerns over civil liberties, we should build in oversight protections, not water down intelligence collection. If our middle-level managers lose their initiative for fear of retribution, they'll revert back to the pre-9/11 timidity that enabled al Qaeda to operate successfully here.

Crush the Cell

Once you know your enemies and can find them, you must render them ineffective. That means putting relentless pressure on both their leadership and their rank-and-file membership, and also limiting their ability to assemble, to communicate, and to procure weapons and dangerous materials.

The emphasis must always be on the offensive—and the offensive in counterterrorism is intelligence operations. It is finding and arresting terrorist operatives in Pakistan, New York, or London. It is breaking up cells that recruit and support terrorist operatives. It is the long-term penetration of radical groups. Major military operations are not counterterrorism. In some special circumstances, such as the takedown of the Taliban, military operations are important aspects of counterterrorism policy, but these are rare indeed.

We need aggressive intelligence operations at home and abroad. This generally does not entail big spending, but there's been a reluctance to push forward due to concerns about civil liberties at home and squeamishness relative to working with unsavory partners abroad. The solution is to create an aggressive system of judicial and congressional oversight to ensure that the executive branch stays focused on violent terrorists and nothing else.

Osama bin Laden remains an important ideological leader and facilitator of terrorism. He's also a murderer of innocents and should be captured or, if he resists, killed. We need to take more risks to eliminate the leadership of the organization, such as bin Laden and his deputy Ayman al-Zawahiri. Previous high-value arrests have been major victories in this struggle and shouldn't be minimized. The arrest of regional leaders such as Hambali in Indonesia and the killing of the thug Abu Musab al-Zarqawi in Iraq were important in stifling al Qaeda's ability to project out of its strongholds in Iraq, Afghanistan, and remote areas of Pakistan. We must continue to target the leadership and their key lieutenants. There's a need for prudent risk-taking in these operations. If we insist on a no-risk attack plan, we'll probably arrive too late and too large, and ultimately be ineffective.

Defensive Strategies

PROTECT THE BORDER

At the border, we need to keep terrorists and would-be terrorists from entering or exiting the country. Although homegrown cells are a serious challenge, their effectiveness can be minimized if their operatives aren't allowed to travel to terrorist camps to get training and further indoctrination. The more isolated the would-be terrorists are from foreign operatives, the better.

Fences work to a certain extent to keep people out. Although they can always be penetrated, they'll go a long way toward bringing some level of control to our porous borders. As a young infantry officer, I served in the demilitarized zone of Korea, which has a 155-mile-long patrolled fence that keeps North Korea and South Korea very much separated. If we really want our borders solidified, fences such as this can work. But they work only when both sides take draconian measures, a requirement America may not yet be ready to face.

As we tighten up our coastlines, weekend boaters may have to give up some of their unregulated privileges so that the Coast Guard can track and identify all boats in U.S. waters. The technology exists to enable all ships to emit a beacon that, in addition to helping track terrorists, would also be a tremendous safety feature in situations of distress. The installation of beacons is long overdue.

In addition to better controlling our borders, the establishment of a national identity card would also go a long way in controlling who we allow in our midst. Again, it's no panacea, but the creation of identity cards would help immensely in isolating the purely domestic cells from their much more highly trained and seasoned counterparts abroad. Oddly, Americans don't seem to like the idea of an identity card, even though almost everyone has a driver's license, work ID, Social Security card, and multiple credit cards. France has had a national identification card program since 1940, and twenty-one of the other twenty-seven countries in the European Union have some form of ID card. We need to get over our phobia and create a card program as soon as possible.

Harden Key Vulnerabilities (Transportation, Finance, Special Events)

It's no secret what terrorists generally attack. Their prime target has been transportation: planes, trains, and buses. Their next favorite target is special buildings: government buildings, embassies, financial institutions, or high-profile foreign hotels. They favor large truck bombs against buildings and smaller backpack bombs against transportation. The evil genius of 9/11 lay in targeting transportation and making the vehicle the weapon.

The federal government as well as local governments in large cities will need to work together to protect key buildings without creating an atmosphere of an armed camp. The government will need to continue its partnership with the private sector and the public authorities that man airports, trains, subways, and ferries to establish prudent security measures. Hardening primary and secondary targets doesn't necessarily prevent a terrorist group from attacking, but it helps minimize strategic impact by diverting terrorists to lower-value targets.

Safeguard Dangerous Materials (CBRN and Explosive Materials)

The most important national security objective of the late twentieth and early twenty-first centuries is to prevent the use of nuclear weapons. This requires focusing on nuclear nonproliferation within nation-states, managing our relations with nuclear powers, and preventing any nuclear materials from falling into the hands of terrorists. Counterterrorism officials play a major role in preventing terrorists from acquiring a nuclear weapon.

By crushing terrorist organizations and cells, we make it much more difficult for them to get their hands on chemical, biological, or radiological materials from which they can construct a weapon of mass destruction. If terrorists can't sustain low-level attacks in the United States, they'll have to resort to a weapon of mass destruction to have a strategic impact. This calls for much closer regulation of radiological materials such as cesium-137 and cobalt-60. We also need to protect certain chemicals and the storage of biological pathogens in our research hospitals.

ELIMINATE AREAS OF SANCTUARY (COUNTERINSURGENCY STRATEGY)

The United States can't afford for there to be another terrorist sanctuary like pre-9/11 Afghanistan. In Afghanistan, the Taliban protected al Qaeda from the reach of the United States. If a similar sanctuary is established again, it must be eliminated. With Afghanistan and the Taliban, the United States and the rest of the world were too patient and too concerned about international opinion. If terrorist camps threaten our nation and the host country doesn't deal with them, it is our obligation to do so. However, that scenario isn't likely to emerge again. More likely, we'll be faced with camps emerging in areas that are outside the full authority of a country. These would include remote areas or areas wracked by conflict, such as the Afghanistan-Pakistan border, parts of Iraq, Somalia, Chechnya, or Kashmir. To the extent it can, the United States should try to defuse these conflicts and bring some degree of order to these regions. In the interim, we need good intelligence operations and the ability to work with the local authorities to disrupt terrorist cells. If the locals are unable or unwilling to cooperate, we'll need to do this unilaterally and without apology. In fact, the apologies should come from the harboring nation.

Some of these conflicts are classic insurgencies, as we've been facing in Iraq and Afghanistan. Although our initial efforts in these countries were overwhelmingly military, we've learned the hard way (again) that counterinsurgency strategies require a multiagency effort and a military force structure and doctrine equipped to handle unconventional warfare—not just tanks in the desert.

Don't Terrorize Ourselves

The United States *will* be attacked by terrorists again. I'm not sure when the attack will occur or what its exact shape will be, but I firmly believe that another attack is inevitable. However, as a people and as a nation, the manner in which we respond to the next attack is entirely up to us. Remembering that the primary target of a terrorist attack is our psyche, we should never allow terrorists to have an inordinate impact on our national consciousness. If we do, we play directly into their hands. It's a delicate balance, but we have complete control over our response. Of course, we should express outrage at the attack and sadness at the loss of life it may have caused, but then we must calmly resolve to crush the attackers without panic, hysteria, or overreaction. A controlled reaction should not be confused with complacency; we need to stay focused and relentless, yet at the same time be mindful of our own role in the attack's psychological impact.

In most terrorist attacks, the impact is largely psychological. Even if terrorists strike one of our ports or knock out a major suspension bridge, our economy need not be inordinately disrupted unless we choose to paralyze ourselves in unwarranted panic. America's massive economy is virtually impossible to affect significantly with one physical event. Even after the horrific impact of hurricanes Katrina and Rita in August and September 2005, the nation's economy grew in 2006. It's almost inconceivable that a terrorist attack could have the physical impact of those hurricanes, which virtually destroyed an entire city and shut down the Gulf of Mexico petroleum industry for several days. However, in addition to physical destruction, a terrorist attack engenders psychological fears, which may cause us to terrorize *ourselves*—if we allow it to.

Although the total number of potential terrorist cells in the United States is small, there are enough that one will probably slip through the cracks of our counterterrorism policies and programs. However, I expect that the next attack will be much less horrific than that of September 11, 2001, and certainly nothing of a scale comparable to Hurricane Katrina. Al Qaeda, operating against an alert and focused international and domestic effort, will have a hard time building a cell of the size needed for the 9/11 attack. They may try to launch simultaneous small attacks in multiple locations, but I suspect the next attack will come in the form of a single, midsized attack by an individual cell. The multiple-attacks scenario requires intercell connectivity that may be beyond al Qaeda's current capability in the United States.

Of course, for those killed or injured and their loved ones, a terrorist attack is a tragic event, but the measured response of our political leaders, including the president, Congress, and the local mayor or governor, will determine how quickly the country rebounds from the attack. Al Qaeda's modus operandi indicates that they'll attempt to conduct simultaneous attacks or launch a second attack within a few hours of the initial event. So appropriate levels of increased security will be important as all first responders swing into high alert. However, unless there's specific evidence that the attack is part of a sustained campaign, we should return to normal operating procedures as quickly as possible. What exactly does this mean? It means FBI, CIA, and DHS should operate at their fullest capacity, investigating all potential leads and establishing appropriate security precautions around the country. Obviously, security will be tightened up everywhere, from airplanes to subways, malls, and ports. However, these enhanced measures shouldn't cripple the country. In fact, we should try to return to normal operating conditions as fast as possible. In so doing, we contain the impact of a terrorist strike to the immediate blast radius and strip the acting terrorist organization of its power over us.

After 9/11, NYPD looked around the world for organizations with which to work and discuss the challenges of modern urban terrorism. And it was only natural that we initiated relationships with both Scotland Yard in London and the Israeli National Police, for as I mentioned in the preface, the British and Israelis have lived with the scourge of terrorism for generations. During my first year at NYPD, I went to London personally to get a look at Scotland Yard's new vehicle camera system and I sent a team to Israel to consult with experts there. Although New York City was no stranger to terrorist activity prior to 9/11, we knew that we had a lot to learn from those for whom terrorism is a constant plague.

I sent a second team to Israel a year later that included Mike O'Neil, the very able and experienced Counterterrorism Division commander; Daniel Rudder, who'd written NYPD extremism manual; a civilian analyst, Erin Eizenstat; and another detective. On the second day of the trip NYPD team was alerted that a bomb had exploded near a mall in a neighborhood outside Jerusalem. NYPD team instinctively rushed to the scene, for it's in the DNA of a cop to get to the scene of a crime as soon as possible. Being professionals, they knew their role and made sure to stay out of the way of local investigators. Their mission was to stay plugged into the developing situation and see if there was a New York angle. In this case, the attack was perpetrated by a solitary suicide bomber with no direct or even indirect connection to New York, but Mike O'Neil's detailed report of how the Israelis reacted to the bomb is very illuminating.

Immediately after the bomb exploded, Israeli police and other first responders sprang into action, quickly and efficiently treating the wounded and searching for possible secondary explosions or attacks against the first responders. A crime-scene investigative team sealed off the blast area with yellow tape in much the same way NYPD does, demarcating a police line that only authorized forensic investigators may cross. This was standard procedure to the O'Neil team and would be familiar to the average American TV watcher. However, after the investigators had spent about an hour crawling over the scene on their hands and knees picking up body parts, bomb fragments, and other clues, a portable vacuum cleaner was brought in. O'Neil was initially shocked and concerned that potentially valuable evidence might be lost. But this was the Israelis' method: after the police had conducted a thorough hand and eye search of the ground, they sucked up anything else that might have been missed so it could be brought to the lab in a vacuum bag.

But why so fast? NYPD crime-scene investigators typically close down a scene like this for several days to pick through every possible piece of evidence. O'Neil soon had his answer. In conjunction with the forensic sweep, the Israelis first came through and handled the body parts of the victims in accordance with their religious tradition. Soon afterward, they washed down the crime scene, removing the debris and stains as much as possible. Behind the sweepers, the building was quickly repaired. Plywood was put up where the glass was shattered and, to the extent possible, immediate repairs were made on the storefront. By the next day the mall was open and people were returning to shop.

The Israelis sent many messages with their response. First, to their own population: "These bombs won't defeat us. In fact, they don't even disrupt our way of life. We'll continue to work, to shop, and to invest in Israel. We grieve our dead and wounded with the pain only mothers and family members can know, but we honor their death with life, with resilience against the killers."

The message to the terrorists is equally strong: "Your attack was a waste of life. We have swept off the blood of the suicide bomber just as we've repaired the damage; shortly there will be no evidence of this killer's futile sacrifice. We will continue to live and our economy will continue to expand. Your strategy is ultimately a terrible waste of your own youth." The Israelis were determined not to allow the attack to have an impact beyond the blast radius of the bomb itself.

Contrast this with the American response to 9/11 (although obviously it was a much larger attack). Because we knew how the terrorists had breached our security systems, al Qaeda's ability to replicate this type of attack in the days after 9/11 was virtually zero, yet we still shut down all commercial aviation for four days. In contrast, the British had almost all of their train system up and running within three hours of the attacks of July 7, when three trains and a bus were blown up. Yes, it would have been possible for other attacks to be perpetrated, but the British resolve to get on with life was more important. It's true that our country was in shock following 9/11, but we mustn't allow shock to magnify our response to even the most catastrophic attack. It took almost two years for our economy to recover from 9/11. My argument here is that the psychological effect of the attack, not its physical damage, did the most to harm our economy.

Am I being overly harsh in my criticism of the ways the federal government reacted to 9/11? Perhaps, but it was only because our nation was asleep to the threat of al Qaeda that the thunderclap of the twin towers falling awakened us into a panicked rage. Perhaps overreaction was inevitable, given the spectacular nature of the attack and our role as the sleeping giant. But next time we'll have no excuses. We mustn't allow the next attack to have a greater impact than absolutely necessary. Overreacting gives the terrorists more power and glory than they deserve.

But what if there is more violence on the way? Is it probable that one attack is an indication of much more to come? Not necessarily, unless we find evidence of many more operationally capable cells. I think it's safe to assume, based on al Qaeda's weak performance record in the United States over the past six years, that they do *not* have the capability to sustain further attacks—unless we see clear evidence to the contrary.

Defeating Strategic Terrorism

Terrorism cannot be eliminated from the planet, as some have called for in political rhetoric. Terrorism is a tactic as old as warfare itself, and it will always be an instrument favored by the weak and humiliated. Our goal should be to minimize the impact of terrorism on our lives and to eliminate organizations that can cause strategic damage to the United States and our allies. Al Qaeda has demonstrated that capability in the past and still harbors that intention. They simply must be destroyed as an effective terrorist organization and minimized as a global movement. Al Qaeda is a strong and resilient movement based on the intense grievances of some Islamic radicals, but even so, it can be defeated.

Ultimately, the al Qaeda threat will be defeated at its source: within the Islamic faith. The movement is self-defeating as a result of the moral bankruptcy of its violent methods, and although its ideology has some appeal to those who value Islamic purity and revivalism, it will eventually be rejected by most Muslims. The leadership of most Muslim governments, universities, and mosques will marginalize this small group of fanatics over time. In the interim, we must deal with the immediate threat to our interests and crush those cells that seek our demise. We should try to be as helpful as possible to our Muslim friends who are at the real front line of this threat, and refrain from making the problem worse with ill-conceived anti-Muslim statements, policies, and programs.

Six years after 9/11, there is good news and bad news. First, the good news: al Qaeda has not been able to attack us again inside the United States. Nobody could possibly have predicted this on September 12, 2001, when we looked and felt so vulnerable. In the past six years, al Qaeda has been able to strike the non-Islamic West in only two cities, London and Madrid. Both of those attacks were conducted by local cells with varying levels of connectivity to the central or strategic hub of al Qaeda. No matter how you spin it, and even if they attack again on the day of this book's publication, this isn't an impressive record for an organization that looked so powerful on 9/11. It's important to recognize our success in mitigating al Qaeda's impact on the world—even in the midst of several years of bad news coming out of Iraq and Afghanistan.

In Islamic countries, al Qaeda was initially more active after 9/11, striking in Indonesia, Tunisia, Morocco, Jordan, Saudi Arabia, Turkey, Egypt, and Pakistan. In Russia, Chechnyan terrorists have struck with lethal frequency against airliners, subways, and other targets. In these countries, terrorist cells have suffered from intense pressure brought against them in the wake of these attacks, especially in Saudi Arabia and Pakistan, two countries critical in this struggle. But on the whole, they appear to be in a better position to rebound and sustain operations than in the West.

In the event that the United States sustains another terrorist attack, we must first find and address the killers and their leadership, and then take a closer look at our own leadership. If the attack wasn't part of a strategic threat but falls within the cost of living in a free society—like the disgruntled postal worker who kills five people in his office—we mustn't overreact. In fact, it's in the national best interest to simply get over it. We shouldn't spend huge resources restructuring our international and domestic security apparatus. Instead, we should identify breakdowns in existing counterterrorism programs and hold our national and local leaders accountable as necessary. But before we point the finger of blame, we must distinguish between systemic flaws and failures in leadership, and also factor in the cost of living in an open society in a world where there'll always be a few maniacal killers. If there's been a failure of leadership, those at fault should be fired or voted out of office. If the attacks are sustained over time, then perhaps wholesale change may be required and new leaders should be appointed with a mandate for dramatic change. But adding another national bureaucracy is generally not the solution.

It is time to put the terrorist threat in perspective. Many Americans have grown tired of the endless speculation and posturing regarding the so-called war on terror. The reality is fairly simple: There is a small and determined group of killers out there. They reside both here at home and abroad. They're bent on attacking the United States and our interests, and unfortunately, they're not going to go away anytime soon. No matter what leaders we elect or appoint, no matter what policies we develop, this small and determined group will be set on attacking us for at least another twenty years, probably longer. But we must remember that they're not everywhere and they're not all-powerful. They have limitations—personal, organizational, and ideological—and they've proven their limits by their inability to attack again in the United States since 9/11.

Until this movement subsides—and it may not go away completely for many generations—al Qaeda and related groups will continue their attempts to kill us. We must find and crush their cells at every opportunity, with focused and relentless determination.

Appendix 1: Sheehan's Career Time Line

1973–1977: Cadet, U.S. Military Academy at West Point, New York.

1977–1978: Infantry Basic Course, Ranger Qualification, Infantry Platoon Leader.

1979: U.S. Army Special Forces Qualification (Green Beret), Fort Bragg, North Carolina.

1979–1982: Detachment Commander of a counterterrorism/hostage rescue unit (A Team). C Company, 3rd Battalion, 7th Special Forces Group (also deployed to Honduras, Dominican Republic, and Ecuador on counterinsurgency and counterterrorism missions), Fort Gulick, Panama.

1980: Colombian Special Forces Qualification (Lancero), Tolemaida, Colombia.

1983–1985: Company Commander, 2nd Infantry Division, Korea.

1985–1986: Counterinsurgency Advisor, Chalatenango, El Salvador.

1986–1988: Masters Degree, Georgetown University (thesis work on counterinsurgency and irregular warfare), Washington, D.C.

1988–1989: Defense Intelligence Agency (Central America/counternarcotics), Washington, D.C.

1989–1991: Intelligence Analyst, International Programs, National Security Council Staff (counternarcotics, low-intensity conflict), White House, Washington, D.C.

1991–1992: Masters Degree, U.S. Army Command and Staff College (thesis work on the history of irregular warfare), Fort Leavenworth, Kansas.

1992–1993: Director of International Programs, National Security Council Staff (peacekeeping operations, Somalia intervention), White House, Washington, D.C.

1993–1995: Special Counselor (peacekeeping operations) to U.S. Permanent Representative, U.S. Mission to the United Nations (deployed to Somalia and Haiti). U.S. Mission to the United Nations, New York City.

1995–1997: Director, Global Issues, National Security Council (UN peacekeeping, the Balkans), White House, Washington, D.C.

1997–1998: Deputy Assistant Secretary, Bureau of International Organization Affairs, State Department (UN affairs, peacekeeping operations), Washington, D.C.

1998–2000: Ambassador at Large for Counterterrorism, U.S. Department of State, Washington, D.C.

2000–2003: Assistant Secretary General for Peacekeeping Operations (mission support), United Nations, New York City.

2003–2006: Deputy Commissioner for Counterterrorism, New York City Police Department, New York City.

2006–2008: Fellow, NYU Center for Law and Security. Fellow, USMA Counterterrorism Center, West Point. Terrorism Analyst, NBC News. Partner, Torch Hill Equity Partners, New York City. CEO, The Lexington Group (Security Consultancy).

Appendix 2: Terrorism's Top Ten

Osama bin Laden: Saudi multimillionaire and founder of al Qaeda. Currently at large and believed to be hiding in Western Pakistan.

Ayman al-Zawahiri: Egyptian-born surgeon who became an early leader of Egyptian Islamic jihad. Zawahiri later became deputy to bin Laden. Still at large.

Hassan al-Banna: Influential mid-twentieth-century Egyptian political activist who founded the Muslim Brotherhood in 1928. Assassinated in 1949 by the Egyptian secret police.

Ramzi Yousef: Chief architect of the 1993 World Trade Center bombing and nephew of Khalid Sheikh Mohammed. Born in Kuwait of Pakistani descent, Yousef is currently imprisoned in the United States.

KSM: Khalid Sheikh Mohammed, senior al Qaeda figure and mastermind of the 9/11 attacks. Like his nephew, Ramzi Yousef, KSM is of Pakistani descent but was born and raised in Kuwait. Currently in U.S. custody.

Hambali: Indonesian al Qaeda terrorist connected to numerous attacks, including the USS *Cole* bombing and 9/11, and mastermind of the 2002 Bali bombings. Currently in U.S. custody.

The Blind Sheik: Omar Abdel Rahman, the Egyptian cleric and longtime Islamic radical who provided the spiritual leadership to al Qaeda and the EIJ. Currently imprisoned in the United States for conspiracy in the first World Trade Center bombing.

Sayyid Qutb: Radical Egyptian author and philosopher who is considered one of the intellectual fathers of the jihadist movement. Executed by Egyptian authorities in 1966.

Hassan Nasrallah: Lebanese cleric and current secretary general of Hezbollah.

Imad Mugniyah: Hezbollah terrorist involved in bombings and kidnappings against Western targets throughout the 1980s and 1990s. Killed in Syria in February 2008.

Appendix 3: Key Terrorist Events

January 1979: **Iranian revolution begins.** Mohammed Reza Pahlavi, Shah of Iran, flees into exile, ushering in the Iranian Revolution.

November 1979: **Iranian embassy crisis begins.** Student militants seize the U.S. embassy in Tehran, beginning a 444-day hostage crisis.

December 1979: **Soviet Union invades Afghanistan.** Invasion triggers a decade-long war that attracts jihadists from all over the globe, including Osama bin Laden and Khalid Sheikh Mohammed.

April 1980: **Iran rescue mission fails.** A secret mission to rescue the American hostages in Tehran fails. The mission is aborted when not enough helicopters make it into Iran. Five airmen and three Marines die in an aircraft crash at the Desert One site inside Iran.

October 1983: **Marine barracks bombed.** A suicide truck bomber strikes a U.S. Marine barracks in Beirut, Lebanon, killing 241 service members. Hezbollah is responsible for the attack. The multinational peace-keeping force that the Marines were a part of is withdrawn from Beirut shortly thereafter.

March 1984: **CIA chief kidnapped by Hezbollah.** William F. Buckley, CIA station chief in Beirut, is kidnapped and dies in captivity more than a year later.

June 1985: **TWA Flight 847 hijacked.** Hezbollah-backed operatives en route from Athens to Rome highjack the plane. During the three-day hostage situation that follows, the hijackers torture and then fatally shoot U.S. Navy diver Robert Dean Stethem.

October 1985: **The *Achille Lauro* hijacked.** Passenger ship is hijacked by terrorists from the Palestine Liberation Front. The hijackers murder wheelchair-bound American passenger Leon Klinghoffer and throw his body overboard.

February 1988: **Marine Lt. Col. William Higgins kidnapped.** Hezbollah-backed terrorists kidnap Higgins in southern Lebanon; he is held captive for more than a year before being murdered.

December 1988: **Pan Am Flight 103 bombed.** 270 people are killed when flight is brought down by an onboard bomb over Lockerbie, Scotland. The incident sparks more than a decade of U.S. and UN sanctions against Libya, whose government ultimately accepts responsibility for the actions of its officials in conducting the bombing.

Summer 1991: **Bin Laden begins to mobilize.** Bin Laden moves from Saudi Arabia to Sudan, where he begins to create his global organization, expanding on his Afghan base.

February 1993: **World Trade Center attacked.** The World Trade Center is bombed by Islamic militant Ramzi Yousef. Yousef employs a truck bomb parked in the facility's underground garage. The explosion kills six and injures more than one thousand; Yousef flees to Pakistan immediately after the attack and remains at large until his capture in Islamabad in 1995.

October 1993: **Mogadishu—Black Hawk Down incident causes U.S. withdrawal from Somalia.** U.S. Army Ranger and Delta personnel in Somalia fight a long gun battle with Somali militia forces in Mogadishu after one of their Black Hawk helicopters is brought down in a daytime raid. Eighteen American soldiers are killed in the fighting; images of Somalis dragging the bodies of several of the dead through the streets of Mogadishu are broadcast worldwide. The incident brings an end to the U.S. presence in the country and leads many to conclude that the United States can no longer tolerate casualties, emboldening terrorist groups like al Qaeda.

May 1996: **Bin Laden leaves Sudan.** Al Qaeda's leader takes refuge in Afghanistan and begins serious planning for global terrorism strikes against the United States.

August 1996: **Bin Laden's first *Fatwa* released**. In effect, bin Laden declares war against America.

February 1998: **Bin Laden's second *Fatwa* released**. Bin Laden preview and justification for his terrorist attacks against the U.S. embassy later in the year.

August 1998: **East African embassy bombed.** Al Qaeda operatives conduct near-simultaneous attacks against American embassies in Dar es Salaam, Tanzania, and Nairobi, Kenya. The blasts kill more than two hundred people and injure thousands, mostly local citizens.

October 2000: **USS *Cole* attacked.** The destroyer USS *Cole* is struck by al Qaeda operatives manning a boat loaded with TNT in the Port of Aden, Yemen, killing seventeen sailors.

September 2001: **9/11 attack launched.** Nineteen al Qaeda operatives simultaneously hijack four airplanes over the United States. Two are crashed into the towers of the World Trade Center, one is crashed into the Pentagon, and one is brought down by the actions of the passengers onboard before hitting the hijackers' intended target. The attacks kill nearly three thousand people.

October 2001: **Afghanistan invaded by SOF and CIA.** After weeks of in-country covert operations by U.S. intelligence and Special Forces personnel, American warplanes begin bombing Taliban strongholds in the al Qaeda safe haven of Afghanistan. The Afghan Northern Alliance begins its march toward the capital with the help of American and British ground troops and advisors. Kabul falls in early November, effectively ending the Taliban's control of the country and beginning a troubled American occupation that continues today.

April 2002: **Truck bomb explodes in Tunisia.** An al Qaeda operative drives a suicide truck bomb into a synagogue on the island of Djerba, Tunisia, killing nineteen.

October 2002: **Bali bombings.** Two suicide bombings at nightclubs in Bali, Indonesia, kill 202 people. Islamic militant group Jemaah Islamiyah is responsible for the attacks.

March 2003: **United States invades Iraq.** After a months-long standoff with Saddam Hussein over a suspected Iraqi WMD program, the United States invades Iraq. The invasion, based on flawed and misused intelligence, is followed by a poorly planned occupation and a bloody civil conflict, fueled in part by foreign terrorist groups like al Qaeda. To date, the war has claimed the lives of nearly four thousand American troops and tens of thousands of Iraqis.

May 2003: **Al Qaeda strikes in Saudi Arabia.** Al Qaeda operatives detonate three truck bombs against Western housing facilities in Riyadh, Saudi Arabia. The bombings kill thirty-five, including nine Americans, and wound hundreds.

May 2003: **Bombs blast Casablanca.** A series of suicide bombings rock Casablanca, Morocco, on the night of May 16. The attackers strike two restaurants, a hotel, a Jewish cemetery, and a Jewish community center, killing forty-five (including twelve bombers). All of the attackers were Moroccans who grew up in the same Casablanca shantytown; it is unclear whether al Qaeda had a major role in the attack, though Moroccan authorities believe the group may have financed it.

August 2003: **Marriot Hotel Jakarta bombing.** A suicide car bomb is detonated outside a Marriot hotel in Jakarta, Indonesia, by an operative from the terrorist group Jemaah Islamiyah. The explosion kills twelve people and injures more than one hundred.

November 2003: **HSBC Bank/British Consulate bombing.** Al Qaeda operatives conduct truck bomb attacks against the HSBC Bank and the British Consulate in Istanbul, Turkey, killing thirty people and injuring hundreds. The attacks followed the bombings of two Istanbul synagogues five days earlier that killed twenty-seven.

March 2004: **Madrid trains bombed.** Islamic militants remotely detonate multiple bombs aboard four separate commuter trains in Madrid, Spain. The explosions kill 191 and injure thousands.

July 2005: **London train system bombed.** Suicide bombers strike the London subway and bus systems, detonating four devices and killing fifty-two commuters. Two weeks later, four more explosives are planted at subway and bus stations, but fail to detonate.

Notes

Chapter 1: Al Qaeda: Killers and Bunglers

1. U.S. Department of State, "Report of the Accountability Review Boards, Bombings of the US Embassies in Nairobi, Kenya and Dar es Salaam, Tanzania on August 7, 1998," January 1999.

2. Commission on Presidential Debates, "Debate Transcript, October 17, 2000: The Third Gore-Bush Presidential Debate."

3. Ibid.

4. Ibid.

5. J. Gilmore Childers and Henry J. DePippo, "Testimony Before the Senate Judiciary Committee Subcommittee on Technology, Terrorism, and Government Information Hearing on Foreign Terrorists in America: Five Years After the World Trade Center, February 24, 1998."

6. Simon Reeve, and Giles Foden, "A New Breed of Terror," *The Guardian,* September 12, 2001.

7. National Commission on Terrorist Attacks upon the United States, *The 9/11 Commission Report,* July 2004, 47.

8. Pamela Constable and Kamran Khan, "Suspect Links Embassy Blast to Saudi Exile," *Washington Post,* Monday, August 17, 1998.

9. CNN, "Crippled *Cole* Awaits Tow Vessel," October 23, 2000.

Chapter 2: Know Your Enemies

1. Central Intelligence Agency, *World Factbook 2007.*

2. BBC News, "Hambali: Asia's bin Laden," September 6, 2006.

3. BBC News, "Bali Death Toll Set at 202," February 19, 2003.

4. "Indonesia Arrests Suspect in Hotel Bombing," *New York Times,* October 30, 2003.

5. Carol Rosenberg, "14 Detainees Upheld as 'Enemy Combatants,'" *Miami Herald,* August 9, 2007.

6. Douglas Jehl and David Johnston, "Threats and Responses: Terror Detainee is Seen as Leader in Plot by Qaeda," *New York Times,* August 6, 2004.

7. Brian Glyn Williams and Feyza Altindag, "El Kaide Turka: Tracing an al-Qaeda Splinter Cell," *Terrorism Monitor,* November 18, 2004.
8. BBC News, "Profile: Muktar Ibrahim," July 11, 2007.
9. Kathryn Haahr, "Spain's 9/11: The Moroccan Connection," *Terrorism Monitor,* July 1, 2004; Jennifer Green, "Sept. 11 Figure Is Convicted in Spain," *Washington Post,* September 27, 2005.

Chapter 3: Al Qaeda's Ideology: Why They Kill

1. National Commission on Terrorist Attacks upon the United States, *The 9/11 Commission Report,* July 2004, 380.
2. Daniel Rudder, "The Evolution of Militant Sunni Ideology," New York Police Department Bureau of Counter Terrorism, September 2005.
3. PBS, "Online Focus: Bin Laden's Fatwa," http://www.pbs.org/newshour/terrorism/international/fatwa_1996.html.
4. Ibid.
5. PBS, "Online Focus: al Qaeda's Fatwa," http://www.pbs.org/newshour/terrorism/international/fatwa_1998.html.
6. Ibid.
7. Ibid.

Chapter 4: Iran and Hezbollah: Bloody but Restrained Terrorists

1. Seymour Hersh, "The Coming Wars," *New Yorker,* January 24, 2005.
2. Office of Senator Chuck Schumer, "Schumer: Subway Expulsions Show That NY Is at Security Risk from Iranian Diplomats; Urges Powell to Clean House at Iran Mission," press release, June 30, 2004.
3. William Finnegan, "The Terrorism Beat," *New Yorker,* July 25, 2005.
4. Sari Horwitz, "Cigarette Smuggling Linked to Terrorism," *Washington Post,* June 8, 2004.
5. Mike Shuster, "Origins of the Sunni-Shia Split," National Public Radio, February 27, 2007.
6. PBS, "Frontline Interview: Robert Oakley," September 2001, http://www.pbs.org/wgbh/pages/frontline/shows/target/interviews/oakley.html.
7. Nazila Fahti, "Translation: Text of Mahmoud Ahmadinejad's Speech," *New York Times,* October 30, 2005.
8. CNN, "Iran: Holocaust Remarks Misunderstood," December 16, 2005.

Chapter 5: Lone Wolves, Cults, and Radical Movements

1. Daniel Gross, "Previous Terror on Wall Street—A Look at a 1920 Bombing," TheStreet.com, September 20, 2001.
2. CBS News, "The Lessons of Oklahoma: Tragic Bombing Alerted Americans to Threat of Domestic Terrorism," April 13, 2000.
3. Leslie Maitland, "Another Act in Terrorism's Deadly Drama," *New York Times,* January 9, 1983.
4. Raphael Cohen-Almagor, "Media Coverage of Acts of Terrorism: Troubling Episodes and Suggested Guidelines," *Canadian Journal of Communication* 30 (2005): 383.
5. "Profile: Timothy McVeigh," BBC News, May 11, 2001, http://news.bbc.co.uk/1/hi/world/americas/1321244.stm.
6. Jo Thomas, "2 Sides of Bombing Suspect Are Depicted as Trail Opens," *New York Times,* November 4, 1997.
7. Jeffrey Gettleman and David Halbfinger, "Suspect in '96 Olympic Bombing and 3 Other Attacks Is Caught," *New York Times,* June 1, 2003.
8. Judith Miller, *Germs: Biological Weapons and America's Secret War* (New York: Simon and Schuster, 2001), 14.
9. James F. Jarboe, "The Threat of Eco-Terrorism: Testimony Before the House Resources Committee, Subcommittee on Forests and Forest Health," February 12, 2002.
10. John Miller, Michael Stone, and Chris Mitchell, *The Cell: Inside the 9/11 Plot and Why the FBI and CIA Failed to Stop It* (New York: Hyperion, 2003).

Chapter 6: The U.S. Army Special Forces: Shooters and Advisors

1. Richard J. Newman, "Hunting War Criminals: The First Account of Secret U.S. Missions in Bosnia," *U.S. News and World Report,* June 28, 1998.
2. National Commission on Terrorist Attacks upon the United States, *The 9/11 Commission Report,* July 2004, 130.

Chapter 7: Door Kickers, Diplomats, and Swamp Drainers

1. Robert Oakley, interview with PBS *Frontline,* September 2001, http://www.pbs.org/wgbh/pages/frontline/shows/target/interviews/oakley.html.
2. Ibid.

Chapter 9: Domestic Intelligence: The Spy Game at Home

1. "Pakistan Native Tried in NYC Subway Plot," Associated Press, April 27, 2006.
2. Matthew Verrinder, "NY Subway Bomb Plotter Gets 30 Years in Prison," Reuters, January 8, 2007.
3. Alan Feuer and William K. Rashbaum, "2 Are Charged in Plot to Bomb Herald Sq. Station," *New York Times,* August 29, 2004.
4. Ibid.
5. William K. Rashbaum, "Terror Jury Hears Talk of Bombing Subway Stop," *New York Times,* April 27, 2006.

Chapter 10: CBRN: Real Danger or Overhyped Threat?

1. "Japan Cultists Sentenced to Death," BBC News, July 17, 2000.
2. Kyle B. Olson, "Aum Shinrikyo: Once and Future Threat?", *Emerging Infectious Diseases* 5:4 (1999).
3. "Group Profile: Aum Shinrikyo": Memorial Institute for the Prevention of Terrorism Knowledge Base, http://www.tkb.org/Group.jsp?groupID=3956.

Chapter 11: The Department of Homeland Security: Searching for a Mission

1. Public Law 107–296, "Homeland Security Act of 2002," 107th Congress, 2002, Section 101.
2. Ibid., Section 102.
3. Ibid., Section 101.

Chapter 12: Defending the Big Apple

1. Louis Meixler, "Terror Groups More Decentralized, Attacked More Muslims in Home Countries amid Global Crackdown," Associated Press, December 23, 2003.

Chapter 13: Crush the Cell

1. Robert S. Mueller, "Statement Before the U.S. House of Representatives Committee on Appropriations Subcommittee on Science, State, Justice, Commerce, and Related Agencies," March 28, 2006.

Glossary of Acronyms

ALF: Animal Liberation Front, a loosely knit global network of radical animal rights activists who engage in vandalism and sabotage.

ASG: Abu Sayyaf Group, Filipino Islamic insurgent group that has waged a decades-long war against the government in the Philippines.

ATF: Bureau of Alcohol, Tobacco, and Firearms, U.S. Government agency charged with investigating crimes involving firearms, explosives, arson, and illegal alcohol or tobacco products.

CBP: Customs and Border Protection, the U.S. government agency charged with patrolling the U.S. borders, stopping illegal immigration, and stemming the flow of drugs and illicit goods in and out of the country.

CBRN: Chemical, Biological, Radiological, Nuclear, a term applied to any weapon that might contain these materials and to the threat of these weapons generally.

CIA: Central Intelligence Agency, the primary U.S. foreign intelligence service and the lead collector of human intelligence.

DHS: Department of Homeland Security, the U.S. cabinet department tasked with protecting the U.S. homeland from terrorist attacks and responding to domestic natural disasters. DHS is the parent department to such agencies as CBP, ICE, FEMA, and Coast Guard.

DIA: Defense Intelligence Agency, the branch of the Defense Department tasked with collecting and analyzing intelligence in direct support of the U.S. military.

EIJ: Egyptian Islamic Jihad, terrorist group founded in the 1970s that carried out the 1980 assassination of Anwar Sadat and later allied with al Qaeda in Afghanistan. Al Qaeda leader Ayman al-Zawahiri led EIJ for several years.

ELF: Earth Liberation Front, a U.S.–based environmental terrorist organization.

ESU: Emergency Service Unit, an elite tactical unit of the New York Police Department. ESU is NYPD's S.W.A.T. team.

FBI: Federal Bureau of Investigation, the United States' primary domestic law enforcement and intelligence service.

FEMA: Federal Emergency Management Agency, U.S. agency charged with coordinating response to natural disasters, terrorist attacks, industrial accidents, and other incidents.

HUMINT: Human Intelligence, intelligence collected directly from human sources.

ICE: Immigration and Customs Enforcement, the investigative unit of the Department of Homeland Security. Created in 2002 by the Homeland Security Act, ICE is charged with enforcing immigration and customs laws.

ISA: Intelligence Support Activity, a small and highly secretive unit within the Army Special Forces responsible for intelligence gathering and covert action.

ISI: Inter-Services Intelligence, the foreign and domestic intelligence bureau of Pakistan.

JI: Jammat-e Islami, one of two political movements born out of the fundamentalist Deobandi movement in Pakistan (see Jammat Ulema-e Islam). JI was a precursor to al Qaeda in Pakistan.

JSOC: Joint Special Operations Command, the U.S. military's interservice command structure for Special Operations Forces.

JTTF: Joint Terrorism Task Force, an antiterrorism task force coordinated by FBI that includes personnel from various law enforcement entities, including state and local police departments and other federal agencies.

JUI: Jammat Ulema-e Islam, one of two political movements born out of the fundamentalist Deobandi movement in Pakistan (see Jammat-e Islami). JUI was a precursor to al Qaeda in Pakistan.

NGA: National Geospatial Intelligence Agency, a Department of Defense entity responsible for analyzing imagery intelligence, primarily maps and other geographic images collected by satellites and other aircraft.

NOC: Non-Official Cover, a type of identity assigned to some covert CIA operatives. This kind of cover strips the operative of any affiliation with the U.S. government, presents far greater risks in the event of exposure.

NRC: Nuclear Regulatory Commission, a five-member commission responsible for regulating commercial nuclear reactors, nuclear material used on other applications, and the handling and disposal of nuclear waste.

NSA: National Security Agency, a Department of Defense agency responsible for collecting and analyzing signals intelligence through the use of cryptanalysis, or codebreaking. NSA also encrypts sensitive communications and data.

ODNI: Office of the Director of National Intelligence, office created in 2003 at the recommendation of the 9/11 Commission. DNI is the head of the U.S. intelligence community and collects intelligence from the community's sixteen agencies; DNI also serves as the principal advisor to the president on intelligence matters.

PIJ: Palestinian Islamic Jihad, a Palestinian terrorist group based in Damascus, which has conducted numerous bombings in Israel, Jordan, and Lebanon. The organization was founded as a counterpart to the Egyptian Islamic Jihad (EIJ).

S/CT: State Department Office of the Coordinator of Counterterrorism, the State Department office responsible for advancing the U.S. counterterrorism agenda through interaction with foreign governments, NGOs, and other entities.

SIGINT: Signals Intelligence, intelligence collected by intercepting voice and data communication.

SOD: Special Operations Division, a part of the New York Police Department responsible for providing specialized services such as air support, dive teams, and search/rescue dogs.

SOF: Special Operations Forces, a term applied to specialized units of all the branches of the U.S. military. The term is distinct from "Special Forces" (SF), which normally refers to specific Army units.

SSP: Sipah-I-Sahaba, Pakistani terrorist group created in 1985 to counter growing Shia activism in Pakistan that had been inspired in part by the success of the Iranian Revolution.

TSA: Transportation Security Agency, agency created after 9/11 to perform airport security functions.

Acknowledgments

THIS IS A STORY ABOUT terrorism and counterterrorism based on more than 30 years of government service in the Army, White House, State Department, UN, and NYPD. In my line of work, experience goes hand in hand with many valued friendships. Any success I have had in counterterrorism is a result of trusted relationships with my bosses, colleagues, and subordinates as we worked together in missions that reached far beyond our individual careers. There is no way I can fully express my gratitude to these people, other than to say that our shared commitment to the welfare and safety of the American people shaped this book more than any other factor. All of my former colleagues and comrades were sitting right beside me as I wrote *Crush the Cell.*

My counterterrorism career started in Charlie Company, 3rd Battalion Special Forces in the Panama Canal Zone in 1979. I would like to thank all of C Company, but particularly the men of ODA-17, including my first team leader, Pat McGree, my team sergeants Joe Walker and Sid Jenson, and a range of great Special Forces sergeants, including Fred Horsley, Rick Reiman, John Heimberger, "Wee-wee" Wilson, Roger Bascomb, John Franklin, John Brandon, Steve Tasker, and Raphael Lopez. I also want to thank my battalion commanders, Colonels Chuck Fry and Gene Russell (both of whom pulled me out of the dumps when necessary in these formative years). My company commanders, Majors Cecil Bailey and Bob Watson, were great bosses who became my great friends. I served with them alongside a stellar group of SOF warriors, who went on to make great contributions to our nation's security, including Remo Butler, Carlos Parker, Jeff Lambert, Mike Vickers, Dave Morris, Bob Sawyer, and many others.

During the war in El Salvador, I was bonded to several key NCOs who worked alongside me in Chalatenango. First was my friend and partner Sergeant Juan Gonzalez, who also served with me in Panama, the Dominican Republic, and Ecuador. Also special thanks to my later roommate in Chalatenango, Sergeant Stan Brown, who helped keep me alive during the tough times by instituting an exhausting but effective reverse cycle training (night training around the base). I would also like to thank my Special Ops team of Salvadoran soldiers, who protected me with their lives, especially its commander, Sergeant Chan (his nom de guerre) and Harry Claflin, a former U.S. Marine who served as trainer of that Salvadoran unit and advised me on the art of counterinsurgency combat operations. Finally, my thoughts go out to the family of the late Sergeant Gregory

"Red" Fronius, who was a true hero in a quiet, forgotten war, who gave his life for his country in Chalatenango six months after I departed.

At Georgetown University, I was fortunate to have inspiring and gifted teachers like Madeleine Albright, Ted Moran, and Allen Goodman. Goodman, the dean of the graduate program, helped me expand my knowledge of counterinsurgent warfare through historical case studies. I graduated in 1988 from the Landegger School of Business Diplomacy, and still benefit from the wise counsel of its benefactor, my friend George Landegger.

In the White House, first under George Bush and then Bill Clinton, I had the opportunity to work with three great national security advisors: LTG Brent Scowcroft, Tony Lake, and Sandy Berger, each of whom woke up every morning committed to doing the right thing for his country. I never once felt a political note in the work I did for these three fine men. I would also like to thank Admiral Jon Howe and Lakhdar Brahimi, my two bosses in Somalia and Haiti, who taught me to see the confluence of diplomacy, peacekeeping, and war-fighting. Mr. Brahimi remained a major mentor for me after Haiti and still today, and nobody understands the challenges and opportunities we face in the Middle East better than this man.

My former professor, Madeleine Albright, plucked me out of the Bush National Security Council staff and brought me to the UN and then back to the State Department with her. Although she knew I had very independent leanings on the political front, in the eight years I worked for her she always supported my ideas and my fledgling career, even as I was off in Somalia and Haiti when I was supposed to be working on her staff. She was a tremendous leader and great friend during that whole period. Her spokesman, Jamie Rubin, became a close friend and policy advisor in many of my CT deliberations in Washington. Jamie also read a draft of the book and provided excellent insights. Richard Clarke also was instrumental in my Washington career. I first met Dick on the Bush NSC staff, where he was one of the best bosses I have ever had. He has provided support during key points of my career and remains a colleague and great friend.

Working with NYPD was one of the highlights of my career thus far. First, I want to thank Commissioner Ray Kelly for giving me the opportunity to serve the great city of New York and for his support, guidance, and leadership. Regarding my partner at NYPD and great friend through it all, David Cohen, I can't say enough. He is perhaps the most dedicated, selfless, and talented public servant I have ever known. I was also supported by a group of very hard-working and talented NYPD chiefs, including Phil Pulaski, John Colgan, and Jimmy Waters. Inspector Mike O'Neil, the commander of the counterterrorism division, was a great partner in many initiatives. And last but not least, I could not have survived without a team of detectives who took care of me, kept me sane, and made me laugh: Detectives Anthony Amorese at the beginning, Mike Cole at the end, and Jimmy Fogarty throughout my time at NYPD. When you know these guys, you can't help but love NYPD.

My rather eclectic group of lifelong friends and my six siblings remain a key part of my life; they are smart, funny, and keep me grounded when I get too far adrift in the sometimes surreal world of counterinsurgency and counterterrorism. Friends Hap, Bill, Andy, Gamby, Ross, Kenny, Danny, Bog, Jack, Arlo, Rocky, Fred, Ted, Mel, and siblings Matt, Dennis, Terry, Joe, and Mary Anne, thanks.

I wrote much of this book with headphones on, listening to music while tapping away at the keyboard. Thanks to Bruce Springsteen and the E Street Band, Bob Dylan, Eric Clapton, The Grateful Dead, The Allman Brothers Band, The Marshall Tucker Band, Neil Young, Barenaked Ladies, Brian Wilson, Bob Marley, Natalie Merchant, George Harrison, and others who kept me rocking when I was tired and burned out.

I would like to thank my agent, Len Sherman, and Crown Publishers' vice president and executive editor Rick Horgan for their ideas, support, and encouragement throughout this process. Thanks to Julian Pavia of Crown Publishers for his outstanding editorial contributions as well. I would also like to thank my partners at Torch Hill Equity and Sheehan Associates for being patient with me as I finished this book and prepare for a tour.

I would also like to give special thanks to Karen Greenberg, New York University, and her team at the Center for Law and Security. Karen gave me a quiet place to write at NYU for my first year out of NYPD and was a constant source of encouragement. She also read a first draft and provided excellent advice. My research assistant, Mike Boland, also contributed significantly with long days and nights at various deadlines without complaint, as did Erin Eizenstat, who reviewed my work for errors.

My most important partner on this book was my editor and chief collaborator, Kate Sheehan Roach (who also happens to be my sister). Kate helped me shape the words and thoughts of *Crush the Cell.* She understood immediately what I was trying to do in this book and helped me find the right words to say it. Her hard work, dedication, and talent were absolutely key to me finishing this project. Thank you, Kate. I could not have done it without you.

I would like express special thanks to my parents. My mom, who offered to proofread the manuscript of this book from her hospital bed, was always encouraging and supportive even in the most difficult final days of her life. Of all the people I've encountered in my career, she was one of the toughest. My dad infected our family with a love of reading and instilled in us the confidence to share our opinions even when they go against conventional wisdom. With his inquisitive mind and expansive memory for details, he still keeps us on our toes. Thank you for all of your love and support over the years.

To my loving and patient wife who supported me throughout this ordeal (including proofreading for me), this book would not have been possible without you. And to my daughter, Alexandra, and son, Michael, you are the joy of my life and a constant inspiration for this project and everything I do.

Index